SCANS
KEY TO BIRDWATCHING

VIRGINIA C. HOLMGREN

Illustrated by Florence M. Walker

TIMBER PRESS
Portland, Oregon
1983

Printed in the United States of America.

TIMBER PRESS
P.O. Box 1631
Beaverton, Oregon 97075

Library of Congress Cataloging in Publication Data

Holmgren, Virginia, C.
Scans key to birdwatching.

Includes index.
1. Bird watching. I. Title.
QL677.5.H64 1983 598'.07'234 82-25597
ISBN 0-917304-48-9

Contents

To all the readers of my newspaper birdlore columns whose enthusiastic response for more than twenty-two years persuaded me that this book for birdwatchers would find a welcome. My thanks also to publisher Richard Abel whose guidance has been invaluable.

Part One

WHAT IS BIRDWATCHING?

Birdwatching can be a now-and-then pastime or an absorbing lifetime hobby. You may choose to watch only birds outside your windows or in your own neighborhood or go far afield seeking birds in every setting all across the continent or even around the world.

There are close to 8,700 species (kinds) of birds in the world. Over 650 species have been found nesting in North America north of Mexico in recent years. The number will change if species from Siberia continue to come to Alaska and others from Mexico and the Caribbean continue to come northward to stay instead of making only an occasional visit. More and more European species have been coming here also, and the total number of species that might be seen in North America goes well over 800 if every stray wanderer is counted.

From 300 to 400 species can be seen in almost any quarter of North America during a full year of watching. How many you will see from your windows or in your neighborhood depends partly on where you live and whether your surroundings make birds feel welcome. (*See* Inviting Birds to Your Yard.) But your birding score at home or away depends mostly on how often and how carefully you look and on how patient — and how lucky — you turn out to be.

Whatever area you choose, birdwatching means more than just giving birds an admiring glance. The real joy of watching — and the enduring challenge — is to know birds by name and to get some understanding of their ways. Since each species has its own unique plumage, its own pattern of daily living, its own ways of food-finding, nesting, courtship and song, getting to know even a few species really well can lead to endless adventure.

You can begin your birdwatching without binoculars, but they will add much to your success and to your pleasure. Even a small 4-power or 6-power lens will reveal things you can't see with just your eyes. Most birders prefer a 7-power lens (7×35) — especially one with an *extra-wide* angle of view so that a bird doesn't go out of sight with every flutter and hop.

Whatever the lens power, be sure you can adjust the focus for both eyes at once, with one-finger touch. Try any glass before you buy. Watch something moving inside or outside the store and focus to follow it. Make sure you can focus easily and that the glass is comfortable in your hands — not too bulky or heavy. Make sure it gives you a clear view, no wavy lines, halos or rainbows. Once you have the glasses home, practice focusing on every bird you see — even those you know quite well — until you can follow any bird quickly and easily. When a bird you don't know comes along you want to be able to use the glasses almost without thinking of how to turn and focus. Then you can give all your attention to the colors and clues that will help you match the bird in the yard with a picture in the book and so learn its name.

Until you know a name, any bird is just a UFO — Unidentified Feathered Object. Birds are the only creatures with feathers, and so it is feathers — not flying skill — that puts birds in a class by themselves. Class Aves, the scientists call it, using the Latin name for birds. So, then, feathers make the bird. And the colors of those feathers — along with a bird's general anatomy, actions and appearance — provide the identification (ID for short) that proves one species different from all others, entitled to a name of its own.

One good way to learn birds by name is to begin watching with a friend who can give you each ID at first glance. For instance, you see a small gray bird you can't name, but your friend is right there to point out the clues — black cap and bib — and tell you it's a black-capped chickadee. Then all you have to do is take a good look — and remember clues and name.

But even the kindest friend can't always be with you. So what you really need is the right book — one small enough to carry with you or keep handy beside your best birdwatching window; one that makes it easy to find the right name for every bird you're likely to see.

SCANS *KEY TO BIRDWATCHING* is planned with just these two needs in mind. You'll find the right name easily because the birds pictured and described in the Key pages are arranged by *size* and *color*. To find a name and matching picture for that bird you've just seen, all you do is judge it as small-and-brown or medium-and-yellow or large-and-blue — or any other general size-and-color combination — and then turn to the Key with that same size-and-color label. The Key will then provide you with a description of the markings that help you tell this bird from all others of the same general size and hue. Full information is given on how to use the Keys.

Most bird books are more difficult to use — as you may have discovered — because the birds are arranged according to a scientific system not easy to understand. Birds with the simplest anatomy are placed first, followed in turn by those of more and more complicated structure. So unless you know the sequence of that system, you have to go through the whole book, page by page, picture by picture, hunting for a match. And if the bird you want is way at the back of the book, you may easily be discouraged.

Of course you know that a system is needed for scientific study of bird ways. And it helps even a beginning watcher to know that species alike in a general way are placed together in a group that science calls an "order". Each order is subdivided so that birds even more closely alike can be placed together in a group called a "family". If you know the order or family to which a bird belongs — or can make a good guess — you can find it fairly easily in bird books that follow scientific arrangement.

However, there are 21 orders of birds in North America (28 worldwide) and 66 North American families (154 worldwide); and so without considerable study you can't know just where each one comes in scientific sequence. And it isn't always easy to know even the right order or family for a bird you've never seen before.

In some groups — like ducks and geese — the species are so much alike that you can scarcely miss in naming the order and even the family. But others are grouped — or *classified*, to use the scientific term — by features you can't readily see. What beginner would guess that a meadowlark with its bright yellow breast is in the same family as blackbirds? Or that the starling — which looks and acts much like blackbirds — is in a different family altogether?

So the arrangement in this book by size and color, rather than scientific sequence, really makes things easier for the beginner and for anyone who has trouble using other bird books. Only 200 birds are fully described and pictured here, but they are the birds seen the most often in the most places. Many of them are seen for all or part of the year in all the adjoining 48 states and in much of southern Canada and northern Mexico. Some are also seen in Alaska and northern Canada, at least in summer, and others winter in Caribbean tropics and even farther south. Nearly 400 others seen less often are named and briefly described, but not pictured.

No handy-size bird book can tell everything everybody wants to know about every bird. If you want more information than this book gives, try *The Audubon Society Encyclopedia of North American Birds* by John K. Terres, a large volume of over 1,100 pages. You'll find the most information in a single pocket-size book in *Birds of North America* by Robbins, Bruun and Zim. Most other complete pocket-size books take two volumes, one for eastern birds and one for western, or one for water birds and the second or land birds. (*See* Part Eight for other recommended books and material.) If you see a bird not pictured in this book, you'll find it in one of these other books by matching bird and picture clue by clue in the same trackdown check you'll learn to use here.

The full trackdown check begins with matching bird and picture by size and color first and then by its actions and call notes. **S**ize . . .**C**olors . . . **A**ctions . . . **N**otes. Those are the four main clues you need to tell one bird from another. As you can see, the first letters of these four words can be put together in order to spell **SCAN.** That's the word every good birdwatcher needs to remember.

House finches *have a snack first, then a drink of water.*

Part Two

HOW TO TELL ONE BIRD FROM ANOTHER THE **SCANS** *WAY*

S*C*A*N IS THE CLUE WORD

The word *scan* means to check point by point, like a detective looking for clues to track down a mystery. And that is just what you do to tell one bird from another — you scan for clues, all the differences in Size, Colors, Actions and Notes that make each species unique, one of a kind.

For the most successful birdwatching, keep scanning as long as the bird is in sight. It's likely to stay in sight longer if you are quiet. So no sudden movements, no loud talking and no pointing. If you raise a hand to point, the bird may think you're about to shoot a gun or throw a stone and it will get out of sight fast.

Train yourself to remember each clue you see or hear. Make your mind into a computer with print-out always on tap for instant recall of every important detail. This may not come easy, but keep trying. You'll improve with practice. But if you feel that remembering is really impossible, carry a small notebook and jot down each clue as you see it — or at least as soon as the bird is out of sight and you can stop scanning.

Once you have all possible clues in mind or in your notebook you can begin to make ID trackdown and find the matching Size-and-Color Key. But first you need to know a little more about the kind of clues to look for in each of the four main SCAN System steps.

SCANNING FOR SIZE CLUES

Most books give a bird's length in inches, measuring from beak-tip to tail-tip, with a dead bird stretched out flat on a laboratory shelf. But you will seldom see a live bird in this stretched-out pose. When you see one on the wing or huddled on a perch or even standing in silhouette, it is difficult to judge its length in inches.

So for getting that first Size clue, it's more helpful to make a rough guess of measurement as *small, medium, large* or *very large*. Of course these terms have to be given a fixed measurement, too. But instead of inches, compare them to the three birds almost everyone knows well by sight — house sparrow, robin and common pigeon, our three "measure birds". Make the comparison like this:

SMALL

Smaller than house sparrow, under 6 inches.

MEDIUM

Between house sparrow and robin, 6 to 9 inches.

LARGE

Between robin and pigeon, 9 to 14 inches.

VERY LARGE

Larger than a pigeon, over 14 inches.

In addition to using the Measure Birds you can use your own fingers, hand and arm for comparison. Like this:

SMALL
: Length from thumb tip to wrist, 5 to 6 inches.

MEDIUM
: Length from longest finger tip to wrist — or from wrist to elbow, whichever is closer to 9 inches.

LARGE
: Length from fingertip or knuckles to elbow, about 14 inches.

VERY LARGE
: Anything longer than the Large measurement.

People come in different sizes for fingers, hands and arms, so each birder will need to take his own measurements to find the best match for the sizes needed. You may want to mark down your own "rule of thumb" measurements in this book so they'll be handy to check as needed. Once you have them well in mind, you'll always have a way to make quick size comparison.

However, keeping a good mental image of the three Measure Birds will give you a better judgment, for a bird's bulk — as well as its length — is part of the size estimate. So, along with a guess at length, notice whether a bird is plump or slim. Judge if its tail, bill, neck, legs or feet seem too long — or too short — for its body. Notice if the bird looks "big headed" or if it has an upright crest of feathers on top of its head or perhaps two feather tufts that look like horns or if the bill has an unusual shape. Anything unusual is an important clue.

Size includes head, feet and every other part of the bird as well as over-all length and shape, especially when trying to separate two species of much the same color. For instance, swans, egrets, whooping crane, white ibis, white pelican, wood stork, white heron and snow goose are all white, all Very Large. But each has some further size clue — length or shortness of legs and neck, length and shape of bill, width of wingspread — to help you match each one with picture and description. If you know what clues to look for, you'll name the bird — perhaps not at first glance, but certainly with a long and lucky look.

So, Size is the first clue you'll want to notice. But you need the combination of Size and Color to lead you to the right Key and the right ID.

SCANNING FOR COLOR CLUES

With a little practice you can make it a habit to notice both size and color at first glance. Often it's some bright patch of color trim that first catches your eye, but it's basic body color that will guide you to the right Key. In the SCANS System, the basic body color is the general tone of back, wings and tail — the colors you see as the bird flies away. The colors you see from the front — forehead, throat, breast and belly or underparts — will be secondary ID clues to be used later. The Key color comes from the back, wings and tail.

Birds come in hundreds of colors, if you count every shade as a separate hue. But for SCAN check, every shade comes under one of ten Key colors: browns, grays, blues-to-purples, greens, yellows, orange, reds-to-pinks, black-and-white, black, white. Browns include every shade from deep chocolate to bright cinnamon to pale tan or grayish buff. Grays go from buffy gray to deep slate. Each of the others — except black and white — includes all tones of the Key color, dark or light.

Judging the basic color of the bird's back-wings-tail is the first step, but keep looking for every patch or line of contrasting color — back, front, legs, feet or bill — for any color mark may be a decisive ID clue. Most often the best clue marks are on the head, especially on the top of the head where there is often a bright patch of color like a skull cap. So make it a habit to look first at the top of the head, if you have a choice. Notice whether the cap blends in with the head color or is a contrasting shade. Notice whether it is one color or bordered with a line of white or black or another color. Look for patches or lines of color over the eyes, on the cheeks, throat, breast — especially the breast. The color of the cap — plus the coloring on the breast — combine for the most important Key clue to use after you have the basic color of the back-wings-tail.

The clue colors help you tell one species of bird from another. Often they help you tell a male bird from a female or young birds not yet in adult plumage even though they are adult size. Many males are brightly colored, easily seen by prowling cats, hawks or other enemies and therefore able to lure the invader away from mate and young, both of whom often wear the drab coloring called camouflage, which blends with surroundings. The blending tones give protection, for as long as the drab-feathered ones remain motionless they are almost invisible.

However, some males wear camouflage colors, too, either all year or only in winter when there is no nest to guard. And some females are feathered as brightly as their mates. So the difference between drab and bright does not always mark a difference in sex. Often even the drabbest females and young show some hint of the male's bright color to give you an ID clue.

To tell a full-grown young bird from an adult of the same plumage, look at the color of the mouth lining. In young birds the color is often bright pink or yellow. Nestlings (young still in the nest) and fledglings (young just out of the nest and full-feathered) often have the brightest mouths of all — evidently making a better target for parent birds with food to ram down baby throats.

For a further aid in matching feather color with printed picture, remember that birds in moist climates tend to be darker than the average individual portrayed in the book. Birds in dry desert country tend to be lighter. For both, the tone is a matter of blending with background for better camouflage protection.

Don't forget that feathers may often change in tone to reflect surrounding color. A drab female house sparrow, for instance, may suddenly look quite green as it crouches under a leafy canopy, especially in full sunlight. Or sunlight reflected from a rock or water may make that same sparrow look quite yellow. Often there seems to be a fool-the-eye glint of yellow on the breast or underwing of any bird that darts from some shady perch into the open, even on a somewhat cloudy day, even though no yellow is actually there. Green, gray, blue or tan feathers may all take on much the same tone in poor light for another fool-the-eye trick the birds play on the birdwatcher without meaning to do so.

Each ray of light is made up of all the colors of the rainbow, and the structure of some feather tips will break up the rays into the separate colors much the way an ocean wave breaks up into separate drops as it hits the rocks. Such feathers then have "drops" of color, especially in full sunlight, giving them an iridescent glow. Male blackbirds and male and female starlings have such a sheen. So do most doves and pigeons, the neck feathers of a cock pheasant, the coat feathers of hummingbirds.

Hummingbird throat feathers, the bright ruff called a gorget, have a different structure that makes the colors completely changeable. The red of a hummer gorget is not actual color. The fiery hue comes from light rays broken up and reflected by the tiny — very tiny — transparent prism layers of the feather tips. When light falls directly on the throat, the feathers reflect only the red and shine with fiery radiance. As the bird turns away from the light, the colors suddenly turn to gray or black, with or without any underglow of red or gold.

So do not judge the colors of any bird with just one look. Remember that even the brightest hues may be changed by changing light, changing surroundings. And the very color clue you need most for ID may be hidden for a moment by tightly closed feathers.

SCANNING FOR ACTION CLUES

Birds spend most of their waking hours hunting for food. So the kind of food a bird eats usually determines the typical action clues you're likely to see. Seed-eaters will usually be on the ground gleaning fallen seeds from weeds and wild grasses. Or they may be clinging to weed stalks as they pry open a seed pod. Eaters of insects and other creatures without backbones may be on the ground or on branches or tree trunks or even snatching a meal in midair.

Swifts and swallows, hummingbirds, flycatchers and birds of the nighthawk family all catch insects on the wing, but each has a typical action that helps to identify the family though not the species. Both swifts and swallows swoop, flutter and glide in sky-skimming flight. Hummingbirds dash and dart or hover with furiously beating wings. Flycatchers perch on a bare branch or wire or fence post, dart out to catch whatever insect wings by and then return to their perch. Nighthawks and their kin swoop and glide much like swifts and swallows but their larger size quickly sets them apart.

Vultures, eagles and hawks all soar on outspread wings, riding the rising air currents as they search the ground below for possible prey. But vultures usually soar with wings lifted in an arch, while eagles and most hawks soar with wings out on even keel. Two hawk species — rough-legged hawks and kestrels (also known a sparrowhawks) — often hover low over a field with fast-beating wings as they wait to pounce on any mouse that leaves its cover.

Birds that feed on fish and other underwater animals or plants may just dip their heads below the surface as they swim around or they may completely submerge for deep-water food hunt. Long-legged birds wade out to find a meal, and the longer their legs, the deeper the water where they will feed. Most long-legged birds have long necks and long bills, too, and they use the bills as a scoop or spear, depending on its shape. A long-legged, long-necked bird that flies with neck curved back in an S shape will be in the heron family. Cranes fly with neck outstretched.

Actions yield a clue, too, if you notice whether a bird is alone or usually with others of its kind. Except in migration or during nesting season, a thrush is almost always alone. Sparrows are almost always in a group. Both kinds of dark-eyed juncos — the slate-colored junco of the east and the Oregon junco of the west — are usually with others of their kind. Cedar and Bohemian waxwings, evening grosbeaks, bushtits and pine siskins are usually in a group, too.

Certain birds repeat a typical action so often that the action itself gave them their name. Sometimes that name is a real family exclusive. Woodpeckers, for instance, are the only birds equipped to drill deep into tree trunks for wood-boring insects. Other tree-trunk feeders can only scrape the surface. But the brown thrasher and other birds with thrasher name are not the only ones you'll see "thrashing around" under bushes hunting for bugs or other tasty tidbits. Other species besides the brown creeper "creep" up and down and around tree trunks.

The greater roadrunner is not the only bird that runs along the road, although it certainly does the best job of it. Flycatchers are not the only birds catching flies, nor gnatcatchers the only ones to dine on gnats. Nevertheless, such names as these — and cowbird, dipper, kingfisher, nutcracker, oystercatcher, turnstone, wagtail, sapsucker, skimmer and darter — give you an ID action clue to match their name.

Most small-to-medium size birds hop or run. Most larger birds walk. So if you see any small-to-medium birds walking like crows or barnyard chickens, remember it as a clue. Among the Small walkers are ovenbird, waterthrushes, longspurs. Medium walkers include blackbirds, starling, meadowlarks, horned larks, pipits, wagtails, pinyon jay, pine grosbeak. Walking — any action clue — may not be the only clue you need for full ID, but it can be an important part of the trackdown.

SCANNING BY NOTES — THE SOUND CLUES

Usually only the male birds sing a full song, doing so only in spring and early summer during courtship and nesting, so you may not hear a song clue at other seasons of the year. However, the females of a few species sing, too, and some males sing in autumn, usually in a softer tone called a "whisper song".

But you can hear call notes all year long from most species, from males, females and young. And the N that stands for Notes also stands for any non-vocal Noises that make up the sound clues. You can tell that a hummingbird is around, even without seeing it, when you hear the whirring buzz of air passing through its rapidly beating wings. Other Noise clues include the drumming sound as a ruffed grouse beats its wings without taking flight, the quill rattling of pheasants and other chicken-like birds as they try to startle some nearby enemy into missing its attack, and the softer winnowing sound made by the wings of doves and pigeons as they alight.

Alarm calls and the conversational chirps and twitters sound much the same for a number of different species. This similarity is a safety factor, for a warning given by one species is usually understood by all. Even a budgerigar just escaped from a cage understands a sparrow's alarm signal.

Some species repeat the same song or call notes so often that they have been named to match the syllables. Among birds known by such echoic names are chickadees, flickers, whip-poor-will, willet, curlews, kittiwakes, killdeer, phoebes, pewees, dickcissel, bobwhite, bobolink, scaups, kiskadee, veery, cuckoos and jays. Some of these — cuckoos, jays, curlews, kittiwakes, scaups — are also seen in England and were named there. The rest were named by English-speaking settlers or explorers in North America. Only two imitative bird names — *towhee* and *chewink* — come from the names used by North American Indians. Each echoes a different call from the same bird, the rufous-sided towhee, and though *towhee* is the official name, *chewink* is still a much-used nickname in Eastern states. Two more imitative names — *chachalaca* and *pauraque* — came from Mexican Indians, and *caracara* is from a Brazilian tribe.

Even birds that have non-imitative names may sing a tune or chirp a call-note phrase that is easy to imitate with words, nonsense syllable or whistled notes. The song of the olive-sided flycatcher seems to be an imperious demand for "Quick! Three beers!" MacGillivray's warbler calls, "Sweeter, sweeter, sweeter! Sugar! Sugar!" And instead of repeating its name, the bobwhite may be making a weather forecast — "More wet!" for a rainy day and "No more wet!" for clear skies. At least a dozen sets of words have been suggested to match the plaintive melody of the white-throated sparrow. Canadians hear "Swee-eet Can-a-da, Can-a-da, Can-a-da!" For some New Englanders it's "Ol'Sam Peabody, Peabody, Peabody!"

Some bird songs may echo a tune you already know. By chance, the notes of the golden-crowned sparrow you'll hear on the Pacific Coast are the same mi-re-do of the old English folk tune, "Three Blind Mice". Jerome Kern frankly admits that he found the opening notes for his "I've told every little star" by listening to a song sparrow. Other duplications in hymns, opera and popular music are cited in *Field*

Book of Wild Birds and Their Music by F. Schuyler Matthews (Putnam 1921, Dover reprint 1967). You may want to write these matches — along with your own — in the margin of your bird book or birding notebook as one more ID clue.

Only a few kinds of birds are so much alike on all other counts — Size, Colors, Actions — that Notes have to provide the chief ID clue. But two look-alike flycatchers both small and gray, need the Note check. The alder flycatcher sings a soft three-note chant that sounds like *fee-bee-o*. The look-alike willow flycatcher has a two-note call like a musical sneeze — *fitz-bew!* Both are sometimes named together as a single species, Traill's flycatcher, but the latest decision is that they are two distinct species. Usually you will find the alder flycatcher only in eastern and northern areas of the continent, while the willow flycatcher prefers the west and southwest as a rule. But the two may frequent the same area where those boundaries meet, and so either may turn up in the other's accustomed territory. When that happens, only N for Notes sets them apart.

Two other species — eastern and western meadowlarks — are so nearly alike in Size and Colors and Actions that they almost have to be held in the hand to see the small differences in pattern of face and tail markings. Luckily their songs are quite different. The easterner sings a four-note whistled tune, clear and ringing, with the up-and-down accent on the first and third notes. It makes a match for the happy message: *Spring*time, *sing* time! The westerner needs seven or eight notes for its lilting message. To some it is singing: Isn't this a pretty place! To other ears the comment is: Hope you have a happy day! And your ears may hear something different still.

Of course you always want to see the singer, if you possibly can, to be very sure of your ID. There are several clever imitators in feathers that can fool even the most experienced birder. The northern mockingbird is the most famous among them, but the starling comes a close second. When tamed as a nestling it can even be taught to mimic words or whistle a tune. Several other species — gray catbird, crows, magpies, jays and thrashers — are also adept at this fool-the-birdwatcher game.

Also, individuals of some species — especially white-throated and white-crowned sparrows — often create variations of the typical theme song that are sometimes tricky to identify unless you see the singer. What you think you hear is not always what you'll see when you finally catch the singer in the act.

S*C*A*N WITH AN EXTRA "S" FOR SETTING

Along with Size, Colors, Actions, Notes, you often need to check for the extra S — Setting. Setting includes both habitat and range. *Habitat* is the kind of terrain — field, forest, marsh, shore — where a bird nests and feeds. *Range* is the geographical territory it covers. Some species live within the same geographical range all year. Others migrate, traveling between winter and summer home areas. Fruit-and-insect eating species often nest in northern areas but must migrate south in winter if they are to survive. Seed-eating species often stay north all year, but may summer in the hills and winter in the warmer valleys. (For records of farthest migrants *see* Fastest and Farthest.)

Bird names that include habitat — marsh wren, cactus wren, mountain bluebird, etc. — are usually fairly reliable clues of a likely setting. But geographical labels — California gull, Tennessee warbler, Virginia rail — usually mark only the place where the species was first put on official record. So check range maps and description, not just the name, to learn any bird's home territory or migrant range.

If you think you've found a bird in a completely wrong setting — a cactus wren in Alaska or any species far from the area on its range map — always suspect that you've made a mistake in ID and look for a likelier choice. But birds do stray if troubled by drought, blizzards or hunger, or when frightened by storms, pedators, gunners, low-flying planes or other hazards. Migrating birds are sometimes blown off course by hurricanes or join the wrong flock in sudden flight from danger and so go far from their normal routes.

Also, cage birds may escape from homes or zoos and settle down in the wild. If the climate is suitable, and if they find a mate of their own kind, they may become as much a part of the wild population as any native North American species. Mute swans native to Europe and Asia have escaped from zoos to settle successfully in several areas. Budgerigars, native to Australia and usually called parakeets, have been extremely successful in establishing colonies elsewhere. Wild flocks totaling over 3,000 have settled around St. Petersburg, Florida. Other members of the parrot family and several alien dove species — especially the spotted dove and ringed turtledove — are now very much at home here in several locales.

Alien species have also been released into the wilds on purpose, always with good intention, but not always with good results. Most welcome among them are the ring-necked pheasants from China that first nested successfully in the wild in Oregon in the 1880s. Least welcome — along with house sparrows and common pigeons — are the starlings, first released in New York City in 1890 by a man who thought this country ought to know all the birds mentioned by Shakespeare in his famous plays and sonnets. Most of the other "literary" imports — nightingales, skylarks, Old World thrushes — soon vanished, but the starlings multiplied beyond all reason.

Native American species have also been transported to parts of the continent where they were unknown. Most of these are game birds — turkeys, bobwhite, grouse, etc. In 1940 house finches from California were caught and taken to New York to sell as cage birds. When the pet-shop owner discovered it was illegal to cage or sell any native bird, he turned the birds free on Long Island to fend for themselves. They settled in, began spreading out, and are now found north to Canada, south to the Carolinas and Georgia, inland to Ohio, moving farther each year.

A few species have reached here from other continents on their own wing power. Cattle egrets from Africa were evidently blown across the Atlantic to South America's Caribbean shores and moved on to Florida in 1952, reached Oregon in 1965 and are now seen almost everywhere. Also, in these crowded times when humans are taking over more and more once-wild terrain, many of our native species are being forced out of their old homes. Anna's hummingbirds, which once were seen almost entirely within California boundaries, have been moving out both northward and eastward since the mid 1960s. They now also nest in Oregon, Washington and Arizona and have visited numerous other western states, even British Columbia and Alaska.

So a birdwatcher anywhere may see species where they are not supposed to be according to the bird books, especially older texts. If you check and double-check and are sure you've seen such a rarity, you might contact the local Audubon Society (usually listed in the phone book) and ask for an expert to verify your discovery. Of course, the rare visitor may be gone by the time you look again, but the attempt is worth the effort.

Setting — like any other of the S*C*A*N*S check points — may give the decisive clue that makes final ID. But be very wary of making a decision on one clue alone. And be doubly wary of forgetting to check Size — the clue to start with, the clue you can't do without. So before you go further with S*C*A*N*S trackdown, get well acquainted with the three "measure birds" that will help you make Size judgment.

THE THREE "MEASURE BIRDS"

The three "measure birds" — house sparrow, American robin and common pigeon — are at home almost everywhere in North America, so you may already know them well. To get better acquainted with their size, both length and bulk, compare each of them with things around the yard — a birdhouse or feeder, a pine cone, a flower pot. Then check with a ruler to see how accurate you were in judging the 6-inch=small or 9-inch=medium or 14-inch=large measurement. Also, guess the size of every bird you see and check with our size charts or the inch measurement in other guide books to grade yourself on accuracy.

If you don't see our three measure birds often enough to use them in comparison, you could choose other species of similar size. You could also make it a point to get to know these three better. A brief introduction to each one follows.

***#1 — house sparrow* 5-1/2–6 inches**

***#2 — American robin* ± 9 inches**

***#3 — common pigeon* 13–14 inches**

House Sparrow — Measure Bird #1

Size: House sparrows at 5½ to 6 inches are the measure mark as largest of the Small birds. *Colors:* The female (#1) has no bright colors. Like many females she wears soft tans that blend with the dried grass of her nest for camouflage protection. The male (#16) is handsome in black bib (for full adult), black eye mask, gray cap edged in reddish brown, white cheek patches. *Actions:* House sparrows are native to much of Europe, Asia and North Africa. Science classifies them as weaverbirds, but "sparrow" used to be a common name for all small brown birds, and since the first ones brought to this country came from England they are often known as English sparrows. They arrived in New York in the 1850s, imported by people who thought they would help native birds destroy bugs that harm fruit trees. They do eat a lot of bugs, but they sometimes drive away smaller birds. *Notes:* They have no real song, and their chatter may sound cheerful or just noisy.

American Robin — Measure Bird #2

Size: At 9 inches (or a bit more or less) the robin (#87) is largest of the Medium birds or smallest of the Large birds. *Colors:* Its red breast is so good a color clue that gray back, black-and-white throat and white eye ring are seldom noticed. A male's cap is usually black; a female's grayish. Young birds have a buffy breast well speckled in black dots. *Actions:* Robins enjoy splashing in pool or puddle, and a backyard bird bath will often bring them to nest nearby, even on a windowsill. They feed on worms and on fruits, especially elderberries, firethorn, hawthorn, mountain ash, dogwood, cascara and wild or cultivated cherries. None of this food is available in the north where winter brings continual ice and snow, but northern robins have an inherited pattern that sends them south each autumn. They are among the earliest migrants to return in spring, so in the north they have become the traditional sign of coming warmth. In the south, of course, they are one of the first to herald coming winter. *Notes:* In winter they give only tup-tup chirps as a rule, but in spring they carol their cheer-a-lee tune, usually starting very early in the morning.

Common Pigeon — Measure Bird #3

Size: At 13–14 inches the common pigeon (#134) makes the mark between Large and Very Large in the SCANS System. *Colors:* Most pigeons are bluish gray, but some are reddish-brown, others almost black. Many are well-splashed with white and all have a white rump patch. *Actions:* The common pigeon is an Old World native, once nesting wild along all rocky coasts and inland shores, but tamed in ancient times for food, pets, or message carriers. They have become famous for their homing ability, especially in wartime. In England the original name for the species was rock dove, because the birds nest on rocky cliffs, not in trees like other wild doves. In France the name *pigeon* imitated the peeping cries of nestlings, and was carried to England by Norman-French conquerors. American usage has made *dove* the name for smaller wild species in the family and *pigeon* for this and other large species. However, many bird books prefer to use *rock dove*. The first ones seen in the Americas came with Columbus and others with later settlers, all intended as barnyard birds for food. *Notes:* The male courts the female with repeated *cuckety-coo* calls and much bowing and bobbing.

Do you now have the SCANS System well in mind? Are you ready to apply each step every time you see a new bird, checking for Size, Colors, Actions, Notes and Setting almost automatically? Then it's time to get acquainted with the SCANS Keys and learn how each clue leads to another as you identify each new bird by name.

By the time you can identify fifty species by name, know all the clues for each one, you will be well on your way to becoming an expert. You may want to keep your lifetime list in a loose-leaf notebook with pages for daily or monthly records and added notes.

*A **hairy woodpecker** perched on a suet feeder gives watchers a Size clue.*

Part Three

*THE **SCANS** KEYS*

HOW TO USE THE SIZE-AND-COLOR KEYS

All species of birds commonly seen over a large portion of North America north of Mexico are named and described in the Size-and-Color Keys. Those seen most often over the widest area — along with those most abundant over a lesser area — are also pictured. The black and white pictures included in the Keys and the color pictures are each identified by the same number used in the Key.

To learn the name of a bird you've seen, the first step is to judge it by Size and Color according to the SCANS System explained on the preceding pages. Once you've tagged the bird by Size and Color, find the Key with a matching label. Then check the Key clue by clue to find a description that matches the bird. When you have a complete match, you have a name.

For reminder: the SCANS System rates birds in four sizes: *Small* is smaller than a house sparrow, under 6 inches. *Medium* is between a house sparrow and a robin, 6 to 9 inches. *Large* is between a robin and a common pigeon, 9 to 14 inches. *Very Large* is over 14 inches.

For reminder: the SCANS System determines a bird's basic color by the main color of back, wings, tail. All shades fit in one of these ten color groups: browns, grays, blues-to-purples, greens, yellows, orange, reds-to-pinks, black-and-white, black, white. The colors are always listed in this sequence.

On the following Key pages you will find all Small birds listed first with the colors in this same sequence. Then all Medium birds of every color are listed, then all Large birds, with the Very Large birds last. In each Key the colors are in the same sequence so you will know just about where to find the color you want.

Once you find the right Size-and-Color Key, the first ID clue to match is the color of the bird's cap. The second clue is the coloring of the breast, whether plain or patterned. These two clues are listed together as the first check point. For example:

CAP: PLAIN BROWN — BREAST: PLAIN (WHITE)

The cap colors are listed in the same sequence used for the Keys. So if you're looking for a bird with a green cap, for instance, you'll skip over the entries for brown, gray or blue caps and go straight to the descriptions under *CAP: GREEN* heading.

The breast coloring is called "plain" if it is white or pale buff or gray with no markings. The breast is "patterned" if it has spots, lengthwise stripes or streaks, crosswise bars, patches that look like bibs, belts or lapels or washes of color deeper in tone than the pale gray or buff of a "plain" breast.

Under the cap-and-breast heading you will find a number and the name of a species that fits the cap-and-breast coloring. In the margin is a picture of the species and a map showing its range. Its picture in the Color Key will have the same number for quick identification. Below the heading you will find the clue points to check for further comparison with the bird you've seen. They are:

CAP (border lines, tufts, crest, etc.)
BILL (thick or thin, long or short, curved, etc.)
FRONT (any marks on cheeks, throat, breast, belly, underparts seen from the front, unusual leg color or size)
BACK (any marks on nape, back, rump, wings, tail)
ACTIONS (feeding actions, etc.)
NOTES (songs, calls, other noises)
HABITAT (desert, brush, woods edge, yards, etc.)

If the numbered species can easily be mistaken for another — or several others — these will be named and briefly described as "close look-alikes". Any species only somewhat similar are named and described as "general look-alikes". When Look-Alikes of either kind are involved, make a careful check of each clue point — and try to see the bird again for further check.

Less common birds, but not Look-Alikes, are described briefly under cap and breast color.

To find the right Key page quickly, check the tab with abbreviations for Size and Color on the outer edge of each Key page. Capital letter for Size; small for color, as S/br is Small/brown. If you color each of these tabs with the matching color, you'll find the right page even more easily.

Before you use the Keys to find the name of a bird you don't recognize, make a trial check — or several trial checks — by finding the right entry for a bird you already know. Just remind yourself of the bird's Size and basic back Color and all the other ID clues for cap, breast, bill, front, back, actions, notes and habitat, and then see how quickly you can find the matching description in the matching Key.

You might even work up a "Key That Bird" game to play alone or with others by putting bird pictures or descriptions on cards or slips of paper — without a name, of course — and then draw one at random and time yourself in finding the matching description in the Keys.

Until you are an expert at Key trackdown, you may want to re-read this reminder before each check:

1. At first scan, decide the bird's Size and the Color of back-wings-tail.
2. Keep scanning for all possible clues, especially the color of the cap and whether breast is plain or patterned.
3. Find the matching Size-and-Color Key, then the matching cap-and-breast combination, then the matching clues for cap, bill, front, back, actions, notes, habitat and range.
4. Make a special second check of all points if there are Look-Alikes.
5. If you can't find a match on the first Key you check, try the next Color or the next Size. If still in doubt, look at the bird again or study color pictures of possible species in several books to see it from every angle.

One further hint — memorizing the sequence of the colors will make your check search easier. The sequence is always the same, both for the Keys themselves in each Size group and for the cap colors. However, not every color is needed for the caps in every Key. No small brown bird, for instance, has a green cap. But the colors that are needed appear in the usual sequence and they are listed in the introduction to each Key as a sort of color index for you to check at a glance.

The Keys may seem complicated at first, but they will be easier to use with each trial. You will soon remember the Size and Color sequence and know the right clues to look for at first scanning or when you take that careful second look. If you like both watching birds and solving mysteries, the SCANS System is the way to go.

ABBREVIATIONS USED IN THE KEYS

f	female	ad	adult
m	male	ID	identification
y	young	L-A	Look-Alike
w	winter-autumn	adw	adult in winter
s	spring-summer	ads	adult in summer

f/y/wm female, young, winter male (which often wear the same plumage).

If no letters indicate sex or season, description applies to both adults all year.

cont continent (range covers most of North America).

cont-ex range covers most of continent except part indicated by following letters: *N* for North, *Ar* for Arctic, *Fla* Florida.

'' inches ' feet

See# (plus number) refers reader to the species described under that number (each number is used for one species only).

X (following a number) refers reader to an extra species, not a Look-Alike, described following the information on the species listed under that number.

L-A (following a number) refers to one or more of the species listed as Look-Alikes under that number.

TO READ THE MAPS

Solid black marks area in which species may be seen for all or part of the year.

vvv marks area in which species may come as migrant or irregular wanderer or in expanding range.

Small—Browns S br

Small—Grays S gy

Small—Blues S bl

Small—Greens S gr

Small—Yellows S yl

Small—Reds S rd

Small—Black-and-White or Black S b/w

Medium—Browns M br

Medium—Grays M gy

Medium—Blues M bl

Medium—Greens M gr

Medium—Yellows M yl

Medium—Orange and Black M o/b

Medium—Reds M rd

Medium—Black-and-White or Black M b/w

Large—Browns L br

Large—Grays L gy

Large—Blues L bl

Large—Green-Black, Black L g/b

Very Large—Browns VL br

Very Large—Grays VL gy

Very Large—Blues VL bl

Very Large—Greens VL gr

Very Large—Red to Pink VL r/p

Very Large—Black-and-White VL b/w

Very Large—Black VL bk

Very Large—White VL wh

S br
S gy
S bl
S gr
S yl
S rd
S b/w
M br
M gy
M bl
M gr
M yl
M o/b
M rd
M b/w
L br
L gy
L bl
L g/b
VL br
VL gy
VL bl
VL gr
VL r/p
VL b/w
VL bk
VL wh

Size: SMALL — Color: BROWNS

To tell one small brown bird from another, the first clue is the color of the cap. The cap may be a flat patch — with or without a visor-like patch of contrasting color and with or without border lines of contrasting color. Or it may be an upright crest or two tufts of feathers like horns. In this Key the cap colors in sequence are: plain browns, streaked or striped browns (with buff, gray or white), gray, orange, red or rusty (or rusty and white), black-and-white striped (and black-white-yellow) and all black.

Find the cap color on the Key that matches the cap color of the bird you want to identify. Then for a second clue, match the description of the breast, whether plain or patterned. When you find the right cap-breast combination, check each numbered species and its look-alikes by the clues given, then by the picture and range map on the page and with the color picture on the first plate. Only numbered species are pictured (not the look-alikes) and the same number identifies the matching map, black-and-white picture and color picture.

CAP: PLAIN BROWN — BREAST: PLAIN

#1. house sparrow (f/y)

CAP buffy border line over eye. BILL thick, short. FRONT buffy gray. BACK streaked in darker browns. ACTIONS ground feeder on seeds, insects. NOTES chattery twitter. HABITAT streets, fields, yards. (*See* Measure Bird #1 and male #16.)

CLOSE LOOK-ALIKE **Eurasian tree sparrow (f/y)** introduced only in St. Louis area. GENERAL LOOK-ALIKES **indigo bunting (f/y)** rump and tail faintly blue, breast lightly streaked (male #44). Range East. **lazuli bunting (f/y)** rump and tail faintly blue, breast lightly washed in buff, 2 white wing bars (male #43). Range West. **brown-capped rosy finch** rump and wings faintly rosy (#25 L-A). Range central Rockies. **Arctic warbler** thin bill, slender body. Range Alaska. **snow-bunting (f/wm)** front, outer tail feathers white. Range North.

#2. Bewick's wren

CAP distinct white border line over eye. BILL thin, medium. FRONT clear white. BACK plain, wings faintly barred, outer tail feathers edged in brown-and-white checks. ACTIONS ground and brush feeder on insects. NOTES rolling trill and warble (similar to song sparrow). HABITAT brush, yards, woods edge.

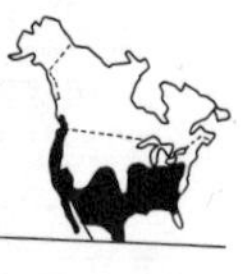

CLOSE LOOK-ALIKE **Carolina wren** throat white, lower breast and underparts darken to cinnamon, tail edges not checked. Notes, triplets in series as if saying "teakettle, teakettle, teakettle". Range East. GENERAL LOOK-ALIKES all 9 species of North American wrens are thin-billed, brown-backed, usually carry tail erect. All are Small except Medium **cactus wren** (#75 L-A). For wrens with patterned breasts, *see* #3, 4, 5. Other plain breasted look-alikes are **canyon wren** cap steaked brown, white border line, underparts streaked cinnamon, tail edges not checked. Range West. **marsh wren (long-billed marsh wren)** cap dark brown, white border line, sides washed in cinnamon, upper back streaked in white, tail edges not checked. Range cont-exN. **sedge wren (short-billed marsh wren)** cap streaked brown and buff, no definite border line, bib cinnamon, tail edges not checked. Range East. **blue throat (f/y)** cap brown, white border line, throat white with black bib line, rusty patch under tail (male #6 L-A). Range, summers in Alaska, may stray south.

CAP: PLAIN BROWN — BREAST: PATTERNED

#3. house wren

CAP very faint buffy border line. BILL thin, medium. FRONT buffy, barred in brown. BACK faintly barred in brown, tail often erect. ACTIONS ground and brush feeder on insects. NOTES rolling, bubbling trill; often scolds. HABITAT underbrush, yards, woods edge.

CLOSE LOOK-ALIKE #4. GENERAL LOOK-ALIKE #2 and L-As.

#4. winter wren

CAP faint buffy border line. BILL thin, medium. FRONT buffy, barred in brown; underparts darker. BACK barred; tail very short, often erect. ACTIONS ground and brush feeder on insects. NOTES rapid trill, often scolds. HABITAT underbrush, yards, woods edge.

CLOSE LOOK-ALIKE #3. GENERAL LOOK-ALIKE #2. Also **rock wren** cap streaked, definite white border line, breast streaked, underpart cinnamon, back streaked and barred, tail feathers have light buffy tips. Range West. **wrentit** faint buffy border line, yellow iris, dark streaked breast, very long tail. Range Pacific coast.

#5. bank swallow

CAP blends, no border line. BILL very short. FRONT white, *brown bib.* BACK plain brown. ACTIONS sky-skimming insect eater; nests in cavity in stream bank or walls of gravel pit. NOTES low buzzy twitter. HABITAT near streams, gravel pits.

CLOSE LOOK-ALIKES **northern rough-winged swallow** no bib, sides of throat buffy. Range cont-exN. **tree swallow (y)** no bib, clear white front, brown of back has greenish tinge (adult #49). Range cont.

#6. northern waterthrush

CAP distinct white or pale buff border line. BILL thin, medium. FRONT entire front streaked in broken lines on white or pale yellow background. BACK plain brown. ACTIONS walks (not hops) bobs and teeters (in spite of name, related to warblers, not thrushes). NOTES lively twitter. HABITAT near woods and water.

CLOSE LOOK-ALIKE **Louisiana waterthrush** throat white, breast and underparts streaked. Range East. GENERAL LOOK-ALIKE **bluethroat (m)** throat and breast blue, central breast patch rusty, bib line black-white-rusty, underparts white, under-tail patch rusty (female #2 L-A). Range, Alaska summer nester, may stray South.

S br | S gy | S bl | S gr | S yl | S rd | S b/w | M br | M gy | M bl | M gr | M yl | M o/b | M rd | M b/w | L br | L gy | L bl | L g/b | VL br | VL gy | VL bl | VL gr | VL r/p | VL b/w | VL bk | VL wh

#7. rufous hummingbird (m)

CAP cinnamon, green visor. BILL long, needle-like. FRONT fiery red throat ruff, white breast and underparts washed in cinnamon (ruff turns dark in poor light, *see* Largest and Smallest Bird). BACK cinnamon, tail dark tipped. ACTIONS darting, hovering, forward-or-backward flight; takes nectar and pollen from flowers, insects from flowers or in midair. NOTES squeaks, tick-tick-chips, humming sound from air moving through feathers. HABITAT wherever there are flowers.

CLOSE LOOK-ALIKE **Allen's hummingbird (m)** cap green, back green, nape and rump cinnamon. Range West Coast. GENERAL LOOK-ALIKES all hummingbirds are alike in actions. (*See* Key for Small and Green, female #53 L-A).

CAP: STREAKED OR STRIPED—BREAST: PLAIN

#8. grasshopper sparrow

CAP pale center stripe, dark border line, pale over eye. BILL thick, short. FRONT buffy. BACK streaked dark and buffy; tail very *short, pointed.* ACTIONS ground feeder on seeds, insects; weak flier. NOTES machine-like, insect-like monotone; throws head back while singing. HABITAT hay and grain fields, country roadsides.

CLOSE LOOK-ALIKES other buffy sparrows with streaked cap and short tail have *streaked* breast, not plain (#11, 12). GENERAL LOOK-ALIKES species with streaked or striped caps and plain breasts have *grayer* plumage and *longer* tails (notched or rounded, not pointed) as **chipping sparrow (y)** white cap border line, gray rump, tail notched (adult #18). **clay-colored sparrow** white cap border line, light center stripe, dark cheek patch, dark whisker line, tail notched. Range central U.S./Can. (spreading). **Brewer's sparrow** cap fine-streaked, no center stripe, tail notched. Habitat sagebrush, desert. Range West. **Bachman's sparrow** back bluish, wing shoulder yellow, tail rounded. Range East. Rare. **Cassin's sparrow** cap fine-streaked, white border line, tail rounded. Range south-central U.S. **golden-crowned sparrow (y)** dark cap border line, center may or may not show yellow, tail notched, over-all size close to Medium (adult #23 L-A). **white-crowned sparrow (y)** cap brown and buff stripes (not streaks), paler border stripe, bill pinkish, tail rounded (adult #23). **white-throated sparrow (y)** cap brown and buff stripes, paler border stripe, bill grayish, throat very white, tail notched (adult #24). (Some adults may have buffy/black striping.) **worm-eating warbler** bill *thin,* cap definite stripes of dark and buff, tail rounded. Tree-feeding insect eater. Range East.

#9. brown creeper

CAP streaked brown and white. BILL thin, slightly down-curved. FRONT white. BACK streaked brown and white, tail pointed. ACTIONS hunts insects on tree *trunk,* usually starting low and working up; uses tail as prop. NOTES high, thin note, single or series. HABITAT woods, yards with trees.

GENERAL LOOK-ALIKES **Bewick's wren** (#2). **snow bunting (f/wm)** paler browns, more white on wings, tail, thick bill. Range North.

#10. song sparrow

CAP grayish border line over eye, dark line through eye. BILL thick, short. FRONT throat white; breast, underparts streaked broken lines, with *central cluster* of spots on breast. BACK streaked browns; tail *long, rounded tip.* ACTIONS ground and bush feeder on seeds, insects. NOTES 3 (sometimes 2) clear melodious notes and trill; often sings all year. HABITAT brush, roadsides, woods-edge, yards.

CLOSE LOOK-ALIKES #11, 12, 13, 76 **(fox sparrow). Lincoln sparrow** fine streaking on upper breast over *buffy wash,* no central cluster. GENERAL LOOK-ALIKES **house finch (f/y)** bill thicker, body chunkier, paler over-all, front fine-streaked throat to underparts (no central cluster), tail notched (male #22). **purple finch (f/y)** bill thicker, body chunkier, fine-streaked breasts and sides, tail notched (male #21). **Cassin's finch (f/y)** bill thicker, body chunkier, very fine streaked front, paler over-all, tail notched (male #21 L-A). **lark sparrow (y)** fine streaking on upper breast over buffy wash, outer tail feathers *white,* rounded (adult #13 L-A). **lark bunting (f/wm/y)** fine streaked breast and sides, white patches on wings, tail edges white, rounded.

#11. Savannah sparrow

CAP faintly striped brown and buff, usually *yellow border line* over eye, light central stripe. BILL thick, short. FRONT streaked broken lines, especially breast and sides; dark triangular cheek patch. BACK streaked browns; tail *short, notched.* ACTIONS ground feeder on seeds, insects; sometimes walks. NOTES musical chips and trills (similar to song sparrow). HABITAT fields, open country, large yards.

CLOSE LOOK-ALIKES #10 and L-A, also #8 and other *short*-tailed buffy sparrows. **Baird's sparrow** center cap stripe *orange-buff,* streaked upper breast. Range midwest plains. **Henslow's sparrow** cap olive-brown and buff, buff border stripe, dark line through eye. Range East. Not common. **LeConte's sparrow** center cap stripe *white* bordered by brown and yellow stripes, upper back purplish, tail short, pointed. Habitat marsh. Range East. **sharp-tailed sparrow** cap plain dark brown with buffy border line, gray cheek patch surrounded by orange-buff, tail short and pointed. Habitat marsh. Range East, Midwest. **seaside sparrow** cap dark gray blending to brown, yellow spot between bill and eye. Range Atlantic and Gulf coasts. **red crossbill (f)** *bill tips twisted,* body all-over streaking with underwash of yellow, rump yellow (male #68). Range North.

#12. pine siskin

CAP finely streaked brown and buff. BILL thin, short. FRONT finely streaked brown and buff. BACK finely streaked brown and buff, *yellow patches* on wings and upper tail; tail short, deeply notched. ACTIONS often in flocks; feeds on seeds of conifers, alder, weeds, etc. and on insects. NOTES lispy twitter. HABITAT woods, fields, yards.

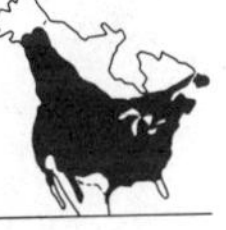

GENERAL LOOK-ALIKES **house** and **purple finches** are larger, chunkier, have thick bill (#21, 22).

#13. vesper sparrow

CAP streaked, buffy border line over eye. BILL thick, short. FRONT throat, breast and sides streaked; dark cheek patch; narrow white eye ring. BACK streaked buff and brown; *outer tail feathers white;* rusty patch on wing shoulder. ACTIONS ground and brush feeder on seeds, insects. NOTES 2 drawled notes and trill. HABITAT fields and roadsides.

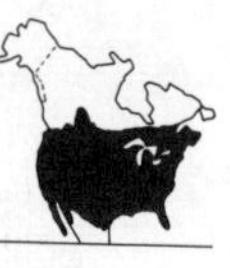

CLOSE LOOK-ALIKES #10, 11, 12 (lack outer white tail feathers). Those with white tail feathers **dark-eyed (Oregon) junco (y)** more heavily streaked, darker, bill lighter (adult #40). Range West. **lark bunting (f/wm)** white (not rusty) wing patches (male #70). Range central. **lark sparrow (y)** tail *rounded,* white all across tip (adult #20). **black-throated sparrow (y)** slaty eye mask. Range West. **sage sparrow (y)** streaked buffy underparts. Range West. **longspurs (f/wm/y)** all four species **(McCown's, Chestnut-collared, Lapland, Smith's)** have long, spurred hind toe, *big feet* and *walk* (#25).

#14. least sandpiper

CAP streaked rusty brown. BILL thin, medium long (short for a sandpiper). FRONT throat white, upper breast streaked over rust wash;, *legs yellowish or yellowish-green.* BACK streaked rusty brown, some feathers white-edged. ACTIONS probes sandy shore or mudflats for food. NOTES thin, two-note cry. HABITAT shores, marshes, mudflats.

CLOSE LOOK-ALIKES two other small sandpipers very similar, but neither has yellowish legs. **western sandpiper** black legs. Range cont. **semipalmated sandpiper** faint wash on upper breast instead of streaks, *black legs.* Range cont-exW. (*See* #78 for similar Medium species).

#15. elf owl

CAP streaked brown, head round, no ear tufts. Bill hooked. FRONT eyes *yellow,* both front-faced; line over eye white; throat, breast and underparts white mottled in buff. BACK mottled brown and buff, some white tips, *tail short.* ACTIONS usually nocturnal; nests (and often sleeps by day) in hole in giant cactus. NOTES rapid squeaky or guttural yelps, whistles. HABITAT southwest deserts, nearby brushy canyons.

CLOSE LOOK-ALIKES (*See* #81 for similar Mediums) **northern pygmy-owl (pygmy owl)** slightly larger, more rusty colored, breast streaked in dark broken lines, *tail long.* Range West (mountains, coast). **flammulated owl** slightly larger, *eyes dark,* grayer overall, small ear tufts. Range West. **ferruginous pygmy-owl** like northern pygmy-owl but lighter breast streaking. Range West lowlands.

CAP: GRAY — BREAST: PATTERNED

#16. house sparrow (m)

CAP gray bordered in rusty line from eye to nape. BILL thick, short. FRONT black mask through eyes, white cheek patch, throat and bib black (less black on younger males). BACK streaked in dark and rusty browns. ACTIONS ground feeder on seeds, insects. NOTES chattery twitter, quarrelsome bickering. HABITAT streets, fields, yards. (*See* Measure Bird #1 and female #1).

CLOSE LOOK-ALIKE **Eurasian tree sparrow (m)** introduced only in St. Louis area. **dickcissel (f/y)** rusty wing shoulder patch, slight tinge of yellow on face and breast. Range East. **dickcissel (m)** bright yellow under black bib, yellow line over eye, rusty shoulder patch. Range East. GENERAL LOOK-ALIKES **Lapland longspur,** other longspurs, #25.

CAP: ORANGE — BREAST: PATTERNED

#17. ovenbird

CAP black border line over eye. BILL thin, medium short. FRONT *white eye ring,* throat and breast heavily streaked, *legs pinkish.* BACK olive brown, plain. ACTIONS *walks,* ground feeder on insects. NOTES seems to say, "Teacher! Teacher! Teacher!" HABITAT woods.

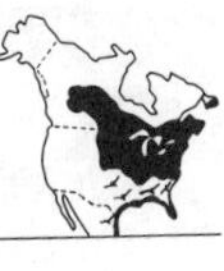

CAP: RED OR RUSTY, RUSTY AND WHITE — BREAST: PLAIN

#18. chipping sparrow

CAP rusty, bordered by *white line, black line* through eye. BILL thick, short. FRONT pale grayish white. BACK streaked, rump gray, tail notched. ACTIONS ground and brush feeder on seeds, insects. NOTES monotonous chips. HABITAT fields, yards.

CLOSE LOOK-ALIKES #19 and L-As. GENERAL LOOK-ALIKE **Swainson's warbler** *thin bill,* eye line buffy (not white), breast buffy (not gray-white). Range East, South to Texas. Not common.

#19. American tree sparrow

CAP rusty, bordered by *gray* line; *rusty* line through eye. BILL thick, short; upper bill dark, lower pale. FRONT pale gray, *one central dark breast spot.* BACK streaked, some white feather edging, tail notched. ACTIONS often in flocks, ground-feeding seed eater. NOTES twitters as it feeds; plaintive trill. HABITAT fields, woods edge, roadsides.

CLOSE LOOK-ALIKES (but no central breast spot) #18. **field sparrow** *white eye ring.* Range East. **swamp sparrow** *black* eye line, *white* throat. Range East (also West in North). **rufous-crowned sparrow** black whisker line on throat, no white feather edging, tail rounded. Range Southwest. GENERAL LOOK-ALIKES (only others with central breast spot, #20 (striped cap), **sage sparrow** (grayish, #27 L-A).

#20. lark sparrow

CAP *striped rusty and white.* BILL thick, short. FRONT throat white, black whisker mark, breast buffy with dark central spot. BACK streaked brown and buff, tail darker, rounded, *white corners.* ACTIONS *walks* or hops; often feeds in flocks on ground. NOTES musical warbling trill (often sings in flight). HABITAT fields, roadsides, parks.

GENERAL LOOK-ALIKES #19, #27 L-A.

#21. purple finch (m)(for female *see* #10 L-A).

CAP purplish red, forms complete hood. BILL thick, short. FRONT cap, cheeks, throat and nape all red; breast fades from red to white. *No striping.* BACK streaked browns, rump matches cap color. ACTIONS ground feeder on seeds, insects; flocks. NOTES bright warble and trill. HABITAT woods edge, yards.

CLOSE LOOK-ALIKES #22. **Cassin's finch** red of cap, throat, rump is rosier, not purplish. Usually in high country. Range West. **common redpoll** smaller, throat is *black,* cheeks brown, nape brown streaked. Range cont-exS. **hoary redpoll** like above except has white rump.

#22. house finch (m)

CAP brown (or reddish brown) with *definite U-shaped visor line* of bright color (usually bright red but may vary from red to pink to yellow to orange). BILL thick, short. FRONT cheeks brown, *throat matches cap and rump, underparts striped* in broken lines. BACK streaked browns, rump matches cap and throat. NOTES bright rolling warble and trill. HABITAT fields, yards, open country.

CLOSE LOOK-ALIKES #21 and L-As, female #10 L-A.

CAP: BLACK-AND-WHITE (OR BLACK-WHITE-YELLOW) — BREAST: PLAIN

#23. white-crowned sparrow

CAP striped, center stripe white. BILL thick, short, *pinkish.* FRONT breast pale gray, throat whitish (*see* #24)). BACK streaked, tail notched. ACTIONS ground feeder on seeds, insects. NOTES plaintive whistling trill; variable, may echo opening notes of "My Faith Looks Up To Thee". HABITAT brushy roadsides, yards.

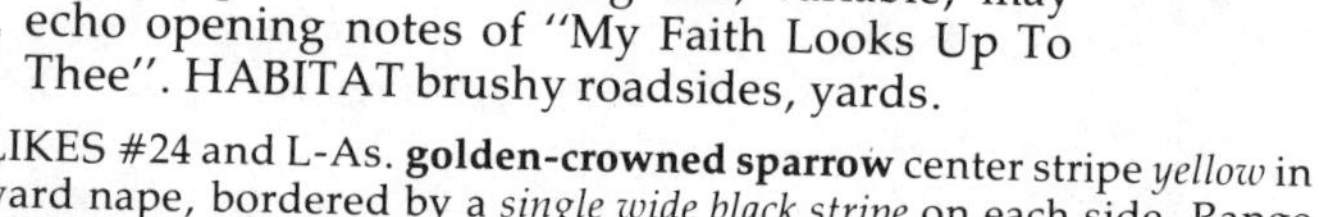

CLOSE LOOK-ALIKES #24 and L-As. **golden-crowned sparrow** center stripe *yellow* in front, whitish toward nape, bordered by a *single wide black stripe* on each side. Range West Coast, Baja to Alaska.

#24. white-throated sparrow

CAP striped, center stripe white. BILL thick, short, *grayish.* FRONT breast pale gray, throat *very white, yellow spot* between eye and bill. BACK streaked, tail notched. ACTIONS ground feeder on seeds, insects. NOTES plaintive trill (two double notes, three triplets). HABITAT brushy roadsides, yards.

CLOSE LOOK-ALIKES #23 and L-A. GENERAL LOOK-ALIKES #25. **chestnut-collared longspur (sm)** *breast black.* **McCown's longspur (sm)** *bib black.* **Smith's longspur (sm)** throat and breast *buff.*

CAP: BLACK — BREAST: PATTERNED

#25. Lapland longspur (sm)

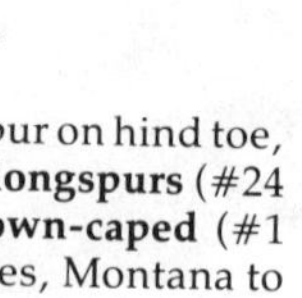

CAP bordered by white line from eye to nape. BILL thick, short. FRONT cheeks, throat, upper breast black; sides streaked. BACK nape rusty, outer tail feathers white. ACTIONS often in flocks; ground feeder on seeds and insects; *walks.* NOTES musical trill. HABITAT fields, prairies.

CLOSE LOOK-ALIKE **Harris's sparrow** nape *gray,* does not have long spur on hind toe, does not walk, no white on tail. **McCown's, Smiths, chestnut-collared longspurs** (#24 L-As). GENERAL LOOK-ALIKE **rosy finch** formerly 3 species — **brown-caped** (#1 L-A) **gray-crowned** (West, north to Alaska) and **black rosy finch** (Rockies, Montana to New Mexico) now considered color phases of one species; all have brownish bodies with wings, rump and sometimes underparts washed in rosy pink; all have dark brown or black visors.

Size: SMALL — Color: GRAYS

To tell one small gray bird from another, the first clue is the color of the cap. The cap may be a flat patch — with or without a visor-like patch of contrasting color and with or without border lines of contrasting color. Or it may be an upright crest or a complete hood. In this Key the cap colors in sequence are: plain brown, gray, green, yellow or yellow-and-orange, red, black.

First find the cap color in the Key that matches the cap color of the bird you want to identify. Then for a second clue, match the description of the breast, whether plain or patterned. When you find the right cap-breast combination, check each numbered species and its look-alikes by the clues listed, then by the picture and range map and by the color picture on the second plate. Only numbered species are pictured (not the look-alikes) and the same number identifies the matching map, black-and-white picture and color picture.

CAP: PLAIN BROWN — BREAST: PLAIN

#26. bay-breasted warbler (m)

CAP reddish brown. BILL think, short. FRONT back eye mask, throat brown to match cap, brown fades to white on breast and sides. BACK streaked gray, nape brown, white corner patches on tail (show usually on underside only). ACTIONS tree feeder on insects. NOTES thin, high monotone. HABITAT forests.

CLOSE LOOK-ALIKE **bay breasted warbler (f/wm)** eye mask is gray (not black), throat white, sides pinkish. GENERAL LOOK-ALIKES (actions differ) **brown-headed nuthatch** (#39 L-A) front white, back bluish-gray, hunts insects on tree trunk. Range East. **pygmy nuthatch** (#39 L-A) cap gray-brown. Range West. **bushtit** (formerly **common bushtit)** front white, tail very long, often in flocks. Most have black eye, some yellow. Subspecies in southwest (**black-eared bushtit**) has black eye mask. Range West. **boreal chickadee** (#38 L-A) cap brown, cheek white, throat black.

CAP: GRAY — BREAST PLAIN

#27. dark-eyed (slate-colored) junco

CAP gray *hood* blends with throat and back. BILL thick, short, *pinkish*. FRONT throat and breast gray, underparts white. BACK gray, *outer white tail feathers*. ACTIONS ground feeder; often in flocks. NOTES sewing-machine monotone. HABITAT fields, roadsides, yards (especially in winter).

CLOSE LOOK-ALIKES **slate-colored** and **Oregon juncos** (#40) were formerly separate species, now rated as color variants of same species, re-named **dark-eyed junco. white-winged junco** 2 white wing bars. Range Rockies and Black Hills. (Now color variant subspecies.) **yellow-eyed junco** front gray, not white, upper back rusty, not gray. Range Southwest forests. GENERAL LOOK-ALIKES **black-chinned sparrow** back and upper wings streaked brown, *throat black,* no white on tail. Range Southwest. **black-throated sparrow** white line over eye and under gray cheek patch, throat black, underparts white. Range Southwest. **sage sparrow** central dark breast spot, broken line streaking down sides, dark cheek patch between white lines. Range West. **Siberian tit (gray-headed chickadee)** cheek white, throat black. Range Alaska/Canadian tundra. **northern wheatear** cap gray, bordered by white line, black mask line through eye, front white, back gray with rump white, tail black center and tip with upper edges white. Range, on East Coast from Canada south as summer visitor; on West Coast Alaska summer visitor, sometimes seen further south. Range expanding both East and West. **black phoebe** (#70 L-A) duplicate of slate-colored junco except that gray is darker (not quite black), bill medium with bristles around base. Typical actions of flycatcher family. Range Southwest, California.

#28. least flycatcher

CAP "big-headed" but not pointed crest. BILL medium, bristles at base. FRONT throat grayish, fading to paler underparts; *white eye ring*. BACK grayish, tail darker, 2 white wing bars. ACTIONS typical actions of family — sits on perch and darts out to catch passing insects. HABITAT brushy places, woods edge, yards.

CLOSE LOOK-ALIKES All 10 members of the genus Empidonax are difficult to tell apart. **Alder** and **willow flycatchers** can be told apart by notes (*see* Scanning for Notes Clues). **Yellow-bellied and Acadian flycatchers** are usually seen only in East. West-only species **dusky, Hammond's, gray, western. buff-breasted.** See *Terres Encyclopedia* or other reference or guide books in bibliography for full descriptions. GENERAL LOOK ALIKES #29, L-As (especially **Hutton's). ruby-crowned kinglet** (#37) does not have "big-headed" look, does not sit upright on branch, may dart out after insects but only a short distance, usually hunts branch to branch. Female lacks distinctive red tuft on cap and male's may not show. Range cont. **blue-gray gnatcatcher** (#42) and **black-tailed gnatcatcher** (#48x) distinguished from Empidonax by slenderer body, very long tail (outer white feathers). Black-tailed range Southwest. Blue-gray East, Southwest. **bushtit** (#26 L-A) long-tailed, gray, not white eye ring.

#29. solitary vireo

CAP white visor line, white eye ring. BILL medium. FRONT throat, breast, underparts white; sides yellow. BACK yellowish gray (Rocky Mt. birds usually lack yellow), 2 white wing bars, rump gray. ACTIONS slower moving than flycatchers. NOTES robin-like. HABITAT woods.

CLOSE LOOK-ALIKES (all vireos alike in slow movements). **gray vireo** no visor line, no wing bars, no yellow. Range Southwest. **Hutton's vireo** smaller by about 1 inch, front dingy. Range West Coast, Mexico. **Bell's vireo** eye ring faint. Range Central, Southwest, California. **white-eyed vireo** visor line and eye ring yellow (not white). Range East. **warbling vireo** eye ring faint, eye line faint, no wing bars. Range cont-exN/Fla.

#30. red-eyed vireo

CAP definite border of thin black line, wider white line, thin black line through eye. BILL medium. FRONT white. BACK olive gray, no wing bars. ACTIONS slower moving than flycatchers. NOTES monotonous series of up-down phrases. HABITAT woods, thickets, yards.

CLOSE LOOK-ALIKES (all vireos alike in slow movements) **black-whiskered vireo** cap similar, black whisker-line on throat. Range Florida coasts.

#31. tufted titmouse

CAP erect *pointed crest*. BILL medium. FRONT cheek patch and throat white, breast whitish, sides of underparts rusty-buff. BACK plain gray. ACTIONS active, acrobatic as searches for insects; often in flocks. HABITAT woods, parks, yards.

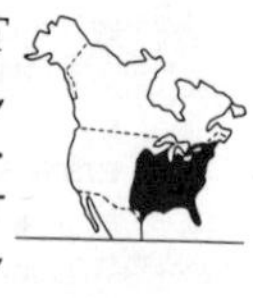

CLOSE LOOK-ALIKES (all with crests) **plain titmouse** pale buffy sides (not rusty). Range Southwest, California to Oregon. **black-crested titmouse** similar except *black* crest. Range Texas-Mexican border (now a subspecies). **bridled titmouse** crest gray in center bordered by triangular black line, white and black lines border triangular white cheek patch, black patch under bill. Range Southwest border. **waxwings** #74 crested, but brown, Medium size.

CAP: GRAY — BREAST: PATTERNED (DARK GRAY)

#32. chimney swift

CAP dark gray. BILL *very short.* FRONT throat paler gray. BACK dark ray; *tail very short,* bristled square tip. ACTIONS sky-skimming flight; clings to vertical surfaces. NOTES rapid ticking chips. HABITAT nests in chimneys, hollow trees, rocky ledges.

CLOSE LOOK-ALIKES All swifts are alike in having wings sweep back from shoulder in *crescent-shape* curve. (Swallow wings angle back in straight line.) **Vaux's swift** throat white, underparts pale. Range West of Rockies. **white-throated swift** (#122X) throat very white, eye line white, *sides patterned* in black and white patches, *tail notched* (6½–7 inches, Medium size). Range West. **black swift** (#122X) all-over dark slate gray that looks black. White visor line visible at close range. *Tail notched* (7–7½ inches, Medium size). Range West.

CAP: GRAY — BREAST: PATTERNED (YELLOW-BLACK TRIM)

#33. magnolia warbler (m)

CAP bordered by white line over eye. BILL thin, medium short. FRONT throat yellow, white half-circle under eye, black eye mask, breast and underparts yellow heavily streaked in black. BACK mottled gray-black, *rump yellow,* wide white patch on wings and on each side of tail (midway, not tip). ACTIONS tree feeder on insects. NOTES softly whistled trill. HABITAT marshy forests, thickets.

CLOSE LOOK-ALIKES **Canada warbler** eye line and full eye ring yellow, no white wing patch, bib of black streaks, *rump gray.* Range East. **Kirtland's warbler** no eye line, full white eye ring, *rump gray,* wing bars *narrow.* Range nests only in jack-pine forests of north-central Michigan (so far as known), winters in Caribbean. Seldom seen in migration. Rare. **yellow-throated warbler** throat and breast yellow but underparts *white,* sides heavily streaked in black, back and rump plain gray, white patch between mask and nape. Range East. **Grace's warbler** throat and breast yellow but underparts white, rump gray, no white on tail, wing bars narrow. Range Southwest. **yellow-rumped warbler** (#36) very similar in over-all pattern, but *cap is yellow, breast black.* **Blackburnian warbler** (#36x) very similar in over-all pattern but cap and throat are *orange* (female #33 L-A).

CAP: GRAY — BREAST: PATTERNED (YELLOW)

#34. Philadelphia vireo

CAP bordered by buffy-white line above eye, black line through eye. BILL medium. FRONT yellow wash throat-to-underparts may be bright or pale; no trim marks. BACK greenish gray; no white on wings, back or tail. ACTIONS slow moving (*see* #29, 30). NOTES monotonous up-down phrases. HABITAT woods edge, thickets.

CLOSE LOOK-ALIKES #29, 30 and L-As. **magnolia warbler (f)** rump yellow (not gray) (male #33). **black-throated blue warbler (f)** yellow front dingier, squarish white wing patch (male #47). (Almost any yellow-breasted warbler in first winter may lack breast trim. Look for faint traces of adult trim.) **American redstart (f/y)** breast white, yellow only at sides, yellow patches also on wings and tail. **Pine siskin** (#12) with similar yellow patches has heavily streaked breast.

CAP: GRAY STREAKED — BREAST: PATTERNED (STREAKED)

blackpoll warbler (f/y) upper breast and sides finely streaked, white "thumbprints" on underside of tail, 2 white wing bars, back finely streaked, front white or buffy. No yellow. Range cont-exSW.

S br | S gy | S bl | S gr | S yl | S rd | S b/w | M br | M gy | M bl | M gr | M yl | M o/b | M rd | M b/w | L br | L gy | L bl | L g/b | VL br | VL gy | VL bl | VL gr | VL r/p | VL b/w | VL bk | VL wh

S br

S gy

S bl

S gr

S yl

S rd

S b/w

M br

M gy

M bl

M gr

M yl

M o/b

M rd

M b/w

L br

L gy

L bl

L g/b

VL br

VL gy

VL bl

VL gr

VL r/p

VL b/w

VL bk

VL wh

yellow-rumped warbler (y) similar to **blackpoll (f/y)** but rump pale yellow, sides faintly yellow, eye ring faint. White thumbprints on underside tail (adult #36).

Cape May warbler (f/y) no eye ring, throat finely streaked, no thumbprints. Range East, Canadian midwest.

red crossbill (f) male #68.

CAP: YELLOW — BREAST: PLAIN

#35. golden-crowned kinglet (m)

CAP center stripe orange (male only) bordered for both male and female by black line and white line over eye, thinner black line through eye. BILL thin, short. FRONT throat, breast white; sides faintly grayish. BACK plain greenish gray, 2 white wing bars; tail short, notched; some white edging on wings. ACTIONS flits among branches hunting insects. NOTES chattery twitter. HABITAT woods (especially conifers) parks, yards.

GENERAL LOOK-ALIKES (#37). **verdin** cap, cheeks and throat yellow, line through eye thin and black, lower breast and underparts white, rusty patch on wing shoulder. Range Southwest. **Brewster's warbler** cap bordered by thin white line, black line through eye. Throat, breast and underparts white except for yellow bib, not always present. Range East. (Hybrid between **blue-winged—golden-winged,** as is **Lawrence's warbler** (#61 L-A).

CAP: YELLOW — BREAST: PATTERNED (YELLOW)

yellow-throated vireo cap greenish-yellow; eye line, eye ring, throat and breast all bright yellow; upper back greenish-gray, rump gray, tail and wing feathers edged in white, 2 white wing bars. Range East.

white-eyed vireo eye ring and visor line yellow, iris white, throat to underparts white but sides yellow, wing and tail feathers edged in yellow. Range East.

Brewster's warbler #35 L-A.

CAP: YELLOW — BREAST: PATTERNED (BLACK)

#36. yellow-rumped warbler (m) [myrtle warbler (East) now combined with **Audubon's warbler** (West.)]

CAP yellow patch encircled in gray. BILL thin, medium short. FRONT throat white (**myrtle**) throat yellow (**Audubon's**), breast for both black, yellow patch at shoulder, white eye ring, underparts white, black streaks at side. BACK black-streaked, rump yellow, tail black with white patches. White wing patch narrow (**myrtle**) wide (**Audubon's**). ACTIONS tree and bush feeder on insects, winter berries. NOTES warbling trill. HABITAT woods, thickets, yards.

CLOSE LOOK-ALIKES #33 and L-As. GENERAL LOOK-ALIKES **golden-winged warbler** eye mask and bib black, white between cap and mask and mask and bib, wing patch yellow. Range East. **hermit warbler** cap *and cheeks* bright yellow, throat *black,* breast and underparts white, black streaking at sides. Female has throat speckled, not solid, black. Range West Coast.

CAP: YELLOW — BREAST: PATTERNED (RUSTY STREAKS)

chestnut-sided warbler cap and nape yellow, narrow black eye mask, black line dividing white cheek and white throat, breast and underparts white, wide rusty stripe at sides. Range East, Midwest.

CAP: ORANGE — BREAST: PATTERNED (ORANGE)

Blackburnian warbler (#33, 36 L-As).
olive warbler (#62 L-A).

CAP: RED OR RUSTY — BREAST: PLAIN

#37. ruby-crowned kinglet (m)

CAP red tuft may be raised or hidden in gray feathers. BILL thin, short. FRONT white eye ring incomplete at top; throat to underparts white or pale grayish. Underparts yellowish in some individuals. BACK grayish, 2 white wing bars, tail short, notched. ACTIONS flits among branches hunting insects. NOTES rippling trill. HABITAT woods, thickets, brushy yards.

CLOSE LOOK-ALIKES #29 and L-As (especially **Hutton's vireo**) and #34 (similar in size and actions, but caps distinctive). **Virginia's warbler** cap rusty-red surrounded by gray, eye ring complete, throat white, breast, rump and under-tail *bright* yellow, no wing bars. Range Southwest. **Lucy's warbler** similar to Virginia's, but front all white, rump rusty-red. Range Southwest. GENERAL LOOK-ALIKE **red-faced warbler** bright red on visor, throat and upper breast always visible, remainder of cap and cheek black, rump white. Range Arizona to Texas on Mexican border.

CAP: BLACK — BREAST: PLAIN

#38. black-capped chickadee

CAP and nape black, cheek patch white. BILL thin, short. FRONT throat black (triangular) breast and underparts grayish-white, sides rusty-buff. BACK wing and tail feathers edged in white. ACTIONS lively flitting tree to tree. NOTES chick-a-dee, dee-dee; whistled plaintive 2-note call in spring courtship: "see-me". HABITAT woods, thickets, yards.

CLOSE LOOK-ALIKES (all have triangular black throat). **Carolina chickadee** sides pale buff, not rusty, no white on wing, throat patch slightly smaller. Range East, south to prairies. **mountain chickadee** black line through eye divides cheek patch, similar to black-throated gray warbler (#38 L-A), sides gray. Range West. **boreal chickadee** cap and back gray-brown, sides rusty-buff. Range Canada to Alaska. **chestnut-backed chickadee** upper back and sides of breast rusty-brown, only chickadee with rusty back,. Range West Coast, California to Alaska. **Siberian tit (gray-headed chickadee)** cap grayish, not black. Range Western Canada and Alaska. GENERAL LOOK-ALIKES #39, 40, 41. **black-tailed gnatcatcher** longer tail, slenderer body, throat white. Range Southwest. **blackpoll warbler** throat white, sides streaked in broken black lines. Range cont-exSW. **black-crested** and **bridled titmice** both have pointed caps. Range Southwest. **black-capped vireo** front white, back greenish-yellowish-gray. Range central, south Texas. **black-throated gray warbler** black cap bordered by white line, *yellow spot* between eye and bill, black eye mask bordered by white chin line, black throat (male only; f/y white), lower breast and underparts white with black broken lines at sides. Range West Coast, British Columbia to Baja.

S br
S gy
S bl
S gr
S yl
S rd
S b/w
M br
M gy
M bl
M gr
M yl
M o/b
M rd
M b/w
L br
L gy
L bl
L g/b
VL br
VL gy
VL bl
VL gr
VL r/p
VL b/w
VL bk
VL wh

#39. white-breasted nuthatch

CAP black extends to nape and upper back, border white. BILL thin, medium long. FRONT all white from cap edge on down. BACK bluish gray, wing and tail feathers edged in white, tail corners white. ACTIONS creeps over tree trunk for insect food, often *head-down*, starting high and working down and around. NOTES "yenk-yenk" or "yank-yank" or churring notes. HABITAT woods, yards with trees, parks.

CLOSE LOOK-ALIKES #38 L-As, #40, 41. **red-breasted nuthatch** (#41) smaller by about 1 inch, white of cheek broken by *black line through eye,* breast rusty-red. Range cont-exSW/Fla. **brown-headed nuthatch** smaller by about 1 inch, similar except cap is brown. Range East Coast and Gulf Coast. **pygmy nuthatch** smaller by about 1 inch, similar except cap is grayish. Range West.

#40. dark-eyed (Oregon) junco

CAP forms complete hood (female hood dark gray). BILL thick, short, *pinkish*. FRONT breast below hood white, sides buffy-rust. BACK upper back rusty, lower back gray, outer tail feathers white. ACTIONS ground feeder, often in flocks. NOTES monotonous trill, twitters. HABITAT woods, roadsides, parks, yards.

CLOSE LOOK-ALIKE #27 and L-As, especially **black-chinned sparrow, black-throated sparrow, sage sparrow** — all westerners. GENERAL LOOK-ALIKES **Lawrence's goldfinch** black cap and throat, gray nape and back, *yellow rump and breast* and wing edges. Range Southwest to California. **white-collared seedeater** *collar and throat white,* bib black, underparts buffy, bill grayish and very stubby. Range Texas along Mexican border.

CAP: BLACK — BREAST: PATTERNED (RUSTY-RED)

#41. red-breasted nuthatch

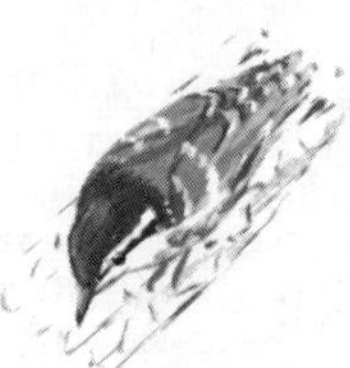

CAP bordered by white line, black line through eye. BILL thin, medium long. FRONT cheek and throat white; breast and underparts pinkish to rusty-red. BACK bluish-gray, tail corners white. ACTIONS creeps over tree trunk hunting insects, often going *headfirst* down and around. NOTES thin, nasal "enk-enk". HABITAT woods, especially conifers, parks, yards.

CLOSE LOOK-ALIKES #38, 39, 40.

Size: SMALL — Color: BLUES

The birds rightfully known as "bluebirds" are all of Medium size, but species both smaller and larger are also feathered in blue. To tell one small blue-feathered bird from another, the first clue is the color of the cap. As it happens, the caps come in only two colors: blue or black.

The second clue is to match the breast coloring: plain (white or pale gray or buff) or patterned (marked or colored). For most small birds in blue, the breast pattern is a wash of color or the accent of black lines or patches.

Throat color makes a third clue. Throats may be blue, yellow, rusty, black, white.

When you find the right combination of colors for cap, breast and throat to match the bird you want to identify, check each numbered species and its look-alikes under that heading until you find the perfect match. Check the black-and-white picture, range map and color picture for final proof.

CAP: BLUE — BREAST: PLAIN

#42. blue-gray gnatcatcher

CAP blue blends with cheek and nape. BILL thin, medium long. FRONT white eye ring. BACK wing feathers edged in white, outer white tail feathers, tail long. Underside of tail is white with central black stripe. ACTIONS flits to catch insects, flicks tail. NOTES whiny, wheezy whistles. HABITAT woods, thickets.

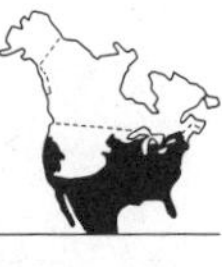

CLOSE LOOK-ALIKES #28 and L-As, #46. **black-tailed gnatcatcher (f/wm)** underside of tail is black with white borders.

CAP: BLUE — BREAST: PATTERNED (CINNAMON)

#43. lazuli bunting (m)

CAP blue hood (cap, nape, throat). BILL thick, short. FRONT throat blue, breast cinnamon, underparts white. BACK blue, black and white edging on wings; rump blue, tail darker, notched. ACTIONS ground and brush feeding seed eater. NOTES two-note whistled series. HABITAT brushy slopes, streambanks, thickets.

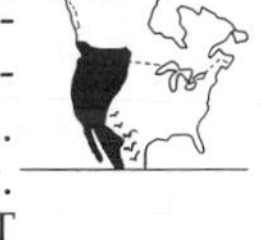

GENERAL LOOK-ALIKES female and young (#1 L-A).**western** and **eastern bluebirds** (#96) are Medium, darker blue.

CAP: BLUE — BREAST: PATTERNED (BLUE)

#44. indigo bunting (m)

CAP blends with cheek, nape. BILL thick, short. FRONT all blue. BACK wing and tail feathers dark edged. ACTIONS ground, brush and tree feeder on seeds, insects, berries. NOTES two-note whistled series, as "see-see, here-here". HABITAT woods edge, thickets, roadsides.

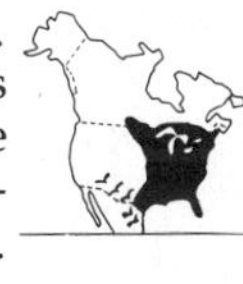

GENERAL LOOK-ALIKES female (#1 L-A). **blue grosbeak** is Medium (#94) brown wing bars. **mountain bluebird** is Medium (#95) white underparts. **eastern** and **western bluebirds** (#96) have rusty breasts.

CAP: BLUE — BREAST: PATTERNED (YELLOW)

#45. northern parula (m) (*warbler* not part of name)

CAP blends with cheek and nape. BILL thin, medium short. FRONT throat and breast yellow, bib line black and rusty, white eye ring, underparts white (female lacks bib). BACK upper back dull yellowish, rump blue, 2 white wing bars, white and black edging on wings and tail. ACTIONS feeds in tree-tops on insects. NOTES sewing-machine trill with final *chip!* HABITAT woods, roadsides, parks, yards with trees.

CLOSE LOOK-ALIKE **tropical parula** black eye mask, no eye ring, no bib mark. Range Texas-Mexican border.

CAP: BLUE — BREAST: PATTERNED (BLACK)

#46. cerulean warbler (m)

CAP blends with cheeks and nape. BILL thin, medium short. FRONT *throat white, bib line black*, breast and underparts white, broken-line streaking at sides. BACK streaked in black, 2 white wing bars. ACTIONS tree-top feeder on insects. NOTES sewing-machine trill. HABITAT woods, roadsides, parks.

CLOSE LOOK-ALIKE female and young lack bib mark.

#47. black-throated blue warbler (m)

CAP blends with nape, visor line black. BILL thin, medium short. FRONT visor, cheeks, throat, upper breast and breast sides black; lower breast, underparts white. BACK blue, black edging on wings, tail; white patch on wing. Female and young brown-backed (#34 L-A). ACTIONS tree-top or brush feeder on insects, seeds, fruit. NOTES sewing-machine trill. HABITAT woods, roadsides, parks, thickets.

CAP: DARK BLUE — BREAST: PLAIN

#48. cliff swallow

CAP may look black or green in certain light; visor patch buffy. BILL very short. FRONT throat and cheeks rusty-brown, bib rusty-black, breast below bib fades to buffy-white underparts. BACK blue-black streaked in white on upper back, rump rusty, tail blue-black with squarish tip. ACTIONS sky-skimmer for insects; builds canteen-shaped nest of mud on cliffs, buildings; nests in colony. NOTES squeaks, churrs. HABITAT open country, canyons, riversides, farms.

CLOSE LOOK-ALIKES **barn swallow** #92. **purple martin** #93. **cave swallow** visor is rusty (not buffy), throat and cheeks buffy (not rusty). Range New Mexico, Texas on Mexican border, spring and summer.

CAP: BLACK — BREAST: PLAIN

black-tailed gnatcatcher (#28 L-A) is also black-capped, told from nuthatches by slender body, long tail.

white-breasted nuthatch (#39) may appear blue or gray.

CAP: BLACK — BREAST: PATTERNED (RUSTY)

red-breasted nuthatch (#41) may appear blue or gray.

Size: SMALL — Color: GREENS

Small green birds come in three shades: bottle green for two swallows, iridescent emerald green for hummingbirds and olive-green — often quite yellowish — for several warblers, finches and buntings, some of which have bright yellow breasts. Since the yellow is much brighter than the olive-green, watchers may count them as yellow and so they will be listed in both Keys.

Swallow caps are bottle green to match the back and both have plain white breasts. Hummingbird caps are purple, green or red. Instead of breast color, their second clue will be *throat* color: white, buffy, gray, blue, purple, green, red, dark dots. Small yellow-green birds have caps of gray, blue, yellow, yellow-green, orange, red, black. Breasts are plain or patterned in yellow, yellow-green, red, black.

When you find the right combination of colors for cap and breast or throat to match the bird you want to identify, check each species under that heading until you find a perfect match on all points. Check the black-and-white picture, range map and color picture for final proof.

SWALLOWS

CAP: BOTTLE GREEN — BREAST: PLAIN

#49. tree swallow

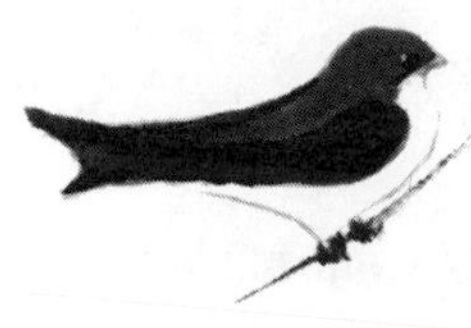

CAP blends with back, *includes eyes*. BILL very short. FRONT very white, throat to underparts. BACK wings and tail brownish, tail notched. ACTIONS sky skimmer for insects; nests in tree cavities or nest box; large flocks in migration, often perches on wires. NOTES musical lispy twitter. HABITAT open country, often near water.

CLOSE LOOK ALIKE **violet-green swallow** cap *does not include eye* (eye area and cheek white, like throat, underparts), two white thumbprints, one on each side of rump, clearly visible in flight. Range West, Mexico to Alaska. GENERAL LOOK-ALIKES #5, 48, 92.

HUMMINGBIRDS

CAP: PURPLE — THROAT: PLAIN (WHITE)

violet-crowned hummingbird (m) upper back green, blending to brownish-green on lower back; wings brown, tail green, throat to underparts very white. Female #53x. Rare. Range Arizona-Mexican border (Guadalupe canyon, etc.).

CAP: PURPLE — THROAT: PURPLE

Costa's hummingbird (m) breast white, sides green, tail *slightly notched,* ruff has *long side feathers*. Only other N.A. hummer with matching cap and throat is larger **Anna's hummingbird** (#54). Range Southwest.

white-eared hummingbird (m) throat purple only in small area under bill, remainder of throat jade green, breast olive-green, curved white line behind eye for "ear" mark, bill bright red. Range Arizona-Mexican border.

CAP: PURPLE — THROAT: GREEN

#50. magnificent hummingbird (m) (Rivoli's)

CAP purple extends just to eye, small white line behind eye. BILL long, dark. FRONT throat-ruff jade green, breast dark green, undertail white, grayish-white. BACK emerald green, tail deeply notched, wings brownish. ACTIONS darts, hovers, feeding on nectar, pollen, insects. NOTES thin chip, tick; humming of wing whir. HABITAT mountain slopes, woods, canyons, gardens. (Individuals extending range and habitat.)

GENERAL LOOK-ALIKES All hummingbirds are alike in actions. **magnificent** is noticeably larger (4½–5 inches) than other hummers with purple caps (3–3½ inches) as described above. Female #53 L-A.

CAP: GREEN — THROAT: BUFFY

Lucifer hummingbird (f) throat and breast buffy, undertail white, bill slightly *down-curved,* tail has rufous, black marks, white tips. Range Texas-Mexican border. Rare.

CAP: GREEN — THROAT: GRAY

blue-throated hummingbird (f) black line through eye, white line over eye, breast pale gray, tail blue, tipped in white. Largest N.A. hummer (5–5¼ inches). Range Southwest. (*See* male below.)

broad-billed hummingbird (f) bill red, black tip (*see* male below).

CAP: GREEN — THROAT: BLUE

blue-throated hummingbird (m) black line through eye, white line over eye, breast greenish-gray, under-tail white, tail blue with white tips on outer feathers. Largest N.A. hummer (5–5¼ inches). Range Southwest. (*See* female above.)

GENERAL LOOK-ALIKE **broad-billed hummingbird (m)** throat *dark* blue blending with dark green of breast, underparts white, small white spot behind eye, bill bright red-orange with dark tip, tail notched, white tipped. Its small size (length 3¼–3½ inches) easily distinguishes this species from the larger **blue-throated hummingbird**. Range Southwest.

CAP: GREEN — THROAT: PURPLE

black-chinned hummingbird (m) upper throat patch small and black, lower throat patch larger and purple, breast white, sides green, undertail white, tail deeply notched or forked. This is the only N.A. hummer with a black throat, but any hummer gorget (especially the red ones) may look black in poor light. (*See* Scanning for Color Clues.) Range West.

Lucifer hummingbird (m) ruff flares with long side feathers, upper breast white, lower breast olive-green (center breast as well as sides). Range Texas-Mexican border. Rare.

CAP: GREEN — THROAT: GREEN

buff-bellied hummingbird (m/f) cap, cheeks, throat and upper breast all green in complete hood; lower breast and underparts buffy, bill bright orange. Range Texas-Mexican border on Gulf Coast.

CAP: GREEN — THROAT: RED

#51. ruby-throated hummingbird (m)

CAP extends to eye, down nape, blends with back. BILL long, dark. FRONT breast white, sides grayish, underparts grayish. BACK tail and wings gray, *tail notched.* ACTIONS darts, hovers, feeding on nectar, pollen, insects; only hummingbird regularly seen in East. NOTES squeaky ticks; humming of wing whir. HABITAT gardens, parks, woods.

CLOSE LOOK-ALIKE **broad-tailed hummingbird (m)** tail feathers even across tip, *not notched,* throat is darker red than **ruby-throated.** Range western mountains. GENERAL LOOK-ALIKES **Calliope** male #52 has *striped* throat. **Anna's** male #54 has red *cap* and throat. **Allen's** male #7 L-A has rusty-cinnamon rump, tail, breast-sides. **Anna's** female #53 L-A. All hummers alike in actions.

#52. Calliope hummingbird (m)

CAP extends to eye, small white spot behind eye. BILL long, dark. FRONT throat ruff *striped* red and white, breast white, sides faintly grayish, underparts white. BACK wings, tail, gray; tail short, square tipped. ACTIONS darts, hovers, feeding on nectar, pollen, insects. NOTES ticks. HABITAT mountains, canyons, woods, yards.

GENERAL LOOK-ALIKES all hummers alike in actions, but **Calliope** is smallest N.A. hummer, only one with *striped* throat. (*See* Largest and Smallest).

CAP: GREEN — THROAT: DOTTED DARK, ON WHITE (females/young)

#53. ruby-throated hummingbird (f)

CAP extends to eye, small white spot behind eye. BILL long, dark. FRONT breast white, sides grayish, throat dotted in dark vertical lines not always easily seen. BACK wings and tail gray, tail black, white tipped. ACTIONS builds and tends nest without help from male; lays 2 white pea-sized eggs; nest is small, cup-shaped, covered in moss, lichens; saddles branch. NOTES squeaky ticks, humming of wing whir. HABITAT gardens, parks, woods.

CLOSE LOOK-ALIKES **ruby-throated** hummer is only hummer seen regularly in East, not seen in West. Other *western* hummers alike in having dotted throat, grayish sides, *no rufous on tail* are **black-chinned (f)** very little buffy-gray on sides. **Costa's (f)** very little buffy-gray on sides. **Anna's (f)** larger (3½–4 inches; others 3–3½) usually has *bright red central throat spot.* **blue-throated (f)** larger (5–5¼ inches) few dots on throat, breast and underparts grayer. **white-eared (f)** dots and sides greenish. **magnificent (f)** most of breast gray, not just sides, larger (4½–5 inches). GENERAL LOOK-ALIKES Other *western* hummers with dotted throat, but sides buffy and *rufous patches* on outer tail feathers above black patches and white tips are **broad-tailed (f)** larger (4–4½ inches). **Calliope (f)** smaller (2¾ inches), slimmer, shorter tailed, *little* rufous on tail. **rufous (f)** breast white, sides cinnamon, often has bright red dots on throat or central spot. **Allen's (f)** cannot be told from female rufous except when seen with male or by smaller size (Allen's 3–3½ inches, rufous 3½–4).

CAP: GREEN — THROAT: WHITE

violet-crowned hummingbird (f) back green, brownish-green; throat and breast and underparts very white (male #49x). Range Arizona-Mexican border (Guadalupe canyon etc.). Rare.

CAP: RED — THROAT: RED

#54. Anna's hummingbird (m)

CAP only N.A. hummer with red cap and red throat. BILL long, dark. FRONT breast white next to throat ruff, then washed in dark gray-green; under-tail white. BACK wings and tail gray; tail notched, *no white*. ACTIONS darts, hovers, feeding on nectar, pollen, insects. NOTES tick-tick; squeaky trill. ACTIONS Only N.A. hummer (male and female) living *year round* north of Mexico and usually remaining in breeding area year round if food available. HABITAT brushy slopes, gardens, canyons.

GENERAL LOOK-ALIKES only other N.A. hummer with matching cap and throat is smaller (3–3½ inch) **Costa's (m)** with cap and throat *purple* (#49X).

WARBLERS, BUNTINGS, FINCHES

CAP: GRAY — BREAST: PLAIN (WHITE)

#55. Tennessee warbler (m)

CAP bordered with white line over eye (female's cap yellow-green). BILL thin, medium short. FRONT throat to underparts white (dingier in winter). BACK greenish, no definite markings, usually pale wing bar ACTIONS tree feeder on insects. NOTES sewing-machine trill, staccato. HABITAT woods, brushy tracts, sometimes yards.

CLOSE LOOK-ALIKES female and young have yellowish front and eye line; #29, 34 (vireos) have back gray, not green; bill medium thick. #56, 62 lack white underparts, eye line, wing bar.

CAP: GRAY — BREAST: YELLOW

#56. mourning warbler (m)

CAP gray extends to throat, nape, upper breast in complete hood (paler on female and young). FRONT gray breast feathers edged in black, lower breast and underparts bright yellow (faint eye ring in fall). BACK uniform greenish-yellow, no definite marking. ACTIONS brush and treetop feeder on insects. NOTES warbling trill. HABITAT woods edge, thickets.

CLOSE LOOK-ALIKES **Connecticut warbler** definite white eye ring all year, male, female, young. Range East, Canadian midwest. **MacGillivray's warbler** definite white eye ring (broken at each side) all year, male, female, young. Range West. GENERAL LOOK-ALIKE **Nashville warbler** cap center *red* (often hidden) surrounded by gray, throat *yellow*, cheeks gray, eye ring white, breast and underparts yellow. Range East, West Coast. **Bachman's warbler (f)** throat and eye ring *yellow*. Range Southwest. Very rare.

CAP: BLUE — BREAST: RED

#57. painted bunting (m)

CAP extends to cheeks, throat, nape in complete hood. BILL thick, short. FRONT eye ring, throat, breast, underparts bright red. BACK yellowish green between blue nape and red rump, wings and tail darker brownish green. ACTIONS ground and brush feeder on seeds, insects. NOTES warbling trill. HABITAT thickets, brushy. clearings, yards.

LOOK-ALIKES none.

CAP: GREEN — BREAST: YELLOW-GREEN

painted bunting (f) only small bird with *thick bill* that comes close to being all olive-green (male #57).

orange-crowned warbler (f) only small bird with *thin bill* that comes close to being all olive-green (male #62). *See also: CAP: GREEN — BREAST: YELLOW.*

CAP: GREEN — BREAST: YELLOW

#58. common yellowthroat (m) (*warbler* not part of name)

CAP olive-green bordered by white line across forehead and over eyes, black visor and eye mask. BILL thin, medium short. FRONT throat, breast bright yellow; underparts white. BACK olive-green, no definite markings. ACTIONS brush and tree feeder on insects; has second-widest range of any warbler in N.A. (1st #61). NOTES warbling trill "witchery-witcher-witchery". HABITAT woods edge, thickets, streambanks, yards.

CLOSE LOOK-ALIKES female similar but lacks mask, throat yellow but breast buffy-yellow. **Kentucky warbler** has black visor, black cheek patch, but area around eye is yellow, not black. Throat, breast, underparts all yellow. Range East. GENERAL LOOK-ALIKES **prairie warbler** black line through eye, black curved line below yellow area around eye, black streakings on sides of breast, white wing bars and feather tips on wings. Range East. **pine warbler** eye mask gray-green, line over eye yellow, breast yellow, faintly streaked, underparts grayish white, 2 white wing bars. Range East. **Wilson's warbler (f)** throat, breast, underparts very yellow; faint yellow eye line, cheek grayish, no back markings (male #66). **hooded warbler (f)** visor bright yellow, cheek bright yellow, outer tail feathers edged in yellow (male #67).

CAP: GREEN — BREAST: BLACK

#59. black-throated green warbler (m)

CAP and nape and cheek patch yellow-green. BILL thin, medium short. FRONT area surrounding *cheek patch yellow,* throat and upper breast solid black, sides lightly streaked in black, lower breast and *underparts white.* BACK faintly streaked in darker tone, wings and tail grayish edged in white, 2 white wing bars. ACTIONS tree-top feeder on insects. NOTES sewing-machine trill "trees, trees, trees, wonderful trees". HABITAT woods, especially pine and cedar.

CLOSE LOOK-ALIKES female and young have less black on throat, but green cheek patch surrounded by bright yellow still evident for clue. **golden-cheeked warbler (f)** greenish eye line, but cheeks are yellow (male #71x). **Townsend's warbler (f/wm)** has green cheek patch, but breast is *yellow* beneath black streaking, not white (male #64 L-A). Range West. **hermit warbler (f/y)** back is gray, not green (male #36 L-A). Range West Coast.

CAP: STREAKED GREEN — BREAST: YELLOW

#60. lesser goldfinch (f)

CAP streaked green includes cheek patch, male (#64) black cap. BILL *thick,* short, pinkish yellow. FRONT yellow throat blends to green on breast, underparts. BACK nape, back and *rump olive-green;* wings and tail black edged in white, 2 white wing bars. ACTIONS seed-eater gleaning fields, yards, roadsides. NOTES plaintive 2-note call.

S br | S gy | S bl | S gr | S yl | S rd | S b/w | M br | M gy | M bl | M gr | M yl | M o/b | M rd | M b/w | L br | L gy | L bl | L g/b | VL br | VL gy | VL bl | VL gr | VL r/p | VL b/w | VL bk | VL wh

HABITAT open country, yards and vacant lots, woods edge.

CLOSE LOOK-ALIKE **American goldfinch (f/y/wm)** slightly larger, more yellow in the olive-green, has *white rump* (male #65). Range cont-exN.

CAP: YELLOW — BREAST: YELLOW

#61. yellow warbler

CAP bordered by lighter yellow line over eye. BILL thin, medium short. FRONT throat yellow, breast lightly streaked in rust (not always visible) underparts yellow. BACK wing and *tail feathers edged in lighter yellow;* no white edging or marks anywhere. ACTIONS tree-top and brush feeder on insects; has widest range of any warbler in N.A. NOTES warbling trill "chee-chee-chee-chee-ah-wee". HABITAT willow thickets, stream banks, yards.

CLOSE LOOK-ALIKES no other yellow or yellowish warbler has yellow tail patches; individuals of Pacific Northwest more greenish than those of East. *See* #58 and L-As. GENERAL LOOK-ALIKES **prothonotary warbler** cap (complete hood) yellow (olive-green in female), back green, wings and tail bluish-gray, extreme underparts white. Range East. **blue-winged warbler** cap, throat to underparts bright golden yellow, back green, wings and tail blue-gray, 2 white wing bars. Range East. **Lawrence's warbler** cheek and throat black divided by bright yellow to match cap, breast, underparts; wings blue-gray, 2 white wing bars. Considered a hybrid of **golden-winged** and **blue-winged warblers,** as is **Brewster's warbler** (#35 L-A). Range East.

CAP: ORANGE — BREAST: YELLOW-GREEN

#62. orange-crowned warbler (m)

CAP tuft of orange feathers surrounded (and often hidden) by yellow-green, eye line lighter yellow. BILL thin, medium short. FRONT cheek patch slightly darker gray-green, eye ring faintly yellow, darker line through eye, lighter line over eye, breast faintly streaked in gray-green. BACK yellow-green, no markings except slightly lighter edging on some wing feathers. ACTIONS insect-eater in brush, thickets, trees; has third widest range of any warbler in N.A. (*see* #58, 61). NOTES sewing-machine trill. HABITAT brushy clearings, slopes, yards.

CLOSE LOOK-ALIKES #61, if greener Northwest race. Female resembles male except lacks orange tuft. Tuft best seen when male dips its head to splash in water. **olive warbler (m)** orange hood complete except for interruption of black eye mask. Back seems more gray than green except under foliage. 2 white wing bars. Female's hood is greenish-yellow, eye mask faint, gray. Range Arizona, New Mexico on Mexican border.

CAP: RED (RUSTY) — BREAST: YELLOW

#63. palm warbler

CAP rusty, bordered by yellow eye-line; dark line through eye. BILL thin, medium short. FRONT throat and breast yellow lightly streaked in dark brown, cheek patch greenish, breast and underparts yellow (fading to white on breast in western race). BACK olive green streaked in brown, rump yellow-green, some light edging on wings, white "thumbprints" on underside of tail. ACTIONS bobs tail, eats insects on bushes, ground. NOTES sewing-machine trill. HABITAT marshy woods.

Nashville warbler small red cap often hidden in surrounding gray, throat yellow, cheeks gray, eye-ring white, breast and underparts yellow. Range West Coast.

CAP: BLACK — BREAST: YELLOW

#64. lesser goldfinch (m)

CAP top of head only, not nape. BILL *thick*, short, pinkish yellow. FRONT plain unstreaked yellow. BACK streaked green, nape to tail, wings and tail black edged in white, 2 white wing bars (*rump olive green*). ACTIONS seed-eater gleaning fields, yards, roadsides. NOTES warbling trill; plaintive 2-note call. HABITAT open country, yards, vacant lots, woods edge.

CLOSE LOOK-ALIKES female #60. **American goldfinch** male is slightly larger, yellower, wears black cap only in summer (#60 L-As, #65) and has white, not green, rump. GENERAL LOOK-ALIKES **Bachman's warbler (m)** bill thin, black cap with *yellow* visor; broad black bib mark. Range East. Rare. **Townsend's warbler (m)** bill thin, yellow line over and under black cheek patch, throat and bib black above yellow breast with black streaks at side, underparts white, wings and tail feathers edged in white, back streaked green. Range West. **Cape May warbler (m)** bill thin, cap bordered by short yellow line over eye, cheek patch rusty against yellow throat and neckside, breast yellow well-streaked in black, back streaked green, wide white wing patch, yellow rump (female #34x). Range East, Canada midwest. **Wilson warbler (m)** #66. **hooded warbler (m)** #67. **golden-cheeked warbler (m)** #71x.

*When a small **warbler** nest is blown from its branch, a young birdwatcher can have a long and wondering look.*

S br | S gy | S bl | S gr | S yl | S rd | S b/w | M br | M gy | M bl | M gr | M yl | M o/b | M rd | M b/w | L br | L gy | L bl | L g/b | VL br | VL gy | VL bl | VL gr | VL r/p | VL b/w | VL bk | VL wh

Size: SMALL — Color: YELLOWS

As every SCANS follower knows, a bird's basic color for Key check is decided by the color of its back, wings, tail. But this rule is often put aside by watchers whose eyes are dazzled by the bright yellow breasts of certain small warblers and finches. The olive-green coloring of each back just seems to vanish, and the watcher instantly, automatically, marks them down in mind as "small and yellow". Later, when binoculars are in focus for careful check, most watchers are really surprised to note that these birds have olive-green backs.

The right place to look for them is in the Key for Small and Green — and that's where they are listed. But because so many watchers think of them as "yellow", the names and numbers — but not full descriptions — will be repeated in this Key. (Repeated numbers are in parentheses.) In addition, the yellowest of the small yellow-green birds will be described here along with one that is truly yellow. Three of these yellowest small ones have yellow caps and three have black caps. As usual, identify them in the Key by the combination of colors for cap and breast.

CAP: GRAY — BREAST: WHITE

(#55) **Tennessee warbler** white line over eye, black line through eye.

CAP: GRAY — BREAST: YELLOW

(#56) **mourning warbler** — cap is compete hood.
LOOK-ALIKES **Connecticut warbler** white eye ring. **MacGillivray's warbler** incomplete white eye ring. **Nashville warbler** white eye ring, red center on cap.

CAP: GREEN — BREAST: YELLOW-GREEN

painted bunting (f) bill thick, narrow yellow eye ring.

orange-crowned warbler (f) bill thin, lighter line over eye, darker line through eye. Male #62.

CAP: GREEN — BREAST: YELLOW

(#58) **common yellowthroat** black mask across eyes and forehead.

Kentucky warbler black visor, black cheek patch, yellow eye patch.

prairie warbler black line through eye, black streaked breast.

pine warbler eye mask gray-green, line over eye yellow.

hooded warbler (f) visor and cheek bright yellow.

CAP: GREEN — BREAST: BLACK

(#59 L-A) **Townsend's warbler (f)** cheek patch green, breast black-streaked yellow, male (#64 L-A) has black cap, eye mask.

CAP: YELLOW — BREAST: YELLOW

(#61) **yellow warbler.**
CAP bordered by lighter yellow line over eye. BILL thin, medium short. FRONT throat yellow, breast lightly streaked in rust (not always visible) underparts yellow. BACK wing and *tail feathers* edged in lighter yellow, no white front or back. ACTIONS tree-top and brush feeder on insects; has widest range of any N.A. warbler. NOTES warbling trill "chee-chee-chee-chee-ah-wee". HABITAT willow thickets, streambanks, yards.
CLOSE LOOK-ALIKES no other yellowish warbler has yellow tail streaks. Eastern individuals less greenish than those of Pacific Northwest. GENERAL LOOK-ALIKES (very bright yellow heads, breasts) **prothonotary warbler** cap (complete hood) golden yellow in male, slightly greenish in female, back of both greenish, wings and tail

bluish-gray, no wing bars, extreme underparts white. Range East. **blue-winged warbler** cap (complete hood except nape) breast and underparts golden yellow, back greenish, wings and tail blue-gray, 2 white wing bars. Range East. **Wilson's warbler (f)** (male #66). **hooded warbler (f)** (male #67).

CAP: ORANGE — BREAST: YELLOW

(#62) **orange-crowned warbler (m)** lighter line over eye, darker line through eye, orange cap not always visible.

CAP: RED OR RUSTY — BREAST: YELLOW

(#63) **palm warbler** cap rusty, bordered by yellow line over eye, dark line through eye, breast streaked.

Nashville warbler small red cap surrounded by gray, white eye ring.

CAP: BLACK — BREAST: YELLOW

(#64 L-A) **Bachman's warbler** visor yellow, throat yellow, bib black.

(#64 L-A) **Townsend's warbler** yellow line over and under black cheek patch, throat black, breast streaked black on yellow.

(#64 L-A) **Cape May warbler** cheek patch rusty, breast streaked in black.

(#64) **Lesser goldfinch (m)** back definitely green, bill thick, has black cap all year. **American goldfinch** (#65) has black cap only in summer.

#65. American goldfinch (m)

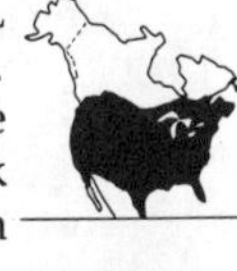

CAP black beak to crown, nape yellow. BILL thick, pinkish. FRONT bright lemon yellow. BACK bright lemon yellow, *rump white,* wide white bar on wing shoulder, wings and tail black edged in white. ACTIONS seed eater; often in flocks. HABITAT fields, roadsides, yards.

CLOSE LOOK-ALIKES winter male lacks black cap, resembles female in paler yellow body color, wing shoulder yellow (female's wing bars narrow white), both have *white rump* (**lesser goldfinch** olive-green rump).

#66. Wilson's warbler (m)

CAP black, visor yellow, yellow line between cap and eye. BILL thin, medium short. FRONT golden yellow from visor to extreme under-tail. BACK olive-green, not white. ACTIONS lively tree and brush feeder on insects. NOTES sewing-machine trill; thin, chattery. HABITAT thickets, streambanks, yards.

CLOSE LOOK-ALIKE female may show a trace of the small black cap or may not, has definite lighter yellow visor and line over eye, faint yellow ring around eye, faint greenish cheek patch. No other yellow-bodied warbler (except **Kentucky** and **hooded**) look so golden-yellow under the tail.

#67. hooded warbler (m)

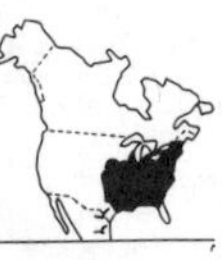

CAP visor golden yellow; cap, nape, neckline and throat continuous black. BILL thin, medium short. FRONT throat and upper breast solid black; cheek, breast, sides, underparts golden yellow. BACK olive-green, no white except as tail streaks. ACTIONS flicks tail open and shut, showing white; insect-eater in trees, brush. NOTES loud musical whistle. HABITAT marshy woods.

S br
S gy
S bl
S gr
S yl
S rd
S b/w
M br
M gy
M bl
M gr
M yl
M o/b
M rd
M b/w
L br
L gy
L bl
L g/b
VL br
VL gy
VL bl
VL gr
VL r/p
VL b/w
VL bk
VL wh

CLOSE LOOK-ALIKE **Kentucky warbler** has black visor, black cheek patch, but area around eye and throat are yellow, not black. Range East. GENERAL LOOK-ALIKE **hooded warbler** female has same golden-yellow visor and underparts but no black hood; green of cap extends to nape, encircling golden cheeks in much the same pattern as male's extended neckline; has faint dark line through eye. Range East.

Size: SMALL — Color: REDS

According to SCANS rule, a bird is Small if it is no larger than a house sparrow, not over 6 inches. It is described as "red" if red is the main color of its back or of back, wings, tail. Only two species pass this size-and-color check — the red crossbill and the white-winged crossbill. SCANS rule also provides that species of the same basic size and color be identified by color of cap and breast for first clue. Since these two species are alike in coloring except for the presence or absence of white wing bars, the wing check makes the ID in this Key only.

The Key also lists certain small birds easily recognized by some bright red or rose coloring elsewhere than on the back — on cap, throat, breast. Also listed are small birds with some red trim on the back or wings, even though red is not the main color. All of these species are also entered in the proper color Key. For other birds in basic red, see Medium-and-Red Key. (Repeated numbers are in parentheses.)

CAP: RED — BREAST: RED

#68. red crossbill (m)

CAP red, blending with nape and throat. BILL tips are crossed for easier extraction of tiny seeds from pine cones. FRONT brick red, females (#12) are streaked yellowish-brown. BACK wings and tail blackish. ACTIONS clings to branches and cones like a parrot. NOTES warbled trill; sharp chips. HABITAT conifer forests.

CLOSE LOOK-ALIKE only other species with *crossed bill* **white-winged crossbill** has 2 wide white wingbars; often found farther north than **red crossbill,** including Alaska.

BIRDS WITH RED TRIM
CAP ONLY

(#37) **ruby-crowned kinglet** red cap not always visible; otherwise seems gray, blends with back. Range cont.

(#37 L-A) **Virginia's warbler** cap visible. Range Southwest.

CAP, BREAST

(#21 L-A) **common redpoll, hoary redpoll** heavily streaked in brown, chin patch black. Range cont-exS.

CAP, BREAST, THROAT

(#37 L-A) **red-faced warbler** visor, throat, upper breast bright red; back gray, lower breast white. Range Arizona to Texas on Mexican border.

(#69x) **vermilion flycatcher** cap, throat, breast, underparts, under-tail patch all bright red; eye mask, nape, wings, back, tail all black. Range Southwest.

CAP, THROAT, RUMP

(#21) **purple finch (m)** back, wings, tail streaked brown. Range cont-exN.

(#21 L-A) **Cassin's finch** similar but rosier. Range West.

(#22) **house finch (m)** red of cap U-shaped visor. Range cont-exCenter.

CAP, THROAT

(#54) **Anna's hummingbird (m)** only N.A. hummer with both cap and throat red. Range West.

CAP, RUMP

(#37 L-A) **Lucy's warbler** cap visible. Range Southwest.

BREAST

(#41) **red-breasted nuthatch** cap black, back blue-gray. Range cont-exFla/Alas.

(#71 L-A) **painted redstart** hood and back black, white on wings, tail. Range Arizona, New Mexico, Texas near border.

BREAST AND RUMP

(#57) **painted bunting (m).**

THROAT

(#7) **rufous hummingbird (m)** back cinnamon. Range West.

(#52) **Calliope hummingbird (m)** throat striped red/white. Range West.

(#51) **ruby-throated hummingbird (m)** back green. Range East.

(#53 L-A) **broad-tailed hummingbird (m)** back green. Range West.

WINGS, RUMP, UNDERPARTS (PINK)

(#1 L-A) **brown-capped rosy finch** cap and body brown, trim rosy. Range Central Rockies.

(#25 L-A) **black rosy finch** cap gray, visor black, body blackish-brown, trim rosy. Range Central Rockies.

(#25 L-A) **gray-crowned rosy finch** cap and nape gray, visor black, body brown. Range Western mountains to Alaska. (These three now classified together as one species, **rosy finch**).

WINGS, TAIL (ORANGE-RED)

(#71) **American redstart (m)** broad patch shoulder, mid-wing; on upper tail at each side.

S br S gy S bl S gr S yl S rd S b/w M br M gy M bl M gr M yl M o/b M rd M b/w L br L gy L bl L g/b VL br VL gy VL bl VL gr VL r/p VL b/w VL bk VL wh

Size: SMALL — Color: BLACK-AND-WHITE or BLACK

For Small birds feathered in black-and-white or whose basic color is black, the first clue to check is the color of the cap. The second clue is the color of the breast. As always, the cap may be a flat patch or a crest and it may or may not match the color of nape and back. It may be a small patch or a complete hood.

For black-and-white birds the caps are orange, black-and-white or white. For birds in black the caps are red or black. The birds listed as "black" may have white marks elsewhere besides the back.

When you find the right combination of cap and breast color, check the descriptions of all birds under this heading until you find a perfect match. Make a final check by picture and range map and by colored picture.

BACKS: BLACK-AND-WHITE
CAP: BLACK/WHITE — BREAST: BLACK/WHITE

#69. black-and-white warbler (m)

CAP center stripe white (lengthwise). BILL thin, medium short. FRONT male has black cheek patch (female faint smudge), male has black streaking on upper breast (female none), lower breast white for both, male has black throat (female white). BACK black and white, no other colors back or front. ACTIONS creeps on tree trunks, branches for insects. NOTES thin sewing-machine trill. HABITAT woods.

CLOSE LOOK-ALIKE none. All other Small birds (except **snow bunting** and **McKay's bunting** in summer only) have some color besides black and white. **snow bunting** (summer) bill thick, cap (hood) white; throat, breast, underparts white; back black, rump white, wings largely white, black patches. Winter, cap cinnamon, back streaked brown (#9 L-A). Range North (summers extreme North). **McKay's bunting** (summer) bill thick, all white except black patches on wing tips. Range Alaska, Bering Sea islands.

BACKS: BLACK
CAP: RED — BREAST: RED

vermilion flycatcher (m) cap is slightly raised crest, bright red; throat, breast, underparts and under-tail all bright red; eye mask, nape, back, tail all blackish. Female brownish, breast streaked, pinkish wash on underparts. Range Southwest.

CAP: BLACK — BREAST: GRAY/YELLOW

bananaquit (Bahama honeycreeper) cap black (slate) bordered in white line over eye, black line through eye, middle breast and rump yellow, underparts white. Range southeast Florida.

CAP: BLACK — BREAST: BLACK

#70. lark bunting (m)

CAP blends with head, front, back. BILL thick, short, gray. FRONT black. BACK black, large white patch covers most of upper wing, lower wing feathers edged in white, tail tips white. ACTIONS ground feeder on seeds, insects; often flocks. NOTES loud musical trill, whistle. HABITAT grasslands, desert scrub.

GENERAL LOOK-ALIKE **bobolink** (m #115) has yellow nape, white rump, slightly larger. **black rail** chicken-like marsh bird with big feet, back and underparts black speckled in white, eye red. Range East. **black phoebe** (#27 L-A) cap (hood), throat, upper breast, nape, back, wings, tail all black, but lower breast and underparts *white;* no large white patches on wings as in lark bunting; bill medium (not thick), bristles at base of bill; sits erect on branch; typical flycatcher behavior. Range Southwest, may stray north to northern California, Utah, Oregon.

#71. American redstart (m)

CAP black (hood). BILL thin, medium short. FRONT throat, upper breast, sides all solid black; lower breast, underparts white. BACK nape, back solid black, wing black with orange-red patch at shoulder and mid-wing, tail black with orange-red patch midway at each side, tail tip black. ACTIONS always flitting, flicking wings, tail; catches insects midair. NOTES sewing-machine trill, high-pitched. HABITAT forest underbrush, thickets, often near water.

CLOSE LOOK-ALIKE **painted redstart** cap (hood) black; throat, nape, back solid black, breast bright red, underparts white, large white patch on wing shoulder, outer tail feathers white. Range mountain forests, canyons Arizona to Texas along border. **golden-cheeked warbler (m)** cap, throat, upper breast and line through eye are all black; lower breast white, streaked in black at sides; *cheeks bright yellow*, nape and back solid black, wing and tail feathers edged in white, underparts white. Female #59 L-A. Not common. Range Texas.

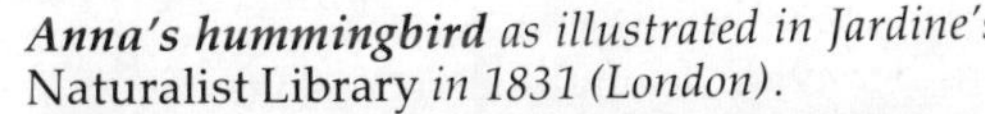

***Anna's hummingbird** as illustrated in Jardine's* Naturalist Library *in 1831 (London).*

S br | S gy | S bl | S gr | S yl | S rd | S b/w | M br | M gy | M bl | M gr | M yl | M o/b | M rd | M b/w | L br | L gy | L bl | L g/b | VL br | VL gy | VL bl | VL gr | VL r/p | VL b/w | VL bk | VL wh

Size: MEDIUM — Color: BROWNS

All Medium brown birds have caps that are also brown, either a plain, solid brown or streaked or mottled. So the first clue to look for is whether the cap is solid color or streaked and whether it blends with the rest of the head or is bordered in contrasting color. The cap may be flat, bushy, a pointed crest or have two upright tufts of feathers like horns.

For a second clue check whether the breast is plain — white or pale gray or buff — or patterned. The pattern may be a black bib or a general wash of color or spots or streaks.

When you find the matching combination of cap and breast description, check every bird listed under that heading until you find a perfect match. Make final check by the picture and range map, if it is a numbered species, and by the color picture identified with the same number. For species not pictured, check with pictures and descriptions in other books if you are not sure of the ID, using the basic SCANS check points.

CAP: PLAIN BROWN — BREAST: PLAIN

ash-throated flycatcher cap (bushy, "big-headed" look) buffy-brown, throat paler than breast, back buffy-brown, wing feathers edged in buff, wing tips in reddish brown, tail feathers streaked in reddish-brown. Underparts may be very pale lemon yellow. Range West.
CLOSE LOOK-ALIKES #74 L-As.

mountain plover visor and line over eye white, black patch between visor and brown cap; back, wings, tail buffy-brown; legs pale, medium long; typical shorebird behavior. In flight shows wings edged in white then dark band on outer edge. Tail spreads to dark band edged in white. Range high deserts, plateaus of West.

CAP: PLAIN BROWN — BREAST: PATTERNED (BLACK BIB)

#72. killdeer

CAP visor small black patch then wider white patch, long white line over eye, short white line under eye. BILL medium thick, medium long. FRONT eye ringed in red, throat and neck white, breast white marked by two wide black semicircular lines, underparts white. BACK nape continues white neck line, back buffy-brown, wings show white bands edged in black in flight, rump and upper tail rusty, edged in black and white. ACTIONS runs across field, lawn, mudflat or stands listening, watching for insects and similar food; lays eggs in depression in pebbles or grass and defends nest and young with pretense of crippled leg or wing to lure enemy away. If lays eggs on gravel roof-top babies will die for lack of food, if not helped to ground, since chicks find own food. NOTES plaintive cries, often on wing, of "kill-dee" or "kill-deer". HABITAT fields, airports, lawns, parking lots, riverbanks, parks.

CLOSE LOOK-ALIKES young has only one bib ring. **Wilson's plover** has only one, very wide black bib ring; smaller than **killdeer.** Range coastal mainland, islands. **semipalmated plover** only one medium-wide black bib ring, smaller than **Wilson's** or **killdeer.** Range cont-exRockies in migration, nests North. **snowy plover** black neck ring only at sides, smaller than semipalmated, back very pale, legs dark. Range West, Gulf Coast to Florida. **piping plover** black bib ring complete or almost complete, about size of **snowy** and as pale but legs yellow. Range East, north-central West. **ruddy turnstone** *splotchy* bib mark, back *rusty,* rump white, wings banded black-white-rusty. Range, nests Alaska and Arctic, winters all coasts.

#73. horned lark

CAP edged in black band that lifts in two feather tufts or horns, bordered by yellow visor and yellow line over eye (or *white* visor and line in many midwest areas). Young birds lack tufts. BILL medium, short. FRONT wide black "comma" line (whisker line) from eye downward, throat yellow, breast below black bib line *white,* sides streaked lightly in buff, cheek behind comma line buffy edged in white. BACK streaked brown, outer tail feathers edged in white. ACTIONS walks, not hops. NOTES warbling trill, high-pitched, often long-continued and given in flight. HABITAT plains, prairies, fields, dirt road edges, golf courses, airports, sand flats.

GENERAL LOOK-ALIKES **meadowlarks** #131 (no horns). **pipits** #79 L-A or **longspurs** #25, 16 L-A (no horns).

CAP: PLAIN BROWN — BREAST: PATTERNED (COLOR WASH)

#74. cedar waxwing

CAP pointed crest. BILL medium, medium short, very slightly hooked at tip. FRONT black mask through eyes, throat black, separated from mask by white line, breast shades from buffy to yellow, extreme *underparts white.* (Breast and underparts streaked on young birds.) BACK wings shade to slate, white feather edges form lengthwise line on either side of rump, bare tips of some wing feathers bright red (look like drops of red wax), tail tips form bright yellow band. NOTES lispy twitter. ACTIONS often in flocks; may perch and dart out for insects like flycatchers or glean berries. HABITAT woods, orchards, yards.

CLOSE LOOK-ALIKE (young have *streaked* breasts) **Bohemian waxwing** wing feathers have *scallops of yellow and white* and white patches as well as waxlike red quill tips, *under-tail rusty,* not white, throat and cheeks have rusty tinge; slightly larger, chunkier than **cedar waxwing.** Range West, north to Alaska, occasional in Northeast. GENERAL LOOK-ALIKES **great crested flycatcher** head is bushy, not pointed crest, *no black eye mask,* throat gray, breast shades gray to yellow, underparts yellow, outer wing tips and tail rusty, bill medium long, medium thick. Range East. **Say's phoebe** head bushy, no mask, throat gray, breast *underparts rusty,* back and wings grayish-brown, tail brown to brownish-black. May nest in building niches or nest box. Range West. **Abert's towhee** *cap flat,* eye mask and underbill patch black, no wing or tail trim. Range Southwest. **brown towhee** *cap flat,* throat streaked, undertail rusty, no mask, no wing or tail trim. Range Southwest. **brown-headed cowbird (f/y)** *cap flat,* blends with gray-brown body color, no black mask, *walks* (male #112). **Brewer's blackbird (f)** cap flat, walks (male #117). **European starling (y)** cap flat, blends with body, no mask, breast may be plain brown or lightly streaked, walks (larger than cowbird), very noisy in clamoring for food from adults (adult #97). **blue grosbeak (f)** *cap flat,* bill thick, short, *2 buffy wing bars* (male #94). **northern shrike (y)** *cap flat,* eye mask black, back brown, rump buffy white, wings and tail black with white edgings. Range cont-exS (more often in West than East). **phainopepla (f)** gray-brown with slender crest, light gray streakings on wings show in flight. Range West. **northern cardinal (f)** (male #108) brown with pointed red crest, thick red bill, red underwash.

CAP: PLAIN BROWN — BREAST: PATTERNED (STREAKED)

#75. sage thrasher

CAP bordered by *buffy-gray* line over eye. BILL medium thin, medium long. FRONT eye *yellow;* throat, breast and underparts well streaked brown on white. BACK plain brown, 2 white wing bars, tail has white outer corners. ACTIONS runs over ground hunting insects, also eats berries; sings from perch or in flight. NOTES warbling trill. HABITAT sage-brush country, valley to foothills.

CLOSE LOOK-ALIKES other thrashers are larger, *see* #124. **cactus wren** cap bordered by distinct *white* line, eye *red,* throat and upper breast splotched in black, back and wing feathers edged in white, tail barred in black, outer feathers checked in white and black (other wrens #2, 3, 4). Range Southwest.

CAP: PLAIN BROWN — BREAST: PATTERNED (SPOTTED)

#76. fox sparrow (western)

CAP chocolate brown, blends with cheeks, nape. BILL thick, short, *lower bill yellow,* upper gray. FRONT throat and breast splotched, central cluster of marks similar to that of smaller **song sparrow** (#10), underparts white (marks usually arrow-shape). BACK plain chocolate brown with rusty tinge, very little contrast of feather edging, seems solid velvety tone. ACTIONS scratches in dirt for seeds, grubs, often with both feet at once in hop-scratch movement. NOTES 2 notes and warbling trill much like song sparrow's. HABITAT woods edge, brush, parks, yards.

CLOSE LOOK-ALIKES **song sparrow** #10 — smaller, tweedier back, not the velvet look, bill all grayish. **fox sparrow (eastern)** basic color *rusty*-brown, well-streaked in other shades, rump and tail bright rusty-brown, light line over eye and under cheek patch, breast marking similar but rustier in tone. Actions, notes, habitat duplicate. Range East-exSFla. **thrushes** *See* #77 — thrush spots are more scattered, not splotches; thrush bills are thin, not thick.

#77. hermit thrush

CAP blends with nape, cheek (olive-brown). BILL medium thin, medium short. FRONT throat, breast white, spotted (some streaking); underparts white, eye ring white. BACK nape, back, wings olive-brown, *tail rusty-brown.* ACTIONS runs along ground, draws up with "puffed up" air; often lifts tail on perch and then lowers it. NOTES clear and flute-like warbled trill with single long-drawn notes between phrases. Often termed most beautiful of all bird songs. HABITAT woods edge, thickets, parks, yards (if secluded).

CLOSE LOOK-ALIKES **wood thrush** *head and nape are bright rusty* — back and tail olive-brown, eye ring white. Most-often-seen thrush of eastern parks and suburbs. Range East. **Swainson's thrush** head, nape, back, wings, tail all buffy olive-brown (no rusty tones); eye ring buffy, not white; throat and breast beneath spots has *yellow wash, cheeks buffy.* Range cont. **gray-cheeked thrush** like **Swainson's** but grayer, cheek definitely gray, *no eye ring,* no rusty tone. Range cont-exWestern States only rarely, nests in western Canada and Alaska, usually migrates east of Rockies. **veery** *rusty-brown* all over head, back, wings, tail; fewer spots on throat and breast than other thrushes; western birds often grayer over all, not so bright; cheek patch *pale buffy,* not gray as in **gray-cheeked.** Range cont-exN/SW/West Coast, may go to Coast and Southwest on

S br
S gy
S bl
S gr
S yl
S rd
S b/w
M br
M gy
M bl
M gr
M yl
M o/b
M rd
M b/w
L br
L gy
L bl
L g/b
VL br
VL gy
VL bl
VL gr
VL r/p
VL b/w
VL bk
VL wh

migration; nests in southern Canada. **brown thrasher** (#124) larger, tail much longer. **fox sparrow** (#76) bill thick, not thin, spots form central cluster on breast.

#78. spotted sandpiper

CAP bordered by definite white line over eye. BILL bright orange-red, dark tipped. FRONT throat, breast, underparts well-dotted in dark *round* spots (not streaks), white eye ring (in winter spots are missing, but throat and upper breast mottled gray). BACK feathers faintly edged in darker tones, in flight shows lower wing edged in black bar between white bars, tail barred in dark bands with white band at tip. ACTIONS bobs and teeters as it walks; flies with vibrating wings, shallow strokes; most often-seen shorebird on inland streams, lakes; often in pairs, small flocks. NOTES whistled cry, "peet-weet" or "weet-weet-weet". HABITAT sandy, muddy or rocky shores, ponds, lakes, streams.

CLOSE LOOK-ALIKES (other sandpipers have bars, streaks, buffy wash, not such round spots as **spotted sandpiper**). **solitary sandpiper** dotted streaks. Range cont. **stilt sandpiper** dotted streaks on throat, crosswise barred scallops on breast and underparts, legs *green*. Range East, Central on migration. **pectoral sandpiper** throat and breast heavily streaked over buffy wash. Range cont on migration. **white-rumped sandpiper** and **Baird's (brown-rumped)** dotted throat and breast, white eye line. Range cont-exW on migration. **sanderling** throat and upper breast dotted streaks over buff, lower breast and underparts white, wing tips white (making band when folded or in flight), runs up and down beach and into waves with twinkling pace. Rusty-brown in summer, pale gray-brown in winter. One of most often-seen sandpipers, always in flocks. Range cont on migration, winters on both coasts, nests in Arctic. **dunlin** throat and breast dotted (lower breast and underparts black in summer), back rusty-brown in summer, gray-brown in winter, bill curves down slightly at tip. Range, winters on both coasts, nests in Arctic, Alaska.

CAP: STREAKED BROWN — BREAST: PATTERNED (STREAKED, MOTTLED, BARRED)

#79. rose-breasted grosbeak (f/y)

CAP center stripe, stripe over eye buffy white, alternate stripes and cheek patch dark brown. BILL thick, short, pale. FRONT breast streaked dark brown over white or buff, wing linings show pinkish-yellow in flight. BACK streaked brown, 2 white wing bars. ACTIONS seed and fruit eater; insects, especially Colorado potato beetle. NOTES lilting robin-like carol (female sings more softly than male, both may sing on nest). HABITAT woods, orchards, yards.

CLOSE LOOK-ALIKE (male #114). **black-headed grosbeak (f/y)** similar markings but on buffy — even orange-buff — background rather than white or pale buff, wing linings deep yellow. (May interbreed where **rose-breasted** and **black-headed** meet.) Range West. GENERAL LOOK-ALIKES **red-winged blackbird (f/y)** *bill medium and pointed,* breast and underparts heavily streaked, *walks.* Year-old males begin to get red on shoulder. Adult male #116. (**tri-colored blackbird** female similar — range West Coast.) **Sprague's pipit** *bill thin, medium,* throat white, back and breast streaked. *Walks;* ground feeder. Short white line behind eye, white outer tail feathers. Range Central. **water pipit** *bill thin, medium,* throat white, breast buffy under streaks, side streaked, back plain and unstreaked, white line over eye, white outer tail feathers. Walks (long claws). Range cont. **bobolink (f/wm)** head striped brown and buff, back heavily streaked, front lightly streaked brown on buff, *narrow pointed tail feathers* (male #115). **yellow-headed blackbird (f)** cap brown, line over eye yellow, throat and upper breast yellow, lower breast streaked, underparts and back brown (male #112x). Range West, wanders east

S br
S gy
S bl
S gr
S yl
S rd
S b/w
M br
M gy
M bl
M gr
M yl
M o/b
M rd
M b/w
L br
L gy
L bl
L g/b
VL br
VL gy
VL bl
VL gr
VL r/p
VL b/w
VL bk
VL wh

in fall. **Willamson's sapsucker (f)** hood brown, breast black, sides barred, center of underparts yellow, back barred, rump white (male #122x). Range West. **yellow-bellied sapsucker (f/y)** cap streaked brown, throat white, breast streaked, back streaked, white and black patches on wings, rump white (male #119). **red-headed woodpecker (y)** head and throat brown streaked, breast white with some brown streaking, large white wing patches, rump white, tail brown (adult #120). **Lewis' woodpecker (y)** head and back brown, breast drab with faint tinge of rose, some mottling (adult #141x).

#80. common nighthawk

CAP mottled, bordered by white line over eye. BILL very short. FRONT throat white in male, buffy in female, breast and underparts of both heavily barred, in flight show white patch in center of *underwing*. BACK wings, back and tail mottled, tail has white bar across above black tip, folded wings longer than tail. ACTIONS sky-skimming flight after insects, prefers dusk or dawn hours or cloudy days, but may fly any time, day or night. HABITAT often in cities chasing insects around street lights.

CLOSE LOOK-ALIKES **lesser nighthawk** smaller by about an inch in length, 2 inches in wingspread, white on underwing *near tip* (instead of center). Range Southwest. **common poorwill** *throat black,* white ring border, folded wings barely as long as tail, smaller over-all by about 1 inch. Range West.

#81. northern saw-whet owl (saw-whet owl)

CAP brown streaked in white, bordered by white line over and between eyes to form a "Y", no tufts. BILL hooked. FRONT throat, breast and underparts streaked, eyes yellow, front-faced, feathers radiate out from eyes, breast and underparts streaked brown (young have unstreaked, buffy breast, cap, facial disks). BACK streaks of white spots on brown, tail short. ACTIONS usually hunts by night, hides by day (sleepiness makes it seem tame, easily approached), feeds more on large insects than on mice, other small rodents or small birds. NOTES rasping call like the sound of someone sharpening (whetting) a saw; 2 notes usually repeated 3 times; seldom heard except in spring courtship. HABITAT woods, especially conifers; swampy woods.

CLOSE LOOK-ALIKES **northern pygmy-owl (pygmy owl)** white lines over eyes, no tufts, *eyes yellow,* bill yellow, breast streaked in *black* on white, sides rusty, nape has oval patch (black circled in white) on each side (looks like eyes in the back of its head), *tail long, barred in white.* Range West. **ferruginous pygmy-owl** similar to **northern pygmy** but tail barred in *black,* breast streaked in *rust.* Range Arizona to Texas along Mexican border. **flammulated owl** only Small or Medium N.A. owl with *dark eyes,* has small tufts, coloring may be rusty-brown or gray with rusty edging, tail short. Range West. Rare. **boreal owl** eyes yellow, face feathers white outlined in black, breast and back splotched rusty and white. Range North (from Oregon to New York) to Alaska. **western screech-owl** similar to **eastern** (#89) but usually brown(not rusty)less often gray and often larger.

#82. sora (*rail* is not part of name).

CAP bordered by gray visor and over eye and cheek. BILL thick, medium long, bright yellow (chicken-like). FRONT black mask extends down throat, bordered by gray, eye bright red, breast gray, underparts barred in white, legs yellow and long, feet large, toes long. BACK mottled brown, feathers edged in white sprinkling, tail pointed (*dark above, white underneath*), may be cocked upright in alarm. ACTIONS thins body to slip through grass or reeds to elude enemy (reason for "thin as a rail" expression), also swims, runs and flies well; eats insects, seeds, mollusks. HABITAT marsh, boggy meadows.

CLOSE LOOK-ALIKE **yellow rail** much smaller, all-over brownish with yellowish-buff background, darker and lighter edging, underparts barred, in flight wide white patch shows on each wing close to body. Range cont-ex N (Arctic/Alaska). Rare. GENERAL LOOK-ALIKE **Montezuma quail (harlequin quail)** clown-patterned face in black and white, back mottled browns; breast black, mottled black-and-white at sides; female all mottled browns. Range Southwest (especially near oaks, pines).

Even eaters of insects and berries like this ***Bohemian waxwing*** *will eat bread in winter when other food is scarce.*

S br | S gy | S bl | S gr | S yl | S rd | S b/w | M br | M gy | M bl | M gr | M yl | M o/b | M rd | M b/w | L br | L gy | L bl | L g/b | VL br | VL gy | VL bl | VL gr | VL r/p | VL b/w | VL bk | VL wh

S br
S gy
S bl
S gr
S yl
S rd
S b/w
M br
M gy
M bl
M gr
M yl
M o/b
M rd
M b/w
L br
L gy
L bl
L g/b
VL br
VL gy
VL bl
VL gr
VL r/p
VL b/w
VL bk
VL wh

Size: MEDIUM — Color: GRAYS

To tell one Medium gray bird from another, the first clue to notice is the color of the cap. It may be plain gray, streaked gray, a tuft of red hidden among surrounding gray, or black. The cap may blend with the rest of the head color or be bordered by a contrasting line or visor. The cap may be flat or bushy, giving a "big-headed" look, or there may be two upright tufts like horns.

For a second clue, check whether the breast is plain — white or very pale gray — or patterned. The pattern may be a black bib or a general wash of gray or another color or streaks.

When you find the matching combination of cap and breast to describe the bird you want to identify, check every bird listed under that heading until you find a perfect match. Make final check by picture and range map and by the color picture identified by the same number as the Key bird.

CAP: PLAIN GRAY — BREAST: PLAIN

#83. northern mockingbird (mockingbird)

CAP bordered by faint white line over eye, very faint dark line through eye. BILL medium thin, medium long. FRONT throat, breast, underparts pale gray to white. BACK wing has 2 white bars, squarish white patch, outer tail feathers white (wing patch and tail feathers show prominently in flight). ACTIONS sings by night or day, often flicks tail or raises wings while on ground; eats insects, fruits, comes to feeding places. NOTES clear musical whistle, rolling warble and trill, imitates other birds, human voices, mechanical sounds, musical instruments. HABITAT thickets, yards, farms, roadsides, streambanks.

CLOSE LOOK-ALIKES #91 **gray catbird. Townsend's solitaire** breast same gray as back, white eye ring, wing patch buffy, not white, but has white outer tail feathers. Range West.

#84. loggerhead shrike

CAP blends with nape. BILL thick, medium, *hooked at tip.* FRONT *black mask* through eyes, breast and underparts pale gray, almost white. BACK *wings and tail black,* rump, wing patch and outer tail feathers white. ACTIONS impales insects, small birds, rodents on thorn or barbed wire for later eating (therefore called **"butcher bird"**). Less often takes frogs, toads, small reptiles. NOTES sewing-machine trills (double) notes), harsh croak. HABITAT open country, fields, orchards, meadows.

CLOSE LOOK-ALIKE **northern shrike** slightly larger, has barred breast, lower half of bill lighter than upper. Young northern shrikes are brown where adults are gray, young loggerheads are gray but with more gray on breast. Range cont-exS.

CAP PLAIN GRAY — BREAST: PATTERNED (COLOR WASH: GRAY)

#85. eastern phoebe

CAP blends with nape, bushy, darker than back. BILL medium (bristles at base), dark-colored. FRONT throat white shading to gray on breast, underparts. BACK some lighter feather edging but no definite wing bars or other markings. ACTIONS bobs tail; waits on perch or wire and darts out after insects. NOTES "fee-bee", 2nd note either higher or lower than 1st. HABITAT farms, roadsides, yards, streambanks.

CLOSE LOOK-ALIKES (*See* #28 for smaller **flycatchers**). **eastern wood-pewee** same bushy cap, coloring, but has light-colored bill, 2 white wing bars. Notes plaintive pee-urr. Range East. **western wood-pewee** breast and sides darker gray than **eastern wood-pewee** or **phoebe,** has light-colored bill, 2 white wing bars. Notes nasal pee-yee. Range West. **olive-sided flycatcher** larger than **phoebe** or **wood-pewee,** breast sides darker than center, white patch on back next to each wing is fluffy, as if peeking from behind wing. Notes three brisk notes, "Quick three beers!" Range cont-exEast Coast, north to Alaska. GENERAL LOOK-ALIKES **Townsend's solitaire** more slender, slightly longer, has white eye ring, white outer tail feathers. Notes robin-like warble. Range West. **Eastern, western, mountain bluebirds (f)** blue-gray, bluer on wings, tail (males #95, 96).

#86. American dipper (dipper)

CAP blends with nape, throat, body. BILL medium. FRONT throat sometimes paler than breast, otherwise all same shade of gray; eye ring white (upper lid). BACK no markings; tail very short, often cocked upright. ACTIONS remarkable for its ability to walk or swim *under water* as it hunts for insects or crustaceans (*see* Most Unusual in Actions), often bobs up and down on rock or bank before going under water. NOTES rolling warbling trill, often compared to song of thrush or wren. HABITAT mountain streams, waterfalls.

common ground dove mottled grayish-brown, shows rusty patch on wing in flight, tail short and dark, feet and legs yellow; bobs its head as it walks. Range south, California to Florida.
CLOSE LOOK-ALIKE **Inca dove** similar but has long tail with white outer corners, slightly larger. Range Arizona to Texas.

CAP: PLAIN GRAY — BREAST: PATTERNED (COLOR OTHER THAN GRAY)

#87. American robin

CAP gray, dark gray or black (males usually darkest). BILL medium, yellow. FRONT throat white striped in black, breast brick red, extreme underparts white (young of year have pinkish breasts covered with dark dots even when full grown). BACK gray, tail and wings darker edging (young have gray backs flecked in buff). Eastern and northwestern birds have tail corners tipped in white; as a rule, western birds lack white tips. ACTIONS hunts worms on lawn, even in city, feeds also on fruits and berries, insects, spiders, caterpillars; often nests on windowsills, porches,

S br · S gy · S bl · S gr · S yl · S rd · S b/w · M br · M gy · M bl · M gr · M yl · M o/b · M rd · M b/w · L br · L gy · L bl · L g/b · VL br · VL gy · VL bl · VL gr · VL r/p · VL b/w · VL bk · VL wh

S br
S gy
S bl
S gr
S yl
S rd
S b/w
M br
M gy
M bl
M gr
M yl
M o/b
M rd
M b/w
L br
L gy
L bl
L g/b
VL br
VL gy
VL bl
VL gr
VL r/p
VL b/w
VL bk
VL wh

city buildings under construction. NOTES warbling trill of "Cheer-up, cheer-a-lee!" for springtime carol, also "Tup-tup!" call. HABITAT yards, parks, roadsides, farms, streambanks, woods edge, orchards, berry patches.

CLOSE LOOK ALIKE #88 (*See* Measure Bird #2)

#88. varied thrush

CAP slate gray bordered by *orange line over eye.* BILL medium, dark. FRONT throat and breast orange, upper breast crossed by black (or slate gray) *bib mark,* underparts buffy to white, *legs orange.* Males usually have darker bib mark than females. Both often miscalled **Oregon robin** or **Alaska robin** because of breast color. BACK gray wings flecked with orange or buffy-orange, outer tail corners have white tips. ACTIONS nests in high forests, especially near lakes; comes to lowland yards in winter, even to city yards. NOTES one long-drawn, quavering whistle, then a pause before a second single note. Sounds like violinist or piper tuning up, note by note. Also makes conversational twitters as birds feed in a flock. HABITAT woods, thickets, especially conifers, in summer; yards, ravines, thickets in winter.

CLOSE LOOK-ALIKES #87. **yellow wagtail** cap gray bordered by definite white line, throat, breast and underparts washed in bright yellow, 2 white wing bars, *long* tail, outer white tail feathers, bobs tail as it *walks.* Nests in Arctic, Alaska, beginning to venture further south. Young buffy instead of yellow. Range North, expanding south. **evening grosbeak (f/y)** beak pale and very thick and short, irregular yellow wash on breast and shoulders, wings and tail boldly patterned in black and white (male #101). Usually with male in flocks.

CAP: STREAKED GRAY— BREAST: PATTERNED (STREAKED, MOTTLED)

#89. eastern screech-owl (also comes in rusty-red, *see* 90x)

CAP two tufts, bordered by slanted white/gray lines over eyes. BILL hooked. FRONT streaked in brownish-gray, feathers of face radiate outward from eyes with curved dark edge, breast streaked to underparts. BACK streaked more darkly than breast, tail short, barred. ACTIONS hunts early dusk to dark, insects, rodents, reptiles, birds, fish; nests in tree cavity; bathes. NOTES not a screech, more a tremolo whistle. HABITAT woods, farms, thickets.

CLOSE LOOK-ALIKE **western screech-owl** (#81 L-A) usually larger, browner, but also has gray phase.

CAP: RED — BREAST: PATTERNED (COLOR WASH, YELLOW)

#90. western kingbird

CAP red (small tuft) remainder gray, bushy. BILL medium. FRONT throat white, breast gray, lower breast and underparts bright (to pale) yellow. BACK nape and back gray, wings and tail dark gray, outer tail feathers white, no wing bars. ACTIONS often boldly attacks crows, ravens, hawks near its nest; darts from perch or wire to catch insects. NOTES chattery twitter, squeaks. HABITAT open country, farms, roadsides.

CLOSE LOOK-ALIKES **eastern kingbird** #111. **Cassin's kingbird** similar coloring but chunkier, has white on tail tips, not sides. Range Southwest.

CAP: RED — BREAST: PATTERNED (STREAKED)

eastern screech-owl (red color phase) *see* #89, substituting rusty-red for gray.

CAP: BLACK — BREAST: PATTERNED (GRAY)

#91. gray catbird

CAP black, bordered by gray visor and gray line over eye. BILL medium. FRONT throat, breast, underparts gray, extreme undertail rusty. BACK gray, no marks, tail blackish, long. ACTIONS flips tail perkily, keeps to underbrush, often sings at night, mimics (but not expertly); eats insects, fruit, comes to feeder. NOTES warbling trill, harsh croaks, mews like a cat, mimics other birds. HABITAT underbrush, farmyards, roadsides.

CLOSE *SOUND*-ALIKE **rufous-sided towhee** also mews like a cat and is called **catbird** as a nickname, but not as official name. Other towhees also mew. *See* #74 L-A for **brown towhees,** #113 for **rufous-sided.** GENERAL LOOK-ALIKES **American dipper** #86 all gray but has very *short* tail, lacks black cap and rusty under-tail patch. **northern mockingbird** #83 has long tail, but has white wing bars and outer tail feathers, light breast. **white wagtail** cap black, visor white, cheeks white, throat and upper breast (bib) black, lower breast and underparts white, back gray, large white patch on wing, tail black, outer white tail feathers white. Range Alaska for summer nesting, may be expanding southward, has been seen on coast down to California.

*You can tell a **varied thrush** from a **robin** by its long orange eyebrow line, not a white eye ring.*

S br · S gy · S bl · S gr · S yl · S rd · S b/w · M br · M gy · M bl · M gr · M yl · M o/b · M rd · M b/w · L br · L gy · L bl · L g/b · VL br · VL gy · VL bl · VL gr · VL r/p · VL b/w · VL bk · VL wh

S br · S gy · S bl · S gr · S yl · S rd · S b/w · M br · M gy · M bl · M gr · M yl · M o/b · M rd · M b/w · L br · L gy · L bl · L g/b · VL br · VL gy · VL bl · VL gr · VL r/p · VL b/w · VL bk · VL wh

Size: MEDIUM — Color: BLUES

All Medium birds in blue wear blue caps. So the first clue to tell one from another is to check the size of the bill — thick or medium-thin or very small. As it happens, the two with the very small bills of the swallow family also have coats of dark blue. The other four have much lighter shades of blue. For these four the color of the breast makes an important clue, along with the size of the bill. You will also want to notice if there is any other color except blue on wings or back.

When you find the right combination of bill size, shade of blue, breast color and back or wing markings to match the bird you want to identify, you will know the right name. Three of them are indeed "bluebirds" by rightful name; the others only share the color and the size. Check the range maps and color pictures for final proof, but these six species will be among the easiest to identify.

DARK METALLIC BLUE

BILL: VERY SMALL — BREAST: BUFFY-RUST

#92. barn swallow

CAP steel blue, visor rusty. BILL very small. FRONT throat, breast, underparts buffy-rust (usually darker, rustier on throat), faint bib mark in blue. BACK nape, back, wings and rump all steel blue, tail steel blue with white steaks (not always visible), *tail deeply forked* (only swallow with deeply forked tail, others only notched). ACTIONS sky-skimming flight after insects; nests on barns, other buildings, sometimes several pairs near each other, sometimes one alone. Plasters nest of straw, grass, mud pellets against vertical wall. Both parents help with nest building and tending young. NOTES much twittering in flight. HABITAT farms, roadside motels and other buildings near open country or water.

CLOSE LOOK-ALIKE #48.

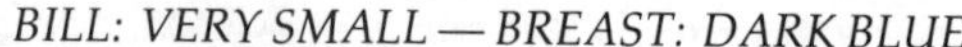

BILL: VERY SMALL — BREAST: DARK BLUE

#93. purple martin (m)

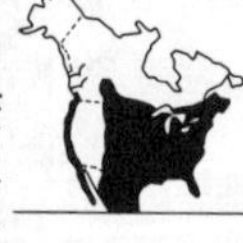

CAP blends with blue-black of nape, throat, body. BILL very small. FRONT throat, breast, *underparts all blue-black* (not purple in spite of name). BACK same blue-black as front, tail notched. ACTIONS sky-skimming flight after insects; nests in cavities, several pairs together, prefer bird houses built "apartment house" style on tall pole. Will use hollowed gourds hung on a cross-bar on tall pole. HABITAT open country, city edge, farms, waterfronts.

CLOSE LOOK-ALIKE **purple martin (f/y)** cap and back same blue-black as male, underparts mottled grayish buff, *larger than any other swallow.*

MEDIUM LIGHT BLUE

BILL: THICK — BREAST: BLUE

#94. blue grosbeak (m)

CAP blends with rich bright blue of nape, throat, body. BILL thick, short, grayish. FRONT throat, breast, underparts all same blue. BACK 2 *rusty-brown wing bars,* some light and dark feather-edging on wings, dark edging on shoulders, remainder same blue (may look black in poor light). ACTIONS ground-feeder, mostly on insects, gleans fresh-plowed fields like cowbirds but *hops,* not walks. HABITAT brush, thickets, streambanks.

CLOSE LOOK-ALIKES #43, 44, 95, 96 (brown female, #74 L-A).

BILL: MEDIUM THIN — BREAST: BLUE

#95. mountain bluebird (m)

CAP turquoise blue, blends with nape, throat, body. BILL medium thin. FRONT throat, breast full turquoise blue, underparts paler, whitish (no brown or rust). BACK all turquoise blue (no brown or rust). ACTIONS feeds chiefly on insects, also berries, fruits; nests in tree cavity; prefers high country. NOTES soft warbling trill, robin-like. HABITAT thickets, farms, mountain meadows, foothills.

CLOSE LOOK-ALIKES #43, 44, 94, 96 (blue-gray female, #85).

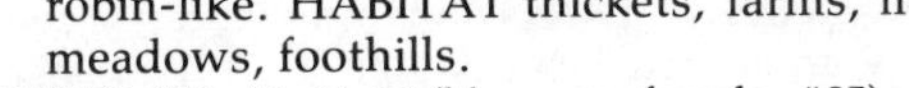

BILL: MEDIUM THIN — BREAST: RUSTY BROWN

#96. eastern bluebird (m)

CAP sky blue, blends with nape, back. BILL medium thin. FRONT *throat, upper breast rusty-brown,* lower breast, underparts white. BACK sky blue (*no rusty-brown*). ACTIONS feeds chiefly on insects, also berries, fruits; nests in tree cavity, very scarce in some areas due to lack of nesting sites; will use nest box 5×5×8'' with $1\frac{1}{2}$'' entry. NOTES 3-note warbling trill "tru-u-ly, tru-u-ly". HABITAT open country, wood's edge, farmland. Will use bird box, *see* Inviting Birds to Your Yard for dimensions.

CLOSE LOOK-ALIKES #43, 44, 94, 95 (blue-gray female, #85). **western bluebird** same appearance as **eastern bluebird** except western has *blue throat* (rusty breast) a *rusty-brown patch on upper back* (female #85 L-A). Range West, north to Canadian border (**mountain bluebird** goes north to Alaska).

S br | S gy | S bl | S gr | S yl | S rd | S b/w | M br | M gy | M bl | M gr | M yl | M o/b | M rd | M b/w | L br | L gy | L bl | L g/b | VL br | VL gy | VL bl | VL gr | VL r/p | VL b/w | VL bk | VL wh

Size: MEDIUM — Color: GREENS

Among the birds that meet the size-and-color description of "Medium and Green" two have dark green backs, one has a brownish-green back and the others are a greenish-yellow or yellowish-green of a shade that makes it difficult to decide whether the yellow or the green is the dominant hue. These half-and-half species will be listed in both Keys. Those with bright yellow breasts are especially likely to be given "yellow" listing.

As usual in our SCANS System, the Key will chart the birds first by cap color — dark green, olive-green or rust — and then by breast color — gray, dark green, yellow-green, yellow or rust-and-white. Find the matching cap and breast colors for the bird you wish to identify and then check each description under that heading until you have a perfect match on each point. Check the pictures and range maps for final proof.

CAP: DARK GREEN — BREAST: PATTERNED (DARK GREEN)

#97. European starling (except winter)

CAP iridescent green-black, blends with head, body. BILL medium thick, medium long, bright yellow (except in winter when it is grayish). FRONT iridescent green-black-purple in good light, seems black in dull light. BACK same as front, but more brown edging on wings, *tail short* (noticeably shorter than other Medium birds that look black). ACTIONS *walks,* gathers with other starlings, blackbirds, grackles in large noisy flocks; strips fruit trees; usurps nesting holes of bluebirds, may destroy nestlings; eats numerous harmful insects including Japanese beetles which most native birds do not eat. Pairs usually separate to nest apart, not in colony. NOTES can imitate other birds, human voices, musical instruments; will learn to talk if trained as nestling; has its own whistles, chatters, trills. HABITAT almost anywhere — farms, cities, orchards; introduced from Europe in the 1890s in New York City, it is now known across the continent, even to Alaska.

CLOSE LOOK-ALIKE in winter, **starling** covered with heavy white speckling, some more densely than others.

CAP: DARK GREEN — BREAST: PATTERNED (RUSTY/WHITE)

green kingfisher big-headed, but no crest; bill long and stout, throat and underparts white, back, wings and tail flecked in white. About half the size of **belted kingfisher.** Female has greenish breast band, not rusty. Range Arizona to Texas along Mexican border.

CAP: RUSTY — BREAST: PATTERNED (GRAY)

green-tailed towhee cap rusty bordered by short white line between bill and eye, gray cheeks, throat white with black stripe down each side, breast gray, underparts white, back, wings and tail olive-green. Like most towhees has a catlike mewing call. *See #74* for other brownish western towhees. Range West.

CAP: OLIVE GREEN — BREAST: PATTERNED (OLIVE-GREEN)

#98. scarlet tanager (f/y/wm)

CAP yellow-green blending with nape, body. BILL medium thick, medium long, grayish. FRONT lighter yellowish-green than back. BACK wings, tail blackish-green (*black for wm*). ACTIONS tree and brush feeder on insects, berries. NOTES call a brisk chip-churr-rr. HABITAT woods, thickets, yards.

CLOSE LOOK-ALIKES (orioles have *pointed* bills, *see* #99). **western tanager (f/y/wm)** 2 *wing bars,* white or yellowish, wings and tail black, front may look more yellow than green (male #102). Range West. **hepatic tanager (f/y)** has *dark bill,* not gray (male #109 L-A). Range Southwest. **summer tanager (f/y)** back is orange-yellow, not greenish, no wing bars (male #109 L-A). Range South, Florida to California, northeast to Great Lakes.

#99. orchard oriole (f/y)

CAP blends with back. BILL medium thick, long and *pointed.* FRONT greenish yellow, throat to underparts. BACK 2 white wing bars. ACTIONS tree and brush feeder on insects, berries; builds hanging nest (not so deep as **northern oriole**). NOTES female does not sing. HABITAT orchards, farms, yards.

CLOSE LOOK-ALIKES (**tanagers** have rounded bill. *See* #98). **Scott's oriole (f/y)** similar coloring, but back is streaked olive-green. Range Southwest. **hooded oriole (f/y)** similar coloring, but more a grayish-green, less yellowish. Range extreme southwest. **northern (Baltimore) oriole (f/y)** front more orange-yellow, less greenish than **orchard** female. Range East, Canadian west. **northern (Bullock's) oriole (f/y)** front is grayish-yellow, back grayish-yellow. Range West.

CAP: GREEN — BREAST: PATTERNED (YELLOW)

#100. yellow-breasted chat

CAP olive-green, bordered by white line over eye. BILL medium. FRONT *white eye ring* joins white eye line, cheek dark gray bordered by white line between cheek and yellow throat, throat and breast bright yellow, underparts white. BACK olive-green, no markings on wings, back, tail; tail long. ACTIONS eats insects, berries; often lurks in thickets and heard but not seen. NOTES chatter, clear whistles, harsh croaks; repeats phrases; may mimic; mews like a cat. May sing at night or on the wing (usually with legs dangling). HABITAT thickets, briar patches, streambanks.

CLOSE LOOK-ALIKES other green-backed, yellow-breasted members of the warbler family (#56-58) are much smaller. **Oriole** and **tanager f/y** duller breast color.

S br · S gy · S bl · S gr · S yl · S rd · S b/w · M br · M gy · M bl · M gr · M yl · M o/b · M rd · M b/w · L br · L gy · L bl · L g/b · VL br · VL gy · VL bl · VL gr · VL r/p · VL b/w · VL bk · VL wh

S br | S gy | S bl | S gr | S yl | S rd | S b/w | M br | M gy | M bl | M gr | M yl | M o/b | M rd | M b/w | L br | L gy | L bl | L g/b | VL br | VL gy | VL bl | VL gr | VL r/p | VL b/w | VL bk | VL wh

Size: MEDIUM — Color: YELLOWS

According to the SCANS System, a bird is counted as "yellow" if that is the main color of its back — not its breast. Therefore you will find the yellow-breasted chat described in the Key for Medium-and-Green (to match its olive-green back) not in this Key. However, female orioles and tanagers which are both of a shade between green and yellow — are in both Keys.

Birds of Medium size whose backs are definitely yellow are easily told apart by the color of the cap — the second important clue, but all these species have yellow (or yellowish) breasts. You will quickly see the other features that set each one apart as you check each point in the usual description — especially the shape and color of the bill. Find the complete match for the bird you want to identify, first by cap and bill and then by other points. Make final check of range map and picture and the color picture numbered to match the Key bird.

CAP: DARK BROWN — BREAST: PATTERNED (YELLOW)

#101. evening grosbeak (m)

CAP visor U-shaped *bright yellow* (wider across forehead). BILL *very thick,* short, pale (almost white). FRONT cheeks and throat shaded (dark over yellow), breast and underparts bright yellow (amount of shading varies). BACK and rump bright yellow, nape and shoulders shaded (more bronze than black), tail black, *wings black with large white patch near body,* tail short and notched. ACTIONS nests in high country, most often in north and west; travels in flocks in winter in all directions, not always on same route each year; comes to feeders for sunflower seeds, also feeds heavily on box elder and maple seeds; usually roosts apart from feeding area (called "evening" because first seen only in evening at roosting area, not in daytime). NOTES loud and clear "yeep" or "yee-ip". HABITAT conifer forests in spring, summer; any place there's food in winter — woods, parks, yards.

CLOSE LOOK-ALIKES **evening grosbeak (f)** has no bright visor, but gray of head and body washed with yellow (brighter on breast and rump), has more white on wings and also white on tail, bill very thick and pale. **white-winged crossbill (f/y)** crossed bill tips and heavily-streaked body give quick ID (male #68 L-A, 110 L-A). **pine grosbeak (f)** bill *black* and *stubby,* yellowish on head and rump, 2 white wing bars (not big patches). Range northeast, northwest, west.

CAP: RED — BREAST: PATTERNED (YELLOW)

#102. western tanager (m)

CAP *hood bright red* (cap, nape, cheeks, throat). BILL medium thick, medium long, *pale.* FRONT breast, underparts bright yellow. BACK black patch across shoulders, bright yellow above and below the patch; tail black, short, notched; wings have 2 white or yellowish bars, some feather edging in white. ACTIONS tree and brush feeder on insects, berries. NOTES robin-like warble, 2 notes, then 3; also "puh-tick". HABITAT woods, wooded slopes, yards with water bowls, feeders with dried fruit, bread.

CLOSE LOOK-ALIKES **western tanager (wm)** red fades on hood, may look orange. **western tanager (f)** no red hood, yellow not bright, has 2 wing bars, bill pale. **scarlet tanager (wm)** basic yellow with black wings but random red patches when changing to adult plumage (summer male #109).

CAP: BLACK — BREAST: PATTERNED (BLACK)

#103. Scott's oriole (m)

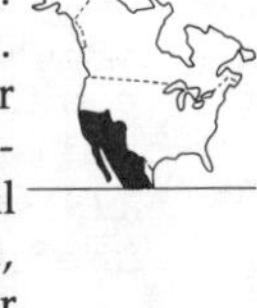

CAP hood black (cap, nape, shoulders, throat). BILL medium thick, medium long, *pointed*, dark. FRONT throat and upper breast black; lower breast, underparts *yellow* (not orange). BACK upper back black, central and lower back *yellow;* tail *yellow* at sides, center and tip black; wings black, 1 white wing bar, some white edging on other feathers. Female (#99 L-A) lacks black. ACTIONS eats insects, probes flowers for nectar (as do most orioles). NOTES clear, lilting whistle (7 or 8 notes much like song of western meadowlark), female also sings near nest. HABITAT wooded canyon slopes.

CLOSE LOOK-ALIKE Only one other male oriole is *yellow* and black (not orange) — the **Audubon's oriole (black-headed oriole).** It is larger than **Scott's** by an inch, has yellow upper back (not black) and is rarer. Range in U.S. only in Texas.

CAP: GREENISH — BREAST: PATTERNED GREENISH (see Green Key*)*

(#98) **scarlet tanager (f/y/wm)**

LOOK-ALIKES (medium bill, not pointed) **western tanager (f/y)** male #102. **hepatic tanager (f/y)** male L-A #109. **summer tanager (f/y)** male L-A #109.

(#99) **orchard oriole (f/y)**

LOOK-ALIKES (medium bill, *pointed*) **Scott's Oriole (f/y)** male #103. **hooded oriole (f/y)** male #103x (*see* next Key). **northern (Baltimore) oriole (f/y)** male #104. **northern (Bullock's) oriole (f/y)** male #105.

Evening grosbeaks *are wanderers but they may stay for weeks — even months — if sunflower seeds are handy.*

S br
S gy
S bl
S gr
S yl
S rd
S b/w
M br
M gy
M bl
M gr
M yl
M o/b
M rd
M b/w
L br
L gy
L bl
L g/b
VL br
VL gy
VL bl
VL gr
VL r/p
VL b/w
VL bk
VL wh

S br · S gy · S bl · S gr · S yl · S rd · S b/w · M br · M gy · M bl · M gr · M yl · M o/b · M rd · M b/w · L br · L gy · L bl · L g/b · VL br · VL gy · VL bl · VL gr · VL r/p · VL b/w · VL bk · VL wh

Size: MEDIUM — Color: ORANGE AND BLACK

No Medium bird has a back of solid orange, but several have a solid orange rump below black patch or streaking. The caps will also be orange or black (or both) and breast color will be orange or orange-and-black. All but one are in the oriole group and so have pointed bills; the other is a grosbeak with a short thick bill.

The description of the cap will be the first clue, with the breast pattern a second clue. The bill and other description will identify each species point by point. One species of oriole will stand apart because the orange of its breast and rump is dark, almost rusty, while the others are all bright. When species look so much alike — all in the family — each small point must be compared carefully.

CAP: ORANGE — BREAST: PATTERNED (BLACK AND ORANGE)

hooded oriole (m) *cap, nape, cheeks orange;* throat, space between bill and eye, center of upper breast black; sides of upper breast, lower breast and underparts orange; shoulders and rump orange, tail black, wings black with 2 white wing bars and some white edging. Range Southwest (California, Nevada, Utah to Texas).

LOOK-ALIKES only two other N.A. orioles have *orange caps* **Altamira (Lichtenstein's) oriole,** seen rarely on Texas border, and **spot-breasted oriole,** introduced in Dade Co. Fla. (recognized by scattering of black spots around the solid black throat and breast patch). Neither is seen often except in a small locale.

CAP: BLACK — BREAST: PATTERNED (BLACK AND ORANGE)

#104. northern (Baltimore) oriole (m)

CAP hood includes *full head* (cap, nape, throat, cheeks). BILL medium thick, medium long, *pointed,* gray. FRONT black of hood comes down to upper breast, from hood's lower edge to underparts bright orange. BACK black of nape comes over shoulders, rump orange, top of tail black, outer feathers of lower half orange, wing has orange bar, *narrower white bar,* some white feather edging. ACTIONS feeds in treetops on webworms, hairy caterpillars and other insects, on wild berries, flower nectar; builds hanging nest 5–6 inches deep, a remarkable structure. NOTES clear, flutelike whistled notes in series. HABITAT woods edge, parks, yards with trees, farms.

CLOSE LOOK-ALIKES #105, 106, 107. **Baltimore oriole** and **Bullock's oriole** *were formerly counted separate species, but interbreed when they meet in the midwest and are now considered one species. Nevertheless, each has distinct markings and should be identified separately.*

#105. northern (Bullock's) oriole (m)

CAP black with *orange visor* and *orange line over eye.* BILL medium thick, medium long, pointed, gray. FRONT *cheeks orange,* throat patch black and narrow, breast orange from cheeks to underparts. BACK nape and shoulders solid black, rump and lower back orange, tail outer feathers orange, center and tip black, wings black with *very wide white patch,* some white edging on other wing feathers. ACTIONS feeds in treetops and thickets, shrubbery on harmful insects (codling moth, weevils, aphids, etc.) on fruit, flower nectar; builds hanging nest similar to **Baltimore oriole's.** NOTES whistled notes similar to **Baltimore's.** HABITAT woods, streambanks, farms, parks, yard with trees.

CLOSE LOOK-ALIKES #104, 106, 107.

CAP: BLACK — BREAST: PATTERNED (ORANGE AND YELLOW)

#106. black-headed grosbeak (m)

CAP hood includes cap, nape, cheeks, upper throat. BILL very thick, pale (not so thick and pale as **evening grosbeak's;** much thicker and shorter than oriole bill). FRONT upper breast and sides clear to underparts orange, central stripe up to midbreast from underparts lemon yellow. Female and young (#79 L-A) patterned brown and buffy orange. BACK orange streaked in black, black nape line irregular, rump orange, wings black, 2 white wing bars, some other white edging, tail black with some white, white "thumbprints" on underside of tail. ACTIONS feeds on seeds, berries, other fruits, codling moths, caterpillars, many harmful insects; likes sunflower seeds, grains; does not gather in flocks at feeder like **evening grosbeaks;** shares incubating duties with female, very protective of mate and nest. NOTES robin-like, but richer, more flowing; female also sings near nest and on nest; call a sharp "eek". HABITAT woods, streambanks, orchards, parks, yards with trees and shrubbery.

GENERAL LOOK-ALIKES orioles are similar in color, but easy to separate by *pointed* oriole beak, *thick* grosbeak. Also, **Bullock's oriole,** which most often shares range, does not have complete black hood.

CAP: BLACK — BREAST: PATTERNED (BLACK AND RUSTY-ORANGE)

#107. orchard oriole (m)

CAP hood includes nape, cheeks, throat, upper breast. BILL medium thick, medium long, *pointed,* gray. FRONT breast to underparts rusty-orange. BACK shoulders and upper back black, lower back and rump rusty-orange, shoulder of wing rusty-orange, tail black, wings black with 1 white wing bar, some white edging on feathers. ACTIONS often keeps to thickets, sings from treetops in courtship; feeds on insects, berries, fruits; pair may nest singly or in a group; builds an open cup-shaped nest, not hanging pouch, between twigs. NOTES robin-like, repeated phrases of 2-notes. HABITAT orchards, farms, quiet yards.

CLOSE LOOK-ALIKES no other oriole has this shade of rusty-orange; no other Medium bird has a similar combination of rusty-orange and black, but **rufous-sided towhee** (#113) has similar look if seen only in profile and without checking shape of bill or color of eye (red for towhee, black for oriole).

S br | S gy | S bl | S gr | S yl | S rd | S b/w | M br | M gy | M bl | M gr | M yl | M o/b | M rd | M b/w | L br | L gy | L bl | L g/b | VL br | VL gy | VL bl | VL gr | VL r/p | VL b/w | VL bk | VL wh

Size: MEDIUM — Color: REDS

Birds of Medium size — between house sparrow and robin — that have red backs also have red fronts, red caps. The cap may be flat or an upright crest, and so it is the shape of the cap — rather than color — that makes the first clue. The shape and color of the bill makes a second clue, since all breasts are red, either entirely or in partial wash, except for two females which have only a hint of the males' bright color. Other females are not red at all and so are in other Keys.

Match the bird you want to identify by cap shape — flat or crest — and by bill shape — short, thick and triangular or medium in length and thickness. Then check other descriptions — especially the color of wings and tail — until you find a perfect match. As always, check the range map and pictures for final proof.

CAP: RED CREST — BILL: THICK, TRIANGULAR

#108. northern cardinal (m) (cardinal, redbird)

CAP all red crest, visor line black. BILL thick, short, triangular, yellowish-red. FRONT black, of visor line extends across eyes and under bill; remainder of throat, breast, underparts all bright red. BACK all red, nape, back, wings, tail. ACTIONS crest may be raised or lowered; ground, tree and brush feeder on insects, fruits, grain; comes to feeder for sunflower seeds, cracked corn and other grain, fruit, suet; nests in thickets; does not usually migrate, even in north, if food available. NOTES loud, musical, 2-note whistle, repeated at length; male and female both sing, but female more softly. HABITAT woods edge, streambanks, parks, thickets, yards.

CLOSE LOOK-ALIKES **northern cardinal (f/y)** over-all color brownish-red that may look just brown from a distance, but quite red (though darker than male) on wings and tail, tip of crest is bright red, bill red, y black mask. **pyrrhuloxia** like female cardinal but grayish instead of brown, male has red wash down center of breast, both sexes have red tip to crest, red eye ring, yellow bill. Range Arizona to Texas on Mexican border.

CAP: RED, FLAT — BILL: MEDIUM LONG AND THICK, GRAY

#109. scarlet tanager (m)

CAP all red, blends with head, body. BILL medium in length, thickness, *pale gray*. FRONT all red, throat to underparts; eye black. BACK all red, nape to rump, but wings and tail *solid black — no white edging*. Female (#98) yellow, no red. ACTIONS tree and brush feeder on insects, berries; male usually arrives in spring before female and claims nesting site by singing, threatening other males. NOTES robin-like song, call notes "chip-churr". HABITAT woods, thickets, yards.

CLOSE LOOK-ALIKES **summer tanager (m)** a rosy red, not the bright fire-engine red of the **scarlet tanager** male, and *no black*. Range Northeast, Southeast, Southwest. **hepatic tanager (m)** more yellowish-red than **summer tanager** but not so bright as **scarlet tanager,** has gray cheek patch, gray-to-black edging on wings and tail. Range Arizona to Texas on border. **scarlet tanager (wm)** keeps black wings and tail but moults each fall, changing red to yellow; may be seen in *half-and-half patchwork red-and-yellow*. **red crossbill (m)** #68 crossed bill tips quick ID.

CAP: RED, FLAT — BILL: THICK, SHORT, TRIANGULAR, BLACK

#110. pine grosbeak (m)

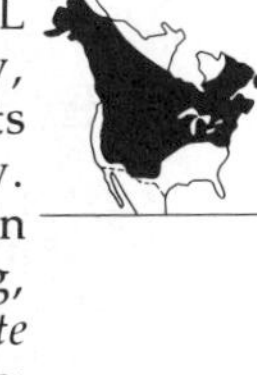

CAP rosy red, blends with cheek, nape. BILL shorter than cardinal bill. FRONT throat gray, breast washed in rosy red, sides gray, underparts gray. Female (#101 L-A) washed in yellow. BACK streaked red nape to rump, rump plain red, tail long and black with some red edging, wings black with *much white edging, two white wing bars.* ACTIONS often seems almost tame; large winter flocks; feeds on seeds of maples, birches, conifers, weeds, on berries, buds, nuts, large insects. NOTES warbling trill, much like purple finch. HABITAT conifer forests, brushy hillsides, woods edge.

CLOSE LOOK-ALIKE male **white-winged crossbill** #68 L-A has similar coloring but is much smaller.

*When a **Steller's jay** comes to the feeder, smaller birds make way.*

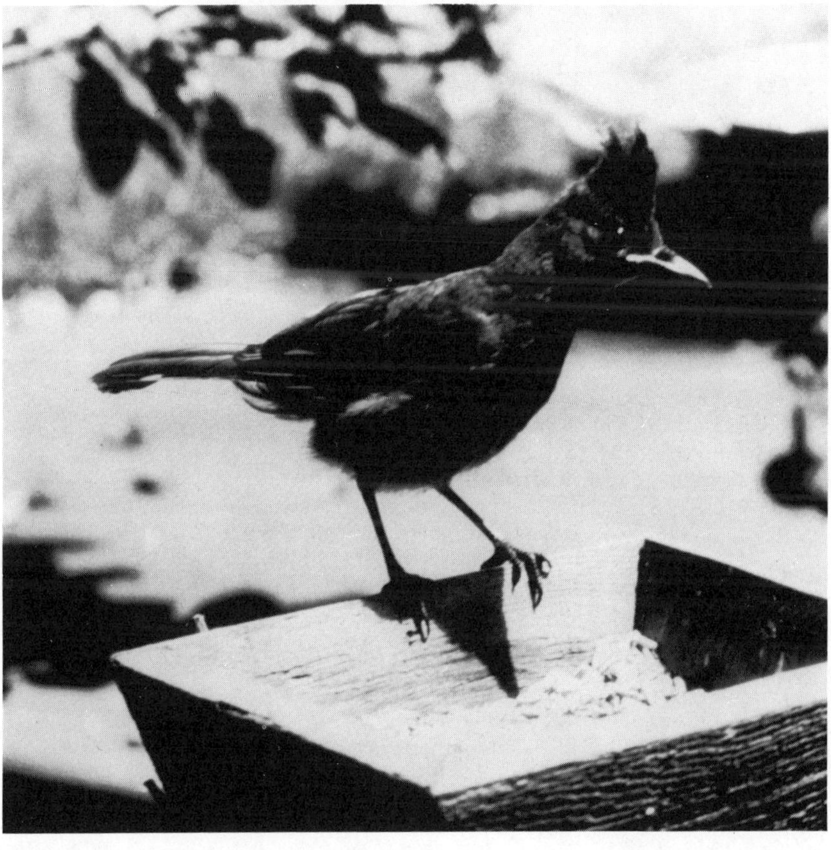

S br · S gy · S bl · S gr · S yl · S rd · S b/w · M br · M gy · M bl · M gr · M yl · M o/b · M rd · M b/w · L br · L gy · L bl · L g/b · VL br · VL gy · VL bl · VL gr · VL r/p · VL b/w · VL bk · VL wh

Size: MEDIUM — Color: BLACK-AND-WHITE or BLACK

Birds of Medium size with black-and-white or all-black backs are easily separated by their actions in food finding. They will be flycatchers, usually snatching insects in mid-air, or ground-feeders such as blackbirds eating mostly seeds and grain, or woodpeckers, or either of two sky-skimming swifts. First, place the bird you want to identify in the right group and then check it by the usual SCANS clues of cap color and breast color. With the woodpeckers you will also want to look for a third clue — the pattern of the back, which may be barred in narrow crosswise lines or patterned in solid patches of black and white. Be very careful with woodpecker clues, for some species have almost identical twins.

Birdwatchers along ocean shores, especially in the Far North and Pacific coasts, will see several kinds of Medium black-and-white birds. Those with chubby bodies and short tails are dovekies, various auklets and murrelets and the slightly larger guillemots — never seen inland. Some sandpipers and other Medium shorebirds such as the black turnstone are black-and-white (or black-white-gray) especially in winter. You'll find them described in books that specialize in sea and shore birds.

FLYCATCHERS

CAP: BLACK — BREAST: PLAIN

#111. eastern kingbird

CAP red central tuft usually not visible amid black. BILL medium, black. FRONT white, throat to underparts; black cap includes eye and upper cheek. BACK black or slate-gray, some feather edging in gray, tail black with *white band across tip*. ACTIONS noisy, often attacks larger birds, even hawks, if they come near nest, has even attacked airplanes; feeds on insects in air and on ground; usually darts out from perch; also eats berries, seeds. NOTES rapid chatter. HABITAT orchards, roadsides, farms, suburbs.

GENERAL LOOK-ALIKE **phainopepla (m)** *breast black,* crest and back black, white patches on wings show in flight, feeds on insects in midair. Female #74 L-A is brown. Range Southwest.

GROUND FEEDERS

CAP: BROWN — BREAST: PATTERNED (BLACK)

#112. brown-headed cowbird (m)

CAP hood, includes nape and throat, upper breast. BILL medium thick, short. FRONT throat and hood dull brown, lower breast and underparts match back in glossy black. BACK glossy black, some iridescence. ACTIONS male courts female (#74 L-A) with much bowing, bobbing; neither adult builds nest or rears young (*see* Most Unusual in Actions); feeds on grain, insects; *walks;* holds head at angle as if in pride. NOTES gurgly squawk, creaking whistle. HABITAT fields, roadsides, yards.

CLOSE LOOK-ALIKE **bronzed cowbird (m)** wings and tail glossy black, body brown, *eye red.* Range Arizona to Texas along border.

CAP: YELLOW — BREAST: PATTERNED (YELLOW)

yellow-headed blackbird (m) cap, nape, throat, breast bright yellow; patch between eye and bill black; underparts black; back, wings, tail black; wing has white patches that show in flight. Female is brown and yellow (#79 L-A). Range West, wanders east in fall.

CAP: BLACK — BREAST: PATTERNED (WHITE AND RED)

#113. rufous-sided towhee (m)

CAP hood, includes cap, nape, throat, upper breast. BILL thick, short. FRONT center breast white, *sides rusty*, under-tail patch rusty, *eye red*. BACK wings black with white patch, white edging (more on western birds than on eastern), outer tail corners white, 2 white "thumbprints" on underside of tail tip. ACTIONS scratches energetically in underbrush for insects, seeds; also eats berries, fruit; western birds come to dooryard, eastern birds usually do not. NOTES vary considerably from one individual to another; westerners slur notes, mew like a cat; easterners enunciate more distinctly (as a rule) saying, "Drink your tea!" or "Tow-*hee*, see tow-*hee*!" Some make it closer to "Too-hee, see too-hee!" or "T'whee!" Eastern birds also give a brisk "Chewink!" Some southern birds call "Jo-ree-ee!" HABITAT thickets, woods edge, clearings, yards.

CLOSE LOOK-ALIKES some individuals in the Southeast have *white eyes* instead of red. Females are the same as males except that they are brownish-black, not jet black. Young towhees, full grown and on their own in first summer, are black flecked over-all in grayish-white; no white on breast, no rusty sides; eyes are brown, not red; have two white "thumbprints" on underside of tail like adults. Adult feathers appear gradually, some rusty patches on sides, some white on breast, full adult plumage by mid-fall. GENERAL LOOK-ALIKES **rose-breasted grosbeak (m)** #114. **orchard oriole (m)** #107.

#114. rose-breasted grosbeak (m)

CAP hood includes, cap, nape, throat. BILL short, thick, triangular, pale. FRONT center of breast bright rose red next to black of throat, narrows to center streak; sides of upper breast and all of lower breast and underparts white to extreme under-tail patch. Female #79 patterned browns. BACK nape, back and shoulders black, rump white, wings black with 2 white wing bars, some white edging; wing linings rose-red, underside of tail white. ACTIONS tree feeder on seeds, blossoms, ground feeder on insects such as grasshoppers, potato beetles. NOTES lilting robin-like carol; male and female both sing, on and off the nest. HABITAT woods, orchards, yards.

GENERAL LOOK-ALIKE **rufous-sided towhee** #113.

CAP: BLACK — BREAST: PATTERNED (BLACK)

#115. bobolink (m)

CAP hood includes cheeks, throat, breast, *not nape*. BILL thick, short, blackish gray. FRONT whole front black from crown of head to underparts. BACK nape buffy-yellow; upper back streaked black, white, yellow-buff; lower back white, upper part of wing white, some buffy edging on black feathers of lower wings, tail black, sharp tipped. Female #79 L-A patterned browns. ACTIONS in summer eats harmful insects, weed seeds, but in winter eats rice growing in fields (called **rice birds** in South) and were once killed in great numbers by rice planters (rice no longer grown in former great quantities). NOTES according to poet William Bryant, song says, "bobolink, bobolink, spink, spank, spink." A bubbling, lilting carol, whatever the words. HABITAT fields, roadsides, marshes.

GENERAL LOOK-ALIKE #70.

#116. red-winged blackbird (m)

CAP blends with head, body. BILL medium, pointed, black. FRONT glossy black. BACK glossy black, shoulder of wing has red patch with yellow lower border (may be hidden). *See* #79 L-A for female, young males — yearling males begin to show red patch and hodge-podge change to adult male plumage. ACTIONS gathers in flocks in winter, smaller flocks in summer; one of the earliest returning migrants in north each spring. NOTES gurgling call, "Cher-o-kee!" HABITAT fields, marshes, streambanks.

CLOSE LOOK-ALIKE **tri-colored blackbird** red wing patch has *white* border instead of yellow. Range mainly California and adjoining states.

#117. Brewer's blackbird (m)

CAP iridescent black, blending with body plumage. BILL medium, pointed, dark. FRONT all iridescent black, *eye whitish-yellow*. BACK purplish-black on head, greenish-black on back, (in winter brownish, barred), tail medium. ACTIONS walks, gleaning insects, weed seeds, grain. NOTES raspy, creaky squawk. HABITAT farms, city parks, fields, roadsides.

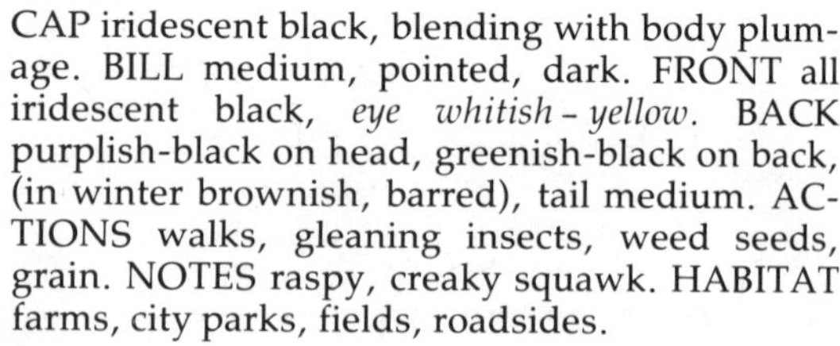

CLOSE LOOK-ALIKE female brownish, dark eye (#74 L-A). **rusty blackbird** not so glossy as **Brewer's,** looks dull black. Range East (west in Canada also).

WOODPECKERS AND SAPSUCKERS

CAP: YELLOW PATCH — BREAST: PLAIN — BACK: BARRED

#118. three-toed woodpecker (northern three-toed woodpecker) (m)

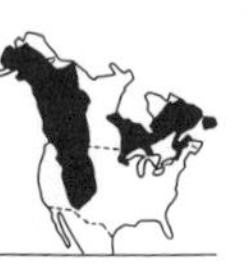

CAP yellow patch bordered in black at sides, visor white; female has black cap. BILL sturdy, medium long. FRONT throat and breast white, sides barred full length, white line over eye and under black cheek patch, black whisker line, bill to shoulder. BACK center of back *barred* black and white, upper wing plain black, lower wing barred in white, outer tail feathers white checked in black. ACTIONS rather slow-moving, unwary; typical woodpecker drilling, tapping for wood-boring insects on tree trunk; also eats wild berries, acorns and other nuts; nests in tree cavity. NOTES drumming and tapping noisier than voice — squeak, hoarse rattle, sharp tick. HABITAT conifer forests.

CLOSE LOOK-ALIKE **black-backed woodpecker (three-toed) (m)** similar in looks except for *solid black back* (not barred) and no black checks on outer white tail feathers. Range similar but not so far north or south.

CAP: RED PATCH — BREAST: PATTERNED — BACK: BLACK

acorn woodpecker cap red, visor white, *eye yellow*, eye mask black, cheek below mask and throat white, bib mark black, breast streaked black on white, rump and wing patches white (show plainly in flight) tail black. *Drills holes in tree trunk* to store acorns and other nuts for future use. Range West — Oregon to California, Arizona to Texas.

white-headed woodpecker red patch cap; white visor, cheeks and throat; breast and underparts black, white lengthwise patch on outer lower wing edge (shows well in flight). Range West Coast in U.S., strays to B.C.

CAP: RED PATCH — BREAST: PATTERNED — BACK: BARRED

#119. yellow-bellied sapsucker

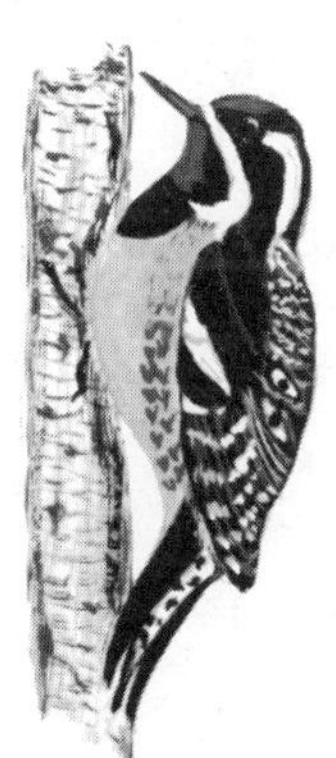

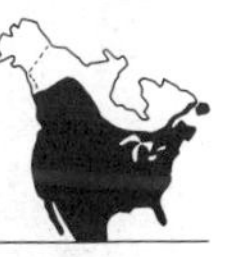

CAP bordered in black, thin white visor line. BILL sturdy, medium long. FRONT throat bright red bordered in black on sides and with black mark, breast streaked in black at sides (female usually has white throat, not red), touches of yellow below bib but entire belly is not yellow in spite of name, only yellowish; cheek striped white and black (black in center). BACK center of back barred black on white, outer edge of folded wing shows *long white patch,* inner edge plain black, lower edges of wing black checked in white, tail black with some white edging, rump white. ACTIONS drills small holes in trunk in fairly regular line to suck sap and nibble inner bark; also eats ants and other insects such as tent caterpillars and some fruit, berries, buds. Comes to feeder in winter for suet, bread, etc. Nests in tree cavity. NOTES nasal mewing whine or churr, hoarse squawk; usual drumming (sometimes on tin roof). HABITAT woods, yards with tall trees, orchards.

CLOSE LOOK-ALIKES **red-naped sapsucker** (subspecies) red halfmoon across nape main difference. Range Rockies to Cascade and Sierra Mts., British Columbia to California, also Texas. **red-breasted sapsucker** (full species) #120 L-A.

CAP: RED HOOD — BREAST: PLAIN — BACK: SOLID BLACK/WHITE

#120. red-headed woodpecker

CAP full red hood covers entire head, nape, throat. BILL sturdy, medium long. FRONT thin black bib line between red hood and white breast, breast to underparts all white. BACK lower half of wing solid white, rump also white making wide band in flight, upper half of wings and tips solid black, tail tip black. ACTIONS formerly abundant, familiar to all, now scarce in some areas (for lack of tall trees or because starlings take over nest holes). Drills for insects on tree trunk or darts out to catch them in midair or on ground; may eat berries, corn, grapes, nuts — and may store such food. Comes to feeder for suet, corn, sunflower seeds, raisins, nuts, bread. Will nest in box. NOTES rattled cluck; whistled "clear, clear-o"; makes usual drumming noises. HABITAT woods and farms with woodlots, yards with tall trees.

CLOSE LOOK-ALIKE no other *eastern* woodpecker has a full red hood (*see* #121 for partial hood) but in west **red-breasted sapsucker** has a full hood (but barred back) and is often miscalled red-headed woodpecker. Formerly subspecies of **yellow-bellied sapsucker,** now given full species rating. Range Pacific Coast, from Cascade and Sierra mountains to the sea, Alaska to Arizona.

CAP: RED HALF-HOOD — BREAST: PLAIN — BACK: BARRED

#121. red-bellied woodpecker

CAP red bordered by buffy-gray visor, gray cheeks; includes cap and nape on male (female *back* of cap and nape). BILL sturdy, medium long. FRONT cheeks, throat, breast, underparts buffy-gray more or less flushed with pink (underparts deeper pink but not bright red). BACK folded wings and back all barred; in flight shows white rump, white wing patch encircled in black on outer edge; central tail feathers barred, outer feathers black. ACTIONS feeds on wood-boring insects on tree trunk, also on ground insects (ants, beetles) nuts, berries; stores any of this food; comes to feeder for suet, peanut butter, nuts, etc. NOTES scolding churr, usual drumming. HABITAT woods, farms with woodlots, yards with tall trees, marshy woods.

CLOSE LOOK-ALIKES **gila woodpecker** red *cap* only; nape, cheeks, visor, throat, breast and underparts all buffy; back barred, white wing patch shows in flight, female similar without red cap. Nests in saguaro cactus. Range Southwest desert. **golden-fronted woodpecker** small red cap but bright yellow-orange on visor and nape; cheeks, throat, breast, underparts all buffy; back barred, rump white, tail black (female has yellow visor and nape but no red cap), shows white wing patch in flight. Range Texas, sw Oklahoma. **ladder-backed woodpecker** red cap extends to upper half of nape, visor red streaked in black, bordered by white line over eye, curving down nape; similar black line through eye and curving down to nape, white cheek patch bordered in black, throat white, upper breast white blending to yellow-buff well streaked in dotted lines, *back barred,* tail black. Range Southwest.

S br S gy S bl S gr S yl S rd S b/w M br M gy M bl M gr M yl M o/b M rd M b/w L br L gy L bl L g/b VL br VL gy VL bl VL gr VL r/p VL b/w VL bk VL wh

CAP: BLACK — BREAST: PLAIN — BACK: WHITE CENTER

#122. downy woodpecker

CAP black, visor white, bordered in wide white line over eye, wide black line through eye; *small red patch* on upper nape of male, remainder of nape black bordered by white (female all black center). BILL sturdy, fairly short. FRONT cheek patch, throat, breast, underparts all white; thin black line between throat and cheek. BACK center from black nape line to gray rump *all white,* upper edge of back plain black, wing splotched in white, tail center black, outer feathers white with small black checks. ACTIONS one of most-often-seen woodpeckers and the smallest in U.S. and Canada; drills tree trunk or large branch for insect food; also eats berries, nuts, seeds, flower buds; comes to feeder for suet, nuts, peanut butter, bread; usually alone except in nesting season. NOTES single-note or quavery screech; sharp tick; usual drumming in long roll. HABITAT woods, gardens, streambanks, parks, yards with trees.

CLOSE LOOK-ALIKE **hairy woodpecker** almost identical except for larger size, *longer bill* (**hairy** 8½-10½″, **downy** 6–7″ in length. To help judge size for **hairy** vs. **downy** ID, measure the side of the feeder or tree trunk where the bird often perches and mark it for comparison. **hairy** has *all white* outer tail feathers (no black check marks) — a clue not always easily seen. Voice of **hairy** is louder. Range similar to **downy's** but extends farther north and south.

CAP: BLACK — BREAST: PATTERNED — BACK: BLACK

Williamson's sapsucker cap black extending to nape, white visor, extending back across black cheek, white line from eye to nape, throat center patch red bordered in black, *upper breast black, lower breast yellow* and barred at sides in black and white, back black, large white patch on upper wing, rump white (show in flight), tail black. Female (#79 L-A) brown head, barred brown-and-white back, yellow belly. Range West.

CAP: BLACK — BREAST: PATTERNED (STREAKED) — BACK: BARRED

Nuttall's woodpecker cap black but lengthwise *nape patch red,* tail black, outer feather white. Range California Coast. Fairly common.

red-cockaded woodpecker cap black, cheek patch white, small red patch at either edge of cap toward nape. Range Southeast, mainly South Carolina to Florida; may stray north or west.

three-toed woodpecker (f) same as male (#118) except cap is black, not yellow.

CAP: BLACK — BREAST: PLAIN — BACK: BLACK

black-backed woodpecker (f) same as male (#118 L-A) **black-backed** except cap is black, not yellow; same as female **three-toed** except has *plain black* back instead of barred back.

SWIFTS

CAP: BLACK — BREAST: PATTERNED (BLACK/BLACK AND WHITE)

white-throated swift throat very white, eye-line white, sides patterned in black patch with smaller white patch, tail notched. Range West.

black swift black or blackish slate-gray over all except for white visor line visible only at close range, tail notched. Range West.

Size: LARGE — Color: BROWNS

Brown birds of any size range in tone from lightest buff to dark chocolate and are often a combination of several dark-to-light shades. Large brown birds range in length from robin to common pigeon. Some will be slender-bodied, others pigeon-plump. Some will have the longer legs of shorebirds and others the very short legs of birds almost constantly a-wing. Three hawks and an owl are also included. You may recognize the family group to which each belongs at a glance, but to know each one by name, look for the same clues you've used to identify smaller birds — color of the cap, color of the breast.

As it happens, all Large Brown birds have brown caps, some plain, others streaked or mottled. Breasts will be plain, washed in color, streaked or barred. First match the bird you wish to identify by cap color, then breast color. Check all the descriptions under the matching cap-breast heading until you have a perfect match. Be sure to check the range, either on the map or in the text so that you know the bird is likely to be in your area. Compare the bird with the picture in this book or in other books for final check.

CAP: PLAIN BROWN — BREAST: PLAIN (WHITE)

#123. yellow-billed cuckoo

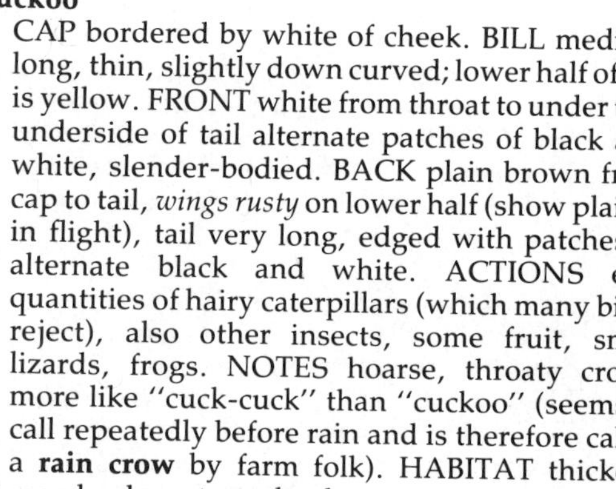

CAP bordered by white of cheek. BILL medium long, thin, slightly down curved; lower half of bill is yellow. FRONT white from throat to under tail, underside of tail alternate patches of black and white, slender-bodied. BACK plain brown from cap to tail, *wings rusty* on lower half (show plainly in flight), tail very long, edged with patches of alternate black and white. ACTIONS eats quantities of hairy caterpillars (which many birds reject), also other insects, some fruit, small lizards, frogs. NOTES hoarse, throaty croak, more like "cuck-cuck" than "cuckoo" (seems to call repeatedly before rain and is therefore called a **rain crow** by farm folk). HABITAT thickets, marsh edge, streambanks.

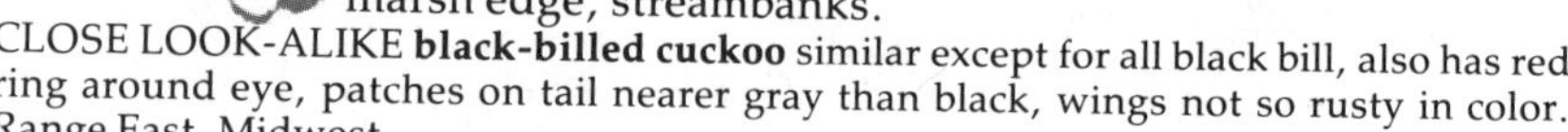

CLOSE LOOK-ALIKE **black-billed cuckoo** similar except for all black bill, also has red ring around eye, patches on tail nearer gray than black, wings not so rusty in color. Range East, Midwest.

CAP: PLAIN BROWN — BREAST: PATTERNED (STREAKED)

#124. brown thrasher

CAP bordered by buffy-gray cheek patch. BILL sturdy, fairly long. FRONT *eye yellow*, breast white heavily *streaked* (not spotted like thrushes), extreme underparts white. BACK nape, back, tail all cinnamon brown; 2 white wing bars, tail long. ACTIONS sings from very top of tree or bush; feeds on ground, scratching and "thrashing" around in leaves as it hunts for insects, tossing leaves aside with bill; walks, runs and hops; also eats berries, small rodents, reptiles, some nuts, corn. NOTES usually repeats each 2-note or 3-note phrase twice in rather bossy tone. Farmers used to say it was giving planting instructions: Drop it, drop it! Cover it, cover it! Also mimics other bird songs. HABITAT thickets, underbrush, woods edge, farms, roadsides, hedgerows.

CLOSE LOOK-ALIKE #75. **long-billed thrasher** more gray-brown than cinnamon, eye bright yellow. Range Texas border. **Bendire's thrasher** paler, grayer than **long-billed** or **brown thrashers;** breast washed in buff beneath streaks; eye yellow. Range Southwest desert. **curve-billed thrasher** bill longer and more down-curved, eye yellow, breast washed in buff beneath streaks. Range Arizona to Texas on border. GENERAL LOOK-ALIKES (bills very long, down-curved). **California thrasher** no breast streaks, washed in gray-brown, throat pale, eye dark. Range California. **LeConte's thrasher** all-over buff, no streaking; eye dark. Range Southwest desert. **crissal thrasher** eye yellow, throat white with black whisker line, under-tail patch rusty. Range Southwest.

#125. American kestrel (sparrowhawk)

CAP cinnamon-brown surrounded by blue-gray. BILL hooked. FRONT cheek and throat white, black "comma" mark in cheek center (under eye) and bordering cheek and nape, breast and underparts buffy, spotted, streaked. BACK *male* shoulders cinnamon-brown barred in black, *pointed wings gray-blue; female* back and wings cinnamon barred in black, also tail; male tail plain cinnamon banded on the tip in wide black above narrow white. ACTIONS feeds on insects, small birds, rodents, reptiles; can hover over field as it hunts. NOTES high-pitched cry of "killy-killy-killy" and so called **killy hawk** by farmers. HABITAT meadows, prairies, deserts, golf courses, yards.

CAP: PLAIN BROWN — BREAST: PATTERNED (MOTTLED)

#126. northern bobwhite (m) (*quail* not part of official name)

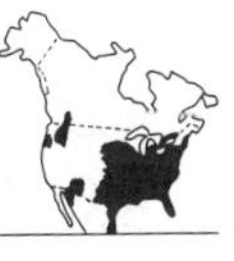

CAP may be raised in tufted look, bordered by white line over eye (male) buffy line (female). BILL thick, short, dark. FRONT curving black line through eye to nape, throat white (male); curving brown line, throat buffy (female); throat edged in irregular dark line, breast mottled and barred in center and streaked at sides in various shades of brown, body plump. BACK nape, back, wings and tail mottled browns, tail short and *dark gray*. ACTIONS winter flocks huddle in circle, tails pointing inward; mated pairs separate in spring; when chased will rise suddenly from cover with loud wing whir ; seldom flies high or far, can run far and fast through fields, both male and female tend brood; feeds on seeds, grain, berries, insects, acorns; comes to gardens for bird seed, cracked grain, water. NOTES whistled call of "bob-white, bob-bob-white!" also conversational clucks and plaintive 3-note rally call. HABITAT farmlands, open country, roadsides; thickets; suburbs with surrounding thickets.

CLOSE LOOK-ALIKES **gray partridge** also called "Hun" for **Hungarian partridge**; cap, back and wings mottled browns, throat plain brown, breast and nape mottled grays, lower breast and underparts rusty and white (center spot, sides barred), tail shows outer feather; *rusty* in flight. Somewhat larger than **bobwhite.** Range introduced both sides Canadian border (more in West than East). **chukar** somewhat larger than **gray partridge**, also shows rusty outer tail feathers in flight, has *bright red* bill, legs and feet, white throat and cheeks bordered in *wide black heart-shape line,* breast gray, sides barred in dark on light, back gray-brown in winter, reddish-brown in spring, summer. Range Asian species introduced in West in rocky, barren country. **ptarmigan** 3 species (**willow, rock** and **white-tailed ptarmigans**) all mottled and barred brown-and-buff in summer, almost all white in winter and a mixture of white (especially on wings) in-between seasons. Range willow and rock only in far north, coast to coast; white-tailed in West only and down into Rockies to New Mexico. **meadowlarks** #131. **prairie chickens** #156 L-A. Other quail **California** #133 and **Gambel's, mountain, scaled** all #133 L-A; **Montezuma,** #82 L-A.

pied-billed grebe water bird of stream, pond, marsh; head, medium-long neck, body all mottled browns; bill pale, chicken-like in shape with black wrap-around stripe in center; black throat stripe; dives quickly, showing white underside of cocky short tail. Range most waterways of U.S. and southern Canada.

CAP: PLAIN BROWN — BREAST: PATTERNED (SPOTTED, BIB)

northern (red-shafted) flicker *See* #132 (yellow-shafted) L-A.

CAP: PLAIN BROWN — BREAST: PATTERNED (COLORED BROWN)

#127. mourning dove

CAP buffy gray-brown with highlights of pastel rose. BILL medium, dark. FRONT eye-ring bluish, iridescent pastel highlights on throat (usually seen only up close), same buffy-gray-brown on throat, breast and underparts; small black patch on cheek, legs and feet pink. BACK buffy-gray-brown nape to tail, several oval black patches on wings, in flight tail shows *zigzag white border,* tail is long, *pointed.* ACTIONS bobs and bows as it walks; builds rather rickety-looking platform nest (male brings twigs, female builds), lives in flocks in winter, pairs in summer; feeds on ground on seeds and grain (especially weed seeds), sometimes on snails and insects, comes to gardens for grain and water. NOTES mournful-sounding call of "ah-coo-coo-coo" is really not evidence of sadness but the usual announcement of territory claim and reassurance to mate. Although all doves are held the symbol of peace, the **mourning dove** and most of its kin can be quite belligerent in defending mate and nest. (*See* #173 for quite different call of **band-tailed pigeon**, an owl-like "oo-hoo".) HABITAT farms, suburbs, open country or woods edge, desert water-holes.

CLOSE LOOK-ALIKES #86x. **white-winged dove** white wing bars show in flight, has *medium fan-shaped* tail, white corners. Range Southeast. **ringed turtle-dove** paler, cream-colored, black nape ring. Introduced California, Florida; occasional escaped cage birds elsewhere. **Inca dove** mottled gray (not brown), tail long, white corners (not zigzag borders), in flight shows rusty wing patches. Range arid southwest.

CAP: MOTTLED BROWN— BREAST: PATTERNED (BLACK)

#128. lesser golden plover (American golden plover)

CAP for summer adults, mottled brown cap bordered by white visor line, white line over eye; for winter adults and young, buffy visor and eye line. BILL medium. FRONT for summer adults, white line over eye curves down around cheek to breast; cheek, throat, breast, underparts *all black;* for winter adults and young, upper breast streaked buff, lower breast buff. BACK nape, back mottled dark-and-light (brown, gold, buff, white), rump dark (same for adults and young). ACTIONS nests on far north tundra, migrating in fall off Atlantic Coast to South America, off Pacific to Hawaii; most return in spring through midland prairies, not coast. NOTES whistled 2-note or 3-note cry. HABITAT on migration over midlands, pastures, mudflats, fields.

CLOSE LOOK-ALIKE **black-bellied plover** cap white, back mottled dark-and-silver. Range, winters on both coasts, Hawaii; migrant over most of continent.

CAP: STREAKED BROWN — BREAST: PATTERNED (STREAKED)

#129. common snipe

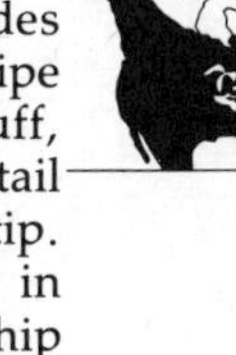

CAP striped *(lengthwise)* buff and brown. BILL straight, long. FRONT throat, breast and sides streaked brown, underparts white, dark stripe goes through eye. BACK streaked browns, buff, white; in flight shows buffy-brown rump, tail rusty-orange with black bands, white tip. ACTIONS usually stays near cover, flies in zigzag pattern, wades in water; in courtship performs sky-dive with tail and wing feathers spread. NOTES harsh churr, plaintive cry; quavery whistle from spread feathers of sky-dive. HABITAT marsh, streambanks, thickets.

CLOSE LOOK-ALIKES **American woodcock** cap bars *crosswise,* visor buff, breast buffy-rust, legs short. Range East. **short-billed dowitcher** rump *white,* winters on ocean beaches of both coasts, nests in far north, crosses inland during migration. **long-billed dowitcher** rump *white,* bill up to 3 inches. Range same as **short-billed dowitcher's. upland sandpiper (upland plover)** buffy line over eye, back and breast mottled. Range East, Canada west to Alaska. **lesser yellowlegs** streaked front and back, rump white. Range, nests Canada to Alaska, winters Atlantic and Gulf Coasts, migrates over continent. **Virginia rail** throat white, breast buffy-rust, underparts barred, back rust. Range cont-exFar North.

#130. burrowing owl

CAP bordered by white or gray-white line V-shape over eyes. BILL hooked. FRONT eyes yellow, front-faced; breast splotched; *legs long,* pale, not heavily feathered. BACK splotched much like breast, tail short. ACTIONS often seen by day standing on ground near burrow or on fence post; bobs and bows; shares terrain with prairie dogs; hovers when hunting for small rodents, insects such as grasshoppers, small birds, reptiles; hunts in early evening or at night more than by day;. NOTES chattery tick-tick-tick, tremolo coo. HABITAT grassland, prairie, farm meadows, desert, river levees; uses vacant rodent burrow for nest.

GENERAL LOOK-ALIKES (fellow predators) **merlin (pigeon hawk) (f/y)** cap streaked brown bordered by buffy line over eye, breast streaked, back and wings brown, tail banded brown and buff with white tip, in flight wings are *long and pointed,* as are all falcon wings. Male adult (#133x) is gray-backed, breast streaked brown on buff. Range cont to Alaska. **sharp-shinned hawk (y)** #150x similar to **merlin (y)** but wings short and rounded. **Cooper's hawk (y)** similar but larger. Range cont to Alaska. **whip-poor-will** similar in actions to smaller **nighthawk** (#80) but has *black* throat bordered by white line, black bib, wings swept back but not pointed, male has large white tail patches (female brown and buff). Call of whip-poor-will led to name. Range East, Southwest. LOOK-ALIKES **common nighthawk** #80. **common pauraque** smaller, has similar black

S br S gy S bl S gr S yl S rd S b/w M br M gy M bl M gr M yl M o/b M rd M b/w L br L gy L bl L g/b VL br VL gy VL bl VL gr VL r/p VL b/w VL bk VL wh

throat. Range West. **chuck-will's-widow** larger, throat brown with white line border, no white in wing, has white streaks, not corners, in tail. Range East.

CAP: STREAKED BROWN — BREAST: PATTERNED (COLOR WASH: YELLOW)

#131. eastern meadowlark

CAP striped brown and buff. BILL medium, sturdy, pointed. FRONT yellow patch between bill and eye, black line from eye to nape, *cheek gray,* throat yellow with black bib (crescent shape), breast yellow, extreme underparts white, some streaking at side of upper breast. BACK wings, back and tail streaked browns, tail's outer feathers white (shows underneath and in flight), tail short. ACTIONS sings from fence posts, rocks; walks; feeds on insects, grain, weed seeds; flies like a quail with a few quick wing flaps then a long glide; nests on ground. NOTES 4-note up-down carol to match "Spring time, sing time!" HABITAT fields, pastures, plains, prairies, overgrown orchards.

CLOSE LOOK-ALIKE **western meadowlark** very little difference in appearance — check **western** has *brown* cheek patch, not gray, and *sides of breast* are *gray streaked* in dark splotches, not yellow. Most easily identified difference is in song — **western** sings a bubbling 7 or 8 note carol to match "Isn't this a pretty place!" Range West, shares territory with **eastern** in southwest and midwest prairie. GENERAL LOOK-ALIKES (similar black bib, *see* #132 L-As).

CAP: GRAY — BREAST: PATTERNED (SPOTTED, BIB)

#132. northern (yellow-shafted) flicker

CAP bordered by buff of cheek patch. BILL fairly long, sturdy. FRONT cheek and throat buff, includes eye; whisker line across cheek from bill thick, black (on male only); both sexes have wide *black bib* (crescent shape) between throat and spotted breast (heavy black spots on pale buff) spotted clear to underparts. BACK nape gray, crossed by *bright red crescent,* back and wings brown barred in black, rump white, lining of wings and tail *bright yellow,* tail black, short and pointed, shafts of feathers also yellow. ACTIONS eats more ants than any other bird, also feeds on other insects, berries, weed seeds; comes to feeder for grain, suet, peanut butter; on ground more than other woodpeckers. NOTES calls rapid "flick-a, flick-a, flick-a", or "flick-flick-flick"; also "clear-*er*!" as if demanding a change in the weather. Usual drumming. HABITAT woods, streambanks, farms, yards.

CLOSE LOOK-ALIKES **red-shafted flicker** formerly counted a separate species, now a color form of **northern (yellow-shafted) flicker**; has brown cap, not gray; red whisker line across cheek, not black; no red crescent on nape (no crescent of any color); lining of wings and tail pinkish-red, not yellow. Range West. **gilded flicker** also now a color form of **northern flicker**; cap brown, whisker line red, no crescent on nape, lining of wing and tail yellow. Range southwest desert. (Other flickers are found in South America, hence "northern" clarifies North American range.) SPECIAL CHECK birds with similar black-bib clue, U or V shaped. **horned lark** #73 breast white. **varied thrush** #87 breast orange. **meadowlarks** #131 breast yellow. **flickers** #132 breast spotted black on buffy-white. **chukar** #126 L-A breast gray. **killdeer** #72 (and 5 Look-Alike plovers) breast white. **dickcissel** #16 L-A breast yellow. **sage grouse (m)** #157 breast buffy-white. **yellow-bellied sapsucker** #119 breast buffy-yellow. **Williamson's sapsucker (m)** #122x **(f)** #79 L-A breast yellow. **blue jay** #139 breast white. **McCown's longspur (sm)** #25 L-A breast grayish white. **Lapland longspur (wm)** #25 breast white, REMINDER **varied thrush, meadowlarks** and **flickers** are often confused by beginning birders who rely on one clue only — the black crescent bib — for ID.

Size: LARGE — Color: GRAYS

Birds that are Large and Gray may be much alike in Size and Color but very different in Actions. Some are plump-bodied, grain-and-insect-eating quails. Two are daylight predators; one a round-winged hawk, the other a pointed-winged falcon. One is the Measure Bird for the entire group, the common pigeon, while another is a little-known western species in the jay-crow family. Two are water birds; one a hook-billed gull, the other a pointed-billed tern. So, many check-points besides basic Size and Color must be made before you learn each one by name.

As usual in the SCANS System, the first ID clues to check — once you've placed a bird in the matching Size-and-Color group — are colors of cap and breast. You'll find each combination listed, as usual, and you'll want to check each species listed under the matching heading before making final ID.

CAP: PLAIN BROWN — BREAST: PATTERNED (MOTTLED)

#133. California quail (m)

CAP *black topknot plume curves forward,* brown cap bordered by white line, *buffy visor patch.* BILL medium thick, short. FRONT cheek and throat black, bordered by very white bib line edged narrowly in black, upper breast plain gray, lower breast and underparts *barred* in brown and buff scallops, sides lengthwise scallops. BACK nape streaked, back shaded grays, tail short. ACTIONS gathers in flocks in fall and winter; usually keeps watch-bird on guard on nearby lookout post while flock feeds, in nesting season male keeps watch, night roost in trees or thickets; usually rests at mid-day, feeding morning and evening on insects, berries, weed seed, grains, acorns; goes to water to drink morning and evening regularly so can often be seen near waterhole; also comes to suburban yards and farmyards for bird seed, grain, water. NOTES rally call for mate or scattered flock is "oh-hi-oh" or "chee-chah-ko" — sometimes plaintive, sometimes brisk; also clucks. HABITAT woods edge, parks, farms, fields with hedges or thickets, yards with shrubbery or water.

CLOSE LOOK-ALIKES **California quail (f)** has shorter plume, no white or black face-and-throat markings, just streaked grays, underparts barred like male's. **Gambel's quail (m)** same black plume, black and white throat markings but *visor is black* not buff, upper breast is gray but lower breast is buff with *large central black splotch* not barred in scallops, sides have large rusty-brown patches beneath white splashes. Female has plain buff underparts, neither black splotch nor scallops. Range Southwest desert country. **mountain quail** black plume is *straight,* not curved forward, white visor line, throat rich brown bordered in white, upper breast bluish-greenish gray, lower breast rich brown widely scalloped in white, under-tail patch rusty. Female similar but paler and with shorter plume. Range brushy mountain slopes, Baja to Canadian border. **scaled quail** has short buffy-gray *tufted crest* not a plume, breast and upper back feather edging outlined in black scallops, underparts in buffy and brown scallops. Range Southwest deserts.

S br | S gy | S bl | S gr | S yl | S rd | S b/w | M br | M gy | M bl | M gr | M yl | M o/b | M rd | M b/w | L br | L gy | L bl | L g/b | VL br | VL gy | VL bl | VL gr | VL r/p | VL b/w | VL bk | VL wh

CAP: PLAIN GRAY — BREAST: PLAIN

Wilson's phalarope in winter, gray mantle, white rump, tail, breast; long, thin bill; in summer rusty wash on neck, back (female more colorful than male). Range, nests Great Lakes, western lakes, marshes (seen inland and on coasts in migration to South America).

CAP: PLAIN GRAY — BREAST: PATTERNED (BARRED IN RED)

sharp-shinned hawk (*see* similar **Cooper's hawk** #168 L-A) cap, back and wing gray, breast *barred* in narrow *red* crosswise lines, eye red, tail faintly banded in black with white tip, tip may be straight across or slightly notched, *not rounded* like larger but almost duplicate **Cooper's hawk.** Young of both species (#130 L-A) are brown-backed with streaked breasts (not barred) and yellow eyes. Range cont.

CAP: PLAIN GRAY — BREAST: PATTERNED (STREAKED)

merlin (pigeon hawk) cap bordered by buffy-gray line over eye, black line (thin) through eye, cheek buffy, breast buffy streaked in darker brown, tail banded plainly, black on light gray, white tips, wings *long, pointed* gray. Young (#130 L-A) are brown, not gray. Range cont.

CAP: PLAIN GRAY — BREAST: PATTERNED (COLOR: GRAY)

#134. common pigeon (rock dove)

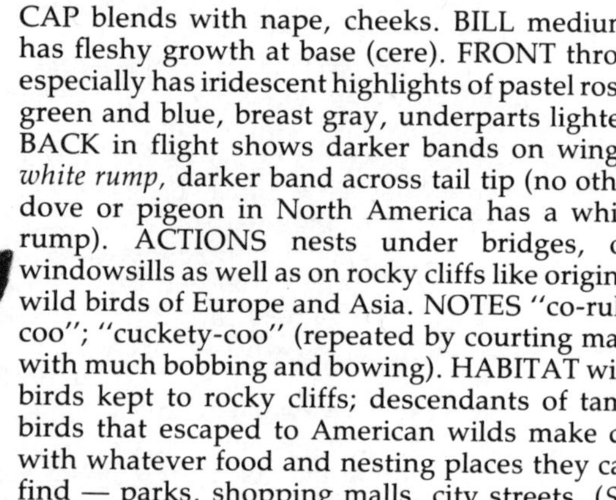

CAP blends with nape, cheeks. BILL medium, has fleshy growth at base (cere). FRONT throat especially has iridescent highlights of pastel rose, green and blue, breast gray, underparts lighter. BACK in flight shows darker bands on wings, *white rump,* darker band across tail tip (no other dove or pigeon in North America has a white rump). ACTIONS nests under bridges, on windowsills as well as on rocky cliffs like original wild birds of Europe and Asia. NOTES "co-ruh-coo"; "cuckety-coo" (repeated by courting male with much bobbing and bowing). HABITAT wild birds kept to rocky cliffs; descendants of tame birds that escaped to American wilds make do with whatever food and nesting places they can find — parks, shopping malls, city streets. (*See* Measure Bird #3.)

CLOSE LOOK-ALIKES #127, #173. Color variants: common pigeon may be a brownish red, very dark gray, almost black, partially white (all have white rump).

#135. gray jay (Canada jay)

CAP gray, white visor. BILL medium, pointed. FRONT visor area large, almost front half of head; cheek and throat white, gray of cap and nape includes eyes breast and entire front white shading to light gray. BACK white of cheek extends to border nape; back, nape, wings and tail all gray, some lighter edging on feathers, nape and wings darker. ACTIONS boldness and hunger of this northern species gave it nickname of **camp robber**. Also called **Whiskey Jack** from a twisting of an Indian name by early loggers. May take food from camper's plate, will eat fat from deer skins spread out to dry in hunter's camp or anything it can grab or beg from picnic or campsite, but does not often come to towns. Feeds in the wild on grasshoppers and other insects, berries, small rodents, small birds and their eggs; often hides food for later eating. NOTES harsh whistle or squawk, softer twittering, may mimic. HABITAT conifer woods.

CLOSE LOOK-ALIKES (young are all gray, no white). **Clark's nutcracker** bill is longer and pointed, visor area white but smaller than **jay's**, nape light gray like cap and back but wings *black* with *white* patch, tail *black* with *white* outer feathers. Range West, especially high mountain forests.

CAP: BLACK — BREAST: PLAIN

#136. Bonaparte's gull (ads)

CAP entire hood (cap, nape, throat) black (in winter, white). BILL medium, *black*. FRONT white breast and underparts, legs and feet red. BACK mantle (expanse of back and spread wings) gray, lower nape white, rump and tail white, outer wing patch white, narrow black edging shows in flight. ACTIONS feeds inland on insects, garbage; at waterfront on fish, marine worms, crustaceans. NOTES nasal churr. HABITAT oceans, bays, rivers, lakes.

CLOSE LOOK-ALIKES **common black-headed gull** bill *red* with black tip, cap brownish-black. Range East Coast, Great Lakes. **Franklin's gull** bill red, breast lightly washed in pink, wing corners black, bordered in white; often follows plow to eat grubs. Range western prairies, marshes. **laughing gull** larger (16–17″), mantle dark gray, not white but on lower wing edges. Range East, Gulf, California coasts. For larger gulls, *see* #171, #191x.

#137. black tern

CAP black hood. BILL medium, pointed, black. FRONT black (white in winter, mixed during molt). BACK dark gray on back, wings and tail, tail short and forked. ACTIONS hovers over marsh waiting to snatch insects or fish, over plowed lands for insects, grubs. NOTE shrill "kree-eek" brisk "krek". HABITAT nests inland near lakes, marshes; migrates on coast and through Mississippi Valley.

least tern black cap, *white visor*, bill pointed, *yellow;* mantle gray, outer wing feathers black, front and tail white, feet and legs yellow. Range Atlantic and Gulf Coasts, coastal rivers, Mississippi Valley rivers, California coast. Once abundant (pre-1880, before killed for feathers to trim women's hats) now scarce. For larger terns, *see* #200.

*A **camp robber** is also a camp helper as it cleans a hunter's deer hide of excess fat. Photo, Donald Fish.*

Size: LARGE — Color: BLUES

No bird in blue of Large size has the official name of bluebird. Five Large and Blue birds in North America are jays, two with crest and three without. One — also with crest, but a shaggy topknot, not sleek and pointed like the jays' — is the kingfisher. Its actions and waterfront habitat quickly set it apart from the jays. Jays have many skills, eat almost anything, but they do not make a daily habit of diving headfirst into deep water after a fish in kingfisher style.

Each jay can easily be told from any other if you get a good look first at the cap — whether crested or flat and of what color — and then at the color and markings of the breast. The cap-breast combination that serves as basic ID clue in each Size-and-Color Key, serves perfectly for large birds in blue. Don't forget that though all five jays are in basic blue, only one — the one first to get on official records — has the official name of blue jay. Each of the others has its own official name for birdwatchers to learn and remember. The purple gallinule, in spite of its name, has a green back and so will be in the next Key.

CAP: BLUE (CREST) — BREAST: PATTERNED (BIB)

#138. belted kingfisher (m)

CAP ragged bushy crest blends with cheek patch. BILL thick, pointed, long. FRONT neck circled in white (throat and nape), wide blue bib for both sexes (female also has lower rust-colored band or "belt"), remainder of breast and underparts white, big-headed in proportion to body. BACK blue, flecked in white on back, wings and tail; tail short. ACTIONS hovers over water on rapidly beating wings searching for fish, then goes for it in headfirst plunging dive, comes up (usually) with fish in bill; also watches for fish from nearby perch, returns to perch to eat, first slamming fish against branch to stun or kill it, then tossing it into air to swallow headfirst. Also eats small reptiles, creatures such as crayfish, small rodents and birds, and large insects. Like most meat-eating birds (hawks, owls, etc.) it disgorges bones, shells and other indigestible parts. Digs tunnel in sandbank for nest or even in gravel pit away from water; may sometimes nest in tree cavity. HABITAT inland rivers, ponds, lakes or seacoast.

GENERAL LOOK-ALIKE **green kingfisher** (#97x) medium size (7–8½") and color and range (Mexican border) quickly separate these two family members.

#139. blue jay

CAP crest sleek, narrow visor black. BILL medium, sturdy, pointed. FRONT cheek white, small patch over eye white, black narrow line through eye, throat white encircled in narrow black bib line which extends up to nape, remainder of breast and underparts white or grayish white. BACK wings and tail patterned in black bars and small white patches, outer tail feathers white, especially at corners. ACTIONS eats nestlings and eggs of other birds but in turn gives them good service in warning them of any enemy approach; also gives warning of its own approach, especially to a backyard feeder; also feeds on acorns and other nuts, corn, seeds, berries, insects. Usually mated pair devoted to each other, male feeds mate on nest. Some recently moving westward. NOTES besides raucous "jay-jay" squawk has other calls, especially soft twitters to mate; mimics other birds. HABITAT woods, thickets, yards.

CLOSE LOOK-ALIKE none. No other North American jay has a *blue crest* and a *white face*. GENERAL LOOK-ALIKES #140, 141.

CAP: BLUE (FLAT) — BREAST: PATTERNED (BIB)

#140. scrub jay (Florida jay combined with **California jay)**

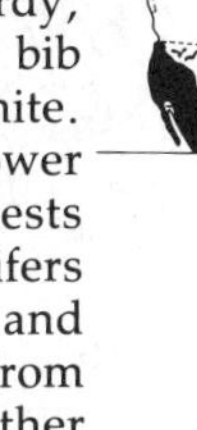

CAP flat, bordered by thin white line over eye and black eye mask. BILL medium, sturdy, pointed. FRONT throat white, incomplete bib mark blue, lower breast and underparts white. BACK nape blue, shoulders buff-gray, lower back, wings and tail bright blue. ACTIONS nests in scrub oak and thickets instead of in tall conifers like **blue jay** (hence name), other actions and food similar to **blue jay's**, often takes food from person's hand. NOTES more rasping than other jays but still has musical undertone in its harsh two-note call, also gives rapid "check-check-check" scolding. HABITAT woods, orchards, thickets, yards.

CLOSE LOOK-ALIKES (no crest). **pinyon jay** *shorter tailed,* no bib, throat only faintly white streaked, breast and *underparts blue, walks* like a crow (other jays hop). Range western sage country, juniper country. **gray-breasted jay (Mexican jay)** throat and breast gray, no bib, shoulders faded blue, not buff-gray in contrast to bright blue. Range Arizona to Texas on border. **California/Florida jay** now considered two geographical races of the **scrub jay.** First reported officially from Florida 1795 and thought to exist only in that area; located in California in 1839 and considered different species by some authors till 1957, ranging up into Oregon and Washington, a few in Idaho, Wyoming — has greatly increased numbers north and east of California in recent years and often ousts **Steller's jay** from former terrain.

CAP: SLATE-BLACK CREST — BREAST: PATTERNED (BLACK/BLUE)

#141. Steller's jay

CAP crest sleek, pointed. BILL medium, sturdy, pointed. FRONT adults usually (not always) have two cobalt blue vertical lines on forehead, short arched blue or white line over eye; remainder of crest, cheek, throat slate-black blending into cobalt blue of breast and underparts. Young birds have same coloring but may lack blue lines and have a softer, less sleek crest. BACK slate-black of nape and shoulders blends into cobalt blue of rump, wings and tail blue barred in thin black lines. ACTIONS similar to **blue jay** in food, actions; will mate with **blue jays** now wandering in west (since 1969) if **blue jay** cannot find mate of own species. **Steller's** only crested jay in most of West, first seen in Alaska in 1741 by Georg Steller, physician-naturalist then sailing with Russian expedition under Bering. Comes to feeder for sunflower seeds, other seeds, grains, often buries or hides surplus food, even burying bread in backyard flowerpot. NOTES typical "jay-jay" squawk (but each jay species has its own tone, soon recognized), talks to mate in soft purring roll, sometimes mimics other birds. HABITAT prefers forests of pine, Douglas fir, sometimes oak or other wooded slopes, visits parks, picnic grounds, camp sites, yards; often takes to high country forests in summer, but not always.

CLOSE LOOK-ALIKE none. No other North American jay has a *slate-black crest and face.*

Size: LARGE — Color: GREEN-BLACK, BLACK

Only one bird of Large size is green — and it is so dark a green that it looks black except in good light. Or perhaps most watchers just expect it to be black because it is a woodpecker and most woodpeckers have black as part of their color scheme.

Sharing this Key is another bird of iridescent black with glossy overtones of purple, blue and green. Two others are black with less iridescence, easily recognized by a thick almost parrot-like bill. This same bill — smooth for one species, carved with grooves for the other — tells these two apart. All of these all-black ones have caps and breasts the same color and so the watcher will have to check the bill, the tail, and actions for ID. Still another with green-black cap and back is the smallest member of the heron family, the only one to be measured as Large instead of Very Large.

CAP: GREEN-BLACK — BREAST: PATTERNED (GRAY)

Lewis' woodpecker dark green cap bordered by red visor, red face and throat, green-black nape, gray of breast encircles neck like a collar, lower breast and underparts rosy pink, wings, rump and tail all dark bottle green that looks black in poor light. Young are brownish-green with pinkish throat and breast. Range Western mountain forests.

CAP: GREEN-BLACK — BREAST: PATTERNED (STREAKED)

least bittern green-black cap bordered by rusty-buff cheek patches, throat white, breast streaked buff on white, wings buff edged in rusty buff, black back shows two buff lengthwise stripes in flight, legs long and yellow. Range reedy marshes; West, East (not midwest plains).

CAP: IRIDESCENT BLACK — BREAST: IRIDESCENT BLACK

common grackle larger than blackbirds (11–14"), eyes yellow, bill long and pointed, females less iridescent than males. Formerly two species — **purple grackles, bronzed grackles** — to describe difference in glossy overtone. Often in winter flocks with blackbirds and starlings and called blackbirds by people who do not notice their larger size. Feeds on beetles, grasshoppers and other harmful insects as well as grain. Range East, but spreading West, especially in Canada, around farmlands.

LOOK-ALIKES **boat-tailed grackle, great-tailed grackle,** both Very Large (16–18") with long tails that dip into a center groove, wide at tip. Females smaller, brownish. Range **boat-tailed** on Atlantic and Gulf Coasts, **great tailed** on Mexican border east to Louisiana.

smooth-billed ani the huge arched bill — somewhat similar in shape to that of parrot or puffin — immediately identifies this bird in black and tells the watcher it is not a **blackbird** or **grackle** (which have pointed bills). Has short rounded wings for futher clue if seen first in flight, and tail is rounded at tip, not wedge-shaped. First reported in Florida in late 1930s, probably blown over from Caribbean islands by hurricane winds. Now nests in much of south Florida, may stray farther North, West. Its whistled call of *queе-ick, quee-ick* distinguishes it from its almost-twin, the **groove-billed ani** whose call is a weak and slurred *plee-oh, plee-oh*.

groove-billed ani deep grooves parallel the curve of the bill's arched outline across the full width of bill. No other easily-seen difference in the two species, so call notes (described above) are ID clue. Range south Texas, some stray west to Arizona, north to Kansas, Nebraska, east to Florida.

Size: VERY LARGE — Color: BROWNS

Most Very Large birds show such easily recognized behavior that you can put them in a matching group by Actions as quickly as by Size and Color. Therefore, in each Color Key you will first match the bird you want to identify with one of the following four Action groups:

long legged (or very-long-legged) waders
short-legged swimmers
hook-billed or pointed-billed hunters, fishers, scavengers
stout-billed seed-and-bud eaters

Once you have matched your bird to the right Action group, follow the usual SCANS System of matching by the color of cap and breast, then by whatever other description is given. Be sure to check the range where the bird is most likely to appear. Double-check any bird out of its usual Setting. (Because sizes vary more for Very Large birds than for other Key size groups, length of each species is given in inches.

LONG-LEGGED WADERS

CAP: PLAIN BROWN — BREAST: PATTERNED (BROWN)

#142. glossy ibis 22–25″

CAP blends with head, neck, body. BILL very long, down-curved, dark; bare *blue* skin at base. FRONT all dark brown, may look black at distance. BACK all dark brown with glossy overtones of green or purple on wings. ACTIONS probes in water or mud for crayfish, small reptiles, insects. First found nesting in N.A. in 1880s on Atlantic Coast. May have been blown across the ocean from Europe. Now found all along the coast and inland to Great Lakes, and spreading. NOTES throaty squawk or grunt. HABITAT dense thickets beside marsh (fresh or salt water).

CLOSE LOOK-ALIKES **white-faced ibis** 22–25″, considered a separate species, only easily seen difference is bare *red* skin around eye in breeding season circled by *wide* white line (**glossy** has blue skin and narrow line). Range West, but in south extends to Louisiana and Florida. **white ibis (y)** 22–28″, head and neck streaked brown, front white, back brown, *bill red*, dark-tipped (adult #197).

sandhill crane (y) 34–48″ brown, not gray like adult (#160) and lacks adult's bright red cap.

king rail 15–19″ long, slightly down-curved bill, rusty-brown cap, cheeks, neck and breast, lower breast and underparts plainly *barred* in dark and light, back streaked, tail short, cocked upright, white underneath. Range East.
CLOSE LOOK-ALIKES smaller **clapper rail** (14–16″), gray-brown, gray cheeks, usually only in salt marshes on all coasts (**king rail** in both salt and fresh). Also still smaller **Virginia rail** (8–10″) #129 L-A.

CAP: STRIPED OR STREAKED BROWN — BREAST: PATTERNED (STREAKED)

#143. long-billed curlew 20–26″

CAP center stripe plain brown, white stripe over eye. BILL very long, down-curved. FRONT throat buffy, streaked at sides, underparts buffy. BACK streaked browns and buff, outer wing shows dark brown patch in flight, wing lining rusty patches next to body, tail barred; largest in sandpiper family. ACTIONS nests in fields, grasslands; very wary due to much hunting; feeds on small reptiles, crustaceans, large insects, berries. NOTES imitated by name — "curloo!" HABITAT marsh, shores, grasslands.

CLOSE LOOK-ALIKES **bristle-thighed curlew** 17″ slightly smaller, shorter down-curved bill. Range Alaska. Rare. **Eskimo curlew** 12–14″ down-curved bill, may be extinct though occasional sightings from Labrador to Texas are reported. **whimbrel** 15–19″ bill down-curved, face and underparts lighter buff. Range both coasts. **marbled godwit** 16–20″ bill almost straight, slightly up-curved. Range both coasts, inland West. **Hudsonian godwit** 13–16″ bill slightly up-curved, neck and breast rusty-buff, tail mostly white, black band across tip. Range nests Arctic, winters S.A. In migration seen inland, coasts. **willet** 14–17″ bill straight, rump white, wings in flight show black patch on outer "shoulder", broad white bands clear across wing above black edging. Range both coasts, nests east coat and beside western lakes, seen inland West on migration. **greater yellowlegs** 14″ neck and breast well streaked in browns, legs yellow (all others in this group have gray or brown legs). Range nests Alaska, northern Canada, winters all coasts. LOOK-ALIKE #129 L-A, **lesser yellowlegs** identified by smaller size, 9½—11″.

#144. American bittern 24–34″

CAP center stripe brown, buffy stripe over eye. BILL fairly long, pointed, fairly slender. FRONT cheek patch *black,* throat *white,* breast and underparts streaked buff and brown on white. BACK streaked browns and buff, wings show wide dark edging in flight, tail short. ACTIONS becomes suddenly thin and motionless among reeds for camouflage, head with bill pointed straight up, seems all but invisible; seldom perches in trees like others of heron family, nests among mounded reeds, not in trees; feeds in marsh on frogs, eels, small fish, reptiles, rodents, water insects. NOTES harsh, throaty, eerie croak; very resonant over water; 3 syllabled "dunk-yer-luck", repeated. HABITAT marsh, reedy bogs, streambanks.

CLOSE LOOK-ALIKES **black-crowned night-heron (y)** 23–28″ lacks black cheek patch, throat streaked, not white (adult #182). Range cont-exN (occasionally wanders to Alaska). **yellow-crowned night-heron (y)** 22–28″ lacks black cheek patch, throat streaked, not white; more gray than young **black-crowned**; thinner neck, longer legs (adult #161). Range East (west to Texas and midwest). **limpkin** 23–28″ more spotted and streaked with white on head, neck, back; walks with limping gait (name means "little limper"), favorite food one species of fresh-water snail, also eats other snails, some insects, worms, small reptiles. Range Georgia, Florida.

SHORT-LEGGED SWIMMERS

CAP: PLAIN BROWN — BREAST: PATTERNED (STREAKED BROWNS)

fulvous whistling-duck (fulvous tree duck) 18–21″ longer legged and somewhat longer necked than other ducks, head, neck, breast and underparts

rusty-buff, back browns and barred, *bill dark*; nests in deep south, coast to coast, often wanders north in fall.
CLOSE LOOK-ALIKE **black-bellied whistling-duck (tree duck)** 18–21″ black underparts, *bill red,* shows wide white wing patches in flight. Range Mexican border. **cinnamon teal (m)** 15–17″ head, neck, breast and underparts rusty-brown, back mottled rusty-brown, shows wide blue wing patches in flight, with smaller emerald green patch. Range West. GENERAL LOOK-ALIKES **blue-winged teal (m)** 14–16″ cap dark brown, white curved patch between bill and eye, breast and underparts mottled buffy-brown. Range cont-exAlaska. **green-winged teal (m)** 13–16″ cap rusty-brown, ovate emerald green patch from eye to nape, breast and back grayish-brown, finely mottled. Range cont.

CAP: STREAKED BROWN — BREAST: PATTERNED (MOTTLED)

#145. mallard (f) 20–28″ (*duck* not part of official name)

CAP bordered by lighter buffy line over eye, darker thin line through eye. BILL dark center, orange edges; flat. FRONT mottled browns over all. BACK mottled browns over all, blue wing patch bordered in thin black line, wider white line (top and bottom), shows plainly in flight, just barely with folded wing, *tail tip white.* ACTIONS often nests near houses; joins captive flocks at zoos, parks; best known, most abundant of all wild ducks; widely domesticated. Feeds by tipping tail up, head down in water (but can dive if necessary), on seeds of wild grasses, water-insects, snails, fish, fish eggs; in fields feeds on grain; will come to yard for bread, grain. NOTES loud quack-quack-quack. HABITAT almost anywhere near water.

CLOSE LOOK-ALIKES *see* #165 for very different **mallard male. American black duck (m/f)** 21-25″, wing patch is purple, bill yellow, over-all mottling darker. Range East. **mottled duck (m/f)** 20″ has white line below blue wing patch but not above, bill yellow, tail brown. Range Florida, Gulf Coast to Texas. **teal females** 14–17″, blue-winged, cinnamon, green-winged, all similar in coloring but smaller. **gadwall** 19–23″, underparts white, wing patch white and brown. Range cont-exN/Fla. **northern pintail (f)** 20–22″, tail dark, *pointed,* wing patch buffy, face darker (male #162). Range cont. **northern shoveler (f)** 17–20″, ID is wider "shovel" bill (male #165 L-A). Range cont-ex eastern Arctic. **eiders (f)** all species of **eiders (common, king, spectacled, Steller's)** distinguished from other ducks by sloping forehead, no blue wing patch, (182x, 183x, 184x). Range extreme north, both coasts.

CAP: BLACK — BREAST: PATTERNED (BROWN)

#146. Canada goose

CAP black. BILL flat, black. FRONT patch cheek-to-cheek and under chin white, neck long and black, breast mottled gray-brown, feather edging gives faint barred pattern, under-tail white. BACK browns, feather edging lighter, wings barred, tail black crossed by V-shaped white band (shows in flight). ACTIONS best known, most abundant of all wild geese; formerly counted as various species due to differences in size (22 to 48 inch length) and darker or lighter coloring, but now all one (white chin strap and white tail V clues for all sizes). Feeds on wild grasses, sprouting grain in fields, underwater plants, small crustaceans. NOTES musical honking cry, nicknamed **honker**. HABITAT near lakes, rivers,

S br | S gy | S bl | S gr | S yl | S rd | S b/w | M br | M gy | M bl | M gr | M yl | M o/b | M rd | M b/w | L br | L gy | L bl | L g/b | VL br | VL gy | VL bl | VL gr | VL r/p | VL b/w | VL bk | VL wh

bays, marshes, grain fields; usually nests on ground but learns to find safer places if flooded out by high water; will accept man-made platforms in trees or on poles, based on wagon wheels, laundry tubs, laundry baskets, etc. and adding nesting material.

CLOSE LOOK-ALIKE **brant** 22–26″ smaller than all but the smallest **Canadas,** has partial white collar on long black neck but not wide white chin strap. Darker individuals formerly counted separate species as **black brant.** Winters in coastal bays, both coasts, nests in Arctic. Range inland, Northeast on migration, Arctic.

#147. ruddy duck (m) 15–16″

CAP black cap and nape bordered by white cheek patch. BILL flat, light blue. FRONT throat, breast, underparts rusty-brown (in winter mottled gray-brown), cheek white, cap black all year. BACK wings, back and rump rusty-brown (gray-brown in winter), tail black, feathers cocked upright and spread in fan-shape, under-tail patch white. ACTIONS cannot walk well on land, cannot take off from water without pattering along surface, dives rather than flies to escape attack, can sink underwater without leaving telltale ripple. NOTES seldom makes any sound, makes chucking talk in courtship. HABITAT freshwater ponds and lakes in summer and winter, in winter also on coast in saltwater bays.

CLOSE LOOK-ALIKE female **ruddy duck** looks like winter male, but has dark line across the middle of her cheek patch.

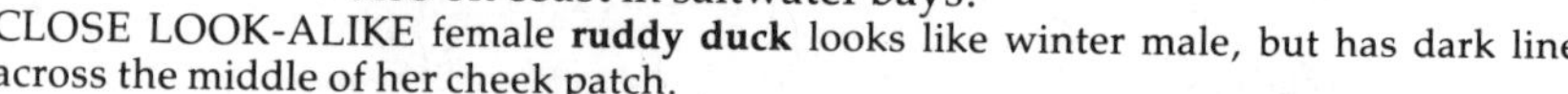

CAP: WHITE — BREAST: PATTERNED (BUFFY BROWN)

#148. American wigeon (m) 18–23″ (formerly spelled *widgeon)*

CAP white. BILL flat, light blue, black tip. FRONT *white cap* best ID plus bright *glossy green patch* from eye back to nape, throat grayish-white, breast buffy brown. BACK brownish with wide white patch on upper part of wing next to body, bordered in black with small white and green patches on lower edge (show in flight), tail pointed, black with white V-shaped line that shows in flight. ACTIONS rises up from water (no need for pattering take-off), rattles wings noisily on take-off if alarmed; dabbles in water to feed on leaves, buds, seeds of underwater plants; also goes inland to feed on sprouting grass and grain, also eats insects. NOTES whistled "whee-you-you". HABITAT freshwater marshes, ponds, bays, fields.

GENERAL LOOK-ALIKES **American wigeon (f)** 18–23″, cap gray, not white, no green patch on head, wing patches same as on male, bill blue with black tip, same as male. **Eurasian wigeon (m)** 18–20″, has buffy cap, not white, face rusty-buff (no green patch), wing patterns similar, females similar. Range, regular winter visitor, both coasts of N.A. occasional winter visitor inland.

HOOKED-BILLED OR POINTED-BILLED HUNTERS, FISHERS, SCAVENGERS

CAP: PLAIN BROWN — BREAST: PATTERNED (BROWN)

#149. golden eagle 30–40″

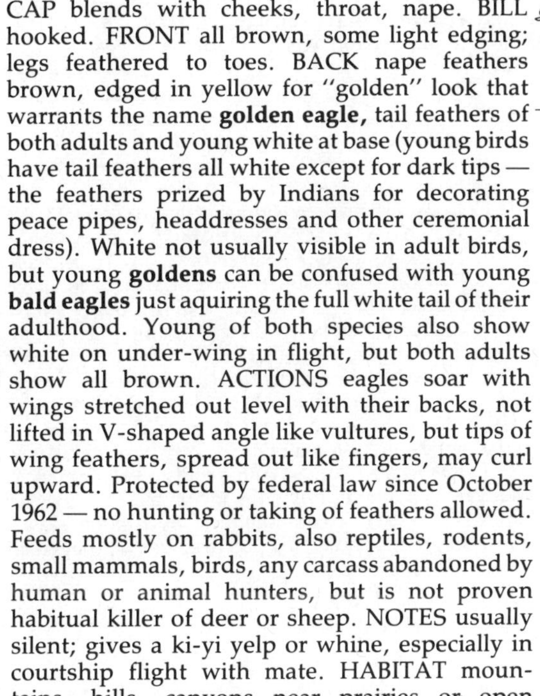

CAP blends with cheeks, throat, nape. BILL hooked. FRONT all brown, some light edging; legs feathered to toes. BACK nape feathers brown, edged in yellow for "golden" look that warrants the name **golden eagle,** tail feathers of both adults and young white at base (young birds have tail feathers all white except for dark tips — the feathers prized by Indians for decorating peace pipes, headdresses and other ceremonial dress). White not usually visible in adult birds, but young **goldens** can be confused with young **bald eagles** just aquiring the full white tail of their adulthood. Young of both species also show white on under-wing in flight, but both adults show all brown. ACTIONS eagles soar with wings stretched out level with their backs, not lifted in V-shaped angle like vultures, but tips of wing feathers, spread out like fingers, may curl upward. Protected by federal law since October 1962 — no hunting or taking of feathers allowed. Feeds mostly on rabbits, also reptiles, rodents, small mammals, birds, any carcass abandoned by human or animal hunters, but is not proven habitual killer of deer or sheep. NOTES usually silent; gives a ki-yi yelp or whine, especially in courtship flight with mate. HABITAT mountains, hills, canyons near prairies or open country.

CLOSE LOOK-ALIKE young **bald eagle** (**golden eagle** leg feathered to toes, **bald eagle** leg only halfway; **golden** under-wing white on lower half, **bald** on upper half; **golden** dark tail tip a definite band, **bald** tail mottled white/dark) **bald eagle** adult #154. GENERAL LOOK-ALIKES **Harris' hawk** 18—29″ has *white* tail tip band with *dark above* next to white rump (reverse of young eagle pattern) and rusty (not white) wing lining. Range Southwest. **short-tailed hawk** 17″ has tail banded all the way in dark and white, may have all white front or all dark. Range Florida (and Mexico, Central America).

CAP: STREAKED BROWN — BREAST: PATTERNED (STREAKED)

#150. red-tailed hawk 19–25″

CAP blends with cheeks. BILL hooked. FRONT comes in dark and light color phases, both streaked browns on white; light-phase wing-lining white with dark feather edging; dark phase mottled brown upper half of wing, white with dark edging on lower half; tail shows red on underside of both. BACK wings, back streaked browns; tail cinnamon red, catches light in sun, fan-shaped in flight; wings in flight broad, not pointed. ACTIONS usually hunts on the wing, soaring over fields looking for rodents, reptiles (has unusually keen eyesight, as do all soaring birds of prey), also small mammals, even insects, only occasionally takes birds, fish; most pairs mate for life; often play in mid-air mock battle with mate or young. NOTES scream or hiss. HABITAT woods, fields, mountains, deserts.

CLOSE LOOK-ALIKES all hawks of the genus Buteo look alike in silhouette in flight with *broad rounded wings* and *fan-shaped tails.* 6 others in brown: **rough-legged hawk** 19–24″, tail white with wide dark tip, lower breast black, head buff streaked in brown (or all brown for dark phase), hovers with fast-beating wings over field on mouse hunt. Range cont-ex Deep South; **ferruginous hawk** 23–25″ tail rusty on lower half, white upper half, shoulders and legs rusty, in flight legs look a dark V against white underparts. Range West, prairie country; **red-shouldered hawk** 17–24″ tail banded white on black, shoulder rusty, underwing rusty (upper half) in flight. Range East, West Coast (becoming scarce); **Swainson's hawk** 19–22″ tail banded black and white, dark phase underparts dark also. Range West to Alaska; **broad-winged hawk** 14–19″ tail banded black and white, breast barred red on white. Range East, Canadian West; **Harris' hawk** 18–29″ #149 L-A.

SPECIAL CHECK all brown hawklike birds look somewhat alike, but each genus has its own distinctive shape: *FALCONS* streamlined, swept-back, *pointed* wings; long, *rectangular* tail; for example **prairie falcon** (#169) 17″ dark "comma" line from eye to neck. Range West. *ACCIPITERS* short, *rounded* wings, long *rectangular* tail; for example **northern goshawk (y)** 20–26″ (adult #168), **Cooper's hawk (y)** 14—20″ (adult #168 L-A), **sharp-shinned hawk (y)** 10–14″ (adult 133x). Young of all three species are brown backed with light fronts streaked in brown, alike except for size. Range cont. *HARRIERS long angled* wings, long rectangular tail. Only N.A. species is **northern harrier,** formerly **marsh hawk,** 17½–24″; female has brown back, a brown-and-buff barred tail, *white rump;* male is gray (#167). *KITES* **snail kite (Everglades kite) (f)** has long angled wings and fan-shaped tail, very hooked bill (male #191x).

ALMOST LOOK-ALIKES most young gulls, even 2 and 3 years old, are mottled brown much like hawks, have slightly hooked bill, but have *webbed feet,* not talons. For adults, *see* #136, #171, #191x. **great skua** and **south polar skua**, sometimes seen offshore, rarely on shore, have white wing patches, wedge-shaped tails for ID clues.

#151. greater roadrunner 20–24″ (roadrunner)

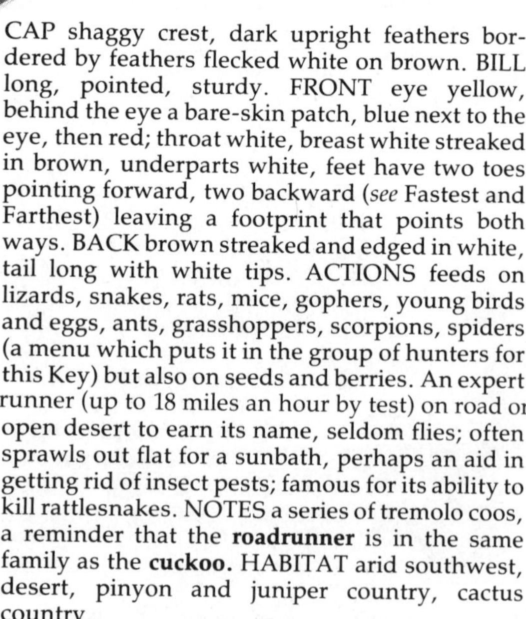

CAP shaggy crest, dark upright feathers bordered by feathers flecked white on brown. BILL long, pointed, sturdy. FRONT eye yellow, behind the eye a bare-skin patch, blue next to the eye, then red; throat white, breast white streaked in brown, underparts white, feet have two toes pointing forward, two backward (*see* Fastest and Farthest) leaving a footprint that points both ways. BACK brown streaked and edged in white, tail long with white tips. ACTIONS feeds on lizards, snakes, rats, mice, gophers, young birds and eggs, ants, grasshoppers, scorpions, spiders (a menu which puts it in the group of hunters for this Key) but also on seeds and berries. An expert runner (up to 18 miles an hour by test) on road or open desert to earn its name, seldom flies; often sprawls out flat for a sunbath, perhaps an aid in getting rid of insect pests; famous for its ability to kill rattlesnakes. NOTES a series of tremolo coos, a reminder that the **roadrunner** is in the same family as the **cuckoo.** HABITAT arid southwest, desert, pinyon and juniper country, cactus country.

GENERAL LOOK-ALIKE **plain chachalaca** 20–24″ (#155x) solid brown, not streaked.

S br | S gy | S bl | S gr | S yl | S rd | S b/w | M br | M gy | M bl | M gr | M yl | M o/b | M rd | M b/w | L br | L gy | L bl | L g/b | VL br | VL gy | VL bl | VL gr | VL r/p | VL b/w | VL bk | VL wh

#152. great horned owl 18–25″

CAP two easily-seen feather tufts or "horns". BILL hooked. FRONT eyes yellow, front-faced, feathers radiate out from eyes to form a disk edged in black; upper breast *streaked,* lower breast and underparts *barred,* throat largely white. BACK streaked browns (darker in moist Pacific Northwest, paler in desert southwest and in Arctic). ACTIONS hunts mostly at night but may hunt by day where there is little human interference; flies almost silently, its wing action muffled by an under-layer of down on flight feathers. Feeds on small and medium mammals (mouse to opossum size), on waterfowl and game birds, barnyard fowls, even sparrows, on fish, frogs, eels and large insects. Takes catch to regular eating perch, spits up skin and bones, feathers, fur, rolled into a pellet by stomach action (typical action for most predators). NOTES hoo-hoo-hoo call led to nickname **hoot owl.** HABITAT woods, thickets, streambanks, open country, cliffs, canyons.

CLOSE LOOK-ALIKES **long-eared owl** 13–16″ considerably smaller but has similar "horns", underparts streaked (not barred). Range cont-ex Far North/Deep South. GENERAL LOOK-ALIKES **short-eared owl** 13–17″ even the so-called short ears do not show in silhouette, smaller but also has round face, yellow eyes and buffy facial disks, breast streaked (not barred). Often hunts in daytime; nests on ground in fields, airports, marshes. In flight, seen from below, a dark patch on the under-wing near the shoulder bend makes an ID clue. Range cont. **barred owl** 17–24″ no ear tufts, *eyes dark,* circled in radiating gray-feather disks, throat and breast barred, lower breast and underparts streaked, voice similar to **great horned owl's** but not so deeply resonant, the hoo-hoo-hoo usually ends with a throaty "hoo-aw" or "who-all". Range East, to midwest in Canada. **spotted owl** 16½–19½″ similar to **barred owl** but limited to West, both breast and underparts barred, eyes dark; has become scarce due to lack of nesting sites in old trees. Range West Coast, Mexican border. **northern hawk-owl** 14½–17½″ facial disks outlined with wide dark bands. Range Canada, Alaska. **great gray owl** 24–33″ larger, grayer, no ear tuft, eyes yellow. Range Canada, Alaska, western mountains.

#153. common barn-owl 14–20″

CAP no tufts, light yellowish brown. BILL hooked. FRONT *face white* and *heart-shaped* with heart outline made by dark line framing face. No other N.A. owl has this heart-shaped face. *Eyes dark.* Throat, breast, underparts white, lightly streaked and dotted with dark brown and yellow-brown under-wash; wing linings also white and entire bird looks white if seen only from below, looking up to it on a perch. BACK yellowish-brown edged in gray, darker brown; may look all yellowish if seen flying away in uncertain light. ACTIONS often sways or bobs head from side to side as it sits on perch; eats rodents, birds (mice and rats chief food), may nest in tree cavity, church tower, man-made nest box. NOTES hisses, snorts. HABITAT fields, farms, country — anywhere it has good food supply.

CLOSE LOOK-ALIKE **snowy owl** 20–27″ (#186) white *barred* breast, not dotted and yellow, has *yellow eyes,* face round, not heart-shaped. Only rarely comes south into **barn owl** terrain.

S br
S gy
S bl
S gr
S yl
S rd
S b/w
M br
M gy
M bl
M gr
M yl
M o/b
M rd
M b/w
L br
L gy
L bl
L g/b
VL br
VL gy
VL bl
VL gr
VL r/p
VL b/w
VL bk
VL wh

CAP: WHITE — BREAST: PATTERNED

#154. bald eagle 30–43″

CAP full hood, head, nape and throat white on adults (fully feathered but looks bald from a distance). BILL hooked. FRONT dark brown from breast to underparts and underwings for adults; young have much white edging on upper half of underwing, brown heads, not white. BACK wings and back brown, tail white for adults, young have dark brown tail well flecked with white that gradually increases in 4-to-5-year-old birds, hood also turns white at same age (young #149 L-A). ACTIONS feeds largely on fish either fresh caught or found dead or dying on the beach or taken from the smaller **osprey** (#155) which in turn robs fish from young eagles in usual predator fashion; also takes some injured waterfowl hunters have abandoned, some small mammals, including those killed on highways. Pair usually mate for life and are attentive mates and parents, often using same nest many years, adding twigs each year. Like **golden eagle**, flies with wings outspread level to body, not raised in V like vultures. Protected by federal law but still being shot for trophy in spite of heavy fine. No longer abundant in any State but Alaska; Florida next with 359 nesting pairs in 1982; some in all States but Vermont, Rhode Island, West Virginia and Hawaii. Efforts to protect and re-establish continue in many areas. NOTES harsh screaming "klee-klee-klee" or throatier "klak-klak-klak" HABITAT usually near water, inland or on coast.

CLOSE LOOK-LIKE adult **bald eagle** with white head and tail cannot be mistaken for **golden eagle** but young birds are confused (*see* explanation #149). **osprey** (#155) has white head but banded tail and is smaller, also has dark line through eye.

CAP: WHITE — BREAST: PLAIN (WHITE)

#155. osprey 21–24½″

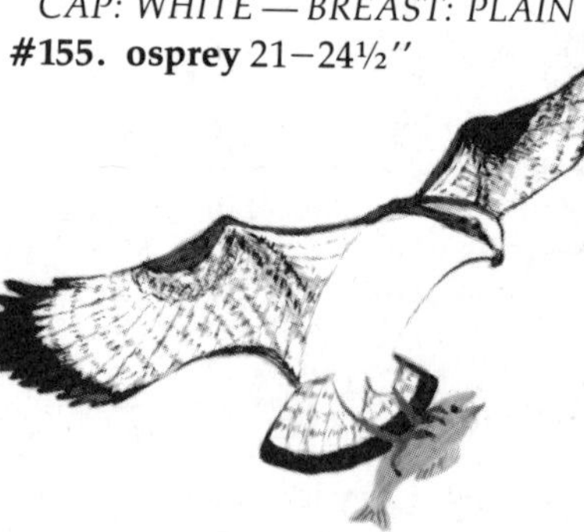

CAP bordered by black line through eye. BILL hooked. FRONT throat, breast, underparts white except for few dark "breast pin" lines, underwings in flight show *black patch* on upper edge at bend of wing, other dark feather edging, dark tips. BACK dark brown except tail banded dark and light. ACTIONS expert at fishing, plunges to catch fish in talons, not bill, has roughened patches on soles of feet to enable it to hold on to catch, always holds fish in both feet, the head pointed forward, as it flies off to eat on nearby perch; may sometimes go clear under water to get its dinner. Has been endangered by pollution in streams but is making come-back with recent added protections and aid in providing nest platforms. HABITAT rivers, lakes, coast.

CLOSE LOOK-ALIKE its white head may lead to confusion with **bald eagle**, but dark line through eye and banded (not all white) tail give quick ID along with smaller **osprey** size and wingspread (eagle wingspread 6½–8 feet, osprey 4½ to 6 feet).

STOUT-BILLED SEED-AND-BUG EATERS

CAP: PLAIN BROWN — BREAST: PATTERNED (BROWN)

plain chachalaca 20–24″ slender, long-tailed bird with much the silhouette of a roadrunner (but *plain dark brown*, not streaked). Name imitates call, coined by Nahuatl Indians of Mexico, but sounds to modern listeners like a repeated request for chocolate (accent on first syllable). Range Texas on Mexican border, wooded country; introduced on some Georgia sea islands.

CAP: STREAKED BROWN — BREAST: PATTERNED (STREAKED)

#156. ruffed grouse 16–19″

CAP ragged crest. BILL thick, short, chicken-like. FRONT both male and female have triangular ruff of dark feathers at each side of neck, throat streaked, breast and underparts barred dark on buff, basic body tone may be grayish-brown or rusty-brown. BACK wings, back and rump streaked brown; tail rusty or gray, barred in black, wider white band then black band at tip — tail spreads out fan-shaped. ACTIONS when startled springs into air with loud wing whir; male beats air with wings for loud drumming sound to attract female in courting season, usually performs this act on a favorite log or stump; fluffs out neck ruffs when excited, raises crest, female may act crippled to distract invader from chicks or nest; feeds on insects, seeds, fruits, some buds and blossoms, occasionally may take small garter snake, frog or toad. Often miscalled a partridge or pheasant — names used since Colonial Days when most people did not know much about birds and their names, since Colonial Days also has been a popular game bird for hunters. NOTES alarm call a brisk "quick-quick" or "quit-quit", male's drumming takes the place of song. HABITAT woodlands, thickets.

CLOSE LOOK-ALIKES all chicken-like game birds — **grouse, partridge, prairie-chickens, ptarmigans, pheasant** — are alike in general appearance and actions, but each has its own ID clues. **blue grouse (f)** 15½–21″ most abundant grouse in western mountains, tail dark with gray band across tip. *See* #172 L-A for sooty-gray male. **spruce grouse (f)** 15–17″ more rusty-brown than **blue grouse** female, rusty band across tail tip. Male #172 is gray. Range North, across continent. **sharp-tailed grouse** 15–20″ mottled buff and browns, longish narrow pointed tail (in flight shows white edging like a mourning dove tail — a clue to distinguish it from female pheasant or prairie chickens or any other grouse), fleshy bare-skin band above eyes in courting season is yellow, male's inflatable neck patches *purple*. Range from Great Lakes, north and west. **greater prairie-chicken** 17–18″ tail short and narrow with *black band* across tip, body *barred* brown and buff, male has long tufts of neck feathers and *yellow* inflatable neck patches in courtship. Range midwest grasslands. Formerly abundant, now uncommon. **heath hen (prairie chicken** subspecies) once common in the East, became rare as early as 1835; last one died on Martha's Vineyard (an island off Massachusetts) in 1932. Another subspecies known as **Atwater's prairie chicken** is rare, found only in Texas and Louisiana. **lesser prairie-chicken** 16″ smaller in length than **greater prairie chicken** by only 2 inches or less, markings identical but paler,, male's inflatable neck patches are *reddish*. Range drylands from southern Colorado to texas, New Mexico. Also rare. **ptarmigans** 3 species — **rock, willow, white-tailed** (#12 L-A) all barred browns in summer, white in winter as camouflage in snow country, *white patches on wings* even in summer. (No grouse has the large white wing patches of the ptarmigans.) All Large (13″) rather than Very Large except **willow ptarmigan** which is 13–17″, range North, across continent, Arctic, Alaska.

S br | S gy | S bl | S gr | S yl | S rd | S b/w | M br | M gy | M bl | M gr | M yl | M o/b | M rd | M b/w | L br | L gy | L bl | L g/b | VL br | VL gy | VL bl | VL gr | VL r/p | VL b/w | VL bk | VL wh

#157. sage grouse (m) 26–30″

CAP bordered by white line over eye. BILL thick, short, chicken-like. FRONT bare-skin patch over eye yellow, line through eye black, curving down to form ragged bib, throat black, line between throat and bib line white, breast white, *underparts black,* sides streaked, wing linings shown in flight white, outer feathers brown. BACK mottled browns, tail long and pointed, in display each pointed tail feather stands apart in fan-shape similar to turkey cock display (but turkey feathers are not separated), also in display shows two inflatable patches (orange-yellow) on breast and white breast feathers are fluffed out. ACTIONS courting display most spectacular of all grouse, all grouse males strut and stomp on display grounds while females watch, all (except **ruffed grouse**) spread tails and hold wings down and out stiffly but only **sage grouse** has long pointed tail feathers and breast patches that swell like balloons (larger than the neck patches of the others), only the **sage grouse** is so large — 26–30″ — compared to 16–18″ for **greater prairie chicken,** 18–21″ for **blue grouse,** while all others are smaller. All in this group eat insects and vegetation in summer, vegetation in winter. **sage grouse** cannot digest hard seeds, feeds on leaves of sagebrush and on leaves, blossoms of certain other dryland plants. NOTES clucks, cackles; in display a bubbling booming note. HABITAT sagebrush country, since sage is both food and shelter.

CLOSE LOOK-ALIKE female 22–23″ has mottled throat, not black; no bib, but large *black patch* on underparts makes instant ID to distinguish from long-tailed hen **ring-necked pheasant** (#158) only slightly larger.

#158. ring-necked pheasant (f) 21–25″

CAP bordered by buffy patch above and below eye. BILL thick, short, chicken-like. FRONT throat, breast buffy; feathers with darker and lighter edging, soft pastel tones visible with binoculars or at close range, especially at sides. BACK mottled browns and buff with washes of pastel tones around nape, rump (rose, lavender) visible with binoculars or at close range, tail feathers mottled with darker edging, long, pointed. ACTIONS 2 or 3 hens usually share the same mate, but each has her own nest, her own roosting places within the cock's territory, but may join others in winter flock; when enemy approaches can rise silently if she and chicks have not been seen or with loud wing whir and clatter of quills to startle the enemy and give herself and chicks time to hide or scatter. NOTES musical clucking call to just-hatched chicks, then less musical clucking for rally call, louder for alarm — a different note to warn of an enemy that comes by air (hawk) from that to warn of one that comes afoot (cat, fox). HABITAT brushy hillsides,

thickets, farmland — usually with water near.

CLOSE LOOK-ALIKE female **sage grouse** (#157 L-A) is closest, but her black belly patch is quick ID; young male **pheasant** similar but soon hints male coloring.

CAP: BLUE-GREEN — BREAST: PATTERNED (VARI-COLORED)

#159. ring-necked pheasant (m) 30–36″

CAP two hornlike feather tufts (held erect in spring courtship) of dark blue, pale green between horns, bordered by dark blue visor and bare-skin red wattles over and around eyes. BILL thick, short, chicken-like, yellow. FRONT eye may be red or yellow; dark blue-green iridescent throat and nape, banded by *white ring collar* (to suggest name); breast and underparts bronze-gold-buff flecked with black edging, darker on underparts. BACK *wing patch gray-blue to match gray-blue rump;* back bronze and buff edged in white, black, brown; tail long, pointed, buff barred in black. ACTIONS male claims territory, then claims hens — fighting rival cock for either if necessary but seldom fights to death (weaker cock yields — and runs), does not help build nest or tend eggs or chicks but guards territory, calling out alarm if he sees hens or chicks in danger (*see* #158 NOTES) and may jet off with quill rattle and wing whir to attract enemy's attention to himself to give mates or young time to escape. Feeds on seeds, buds, insects, grain, nuts, berries; sometimes on mice, snails, small snakes; courts hen with circling "dance" ruffling feathers her way in full spread to look even larger and more brilliant. Not native to this hemisphere; first sent to Oregon from China in the 1880s by Owen Denny, U.S. consul-general in Shanghai; nested successfully. Similar **black-necked pheasants** (without neck ring) discovered by ancient Greeks near Black Sea beside the River Phasis and were therefore called *phasianos ornis,* Greek for "Phasian birds"; introduced throughout Europe by conquering Romans (*pheasant* is an old English version of Greek and Roman *phasianos*). **ring-necked pheasants** now well established in U.S. and southern Canada, but supply for hunting increased each fall by birds reared in game farms. NOTES besides rattling alarm call, cock claims his territory each spring morning (and through the day) with ringing "kok-kok" call followed by a ruffling of wing feathers: usually calls from same look-out post or whenever, wherever, he hears rival cock crow. HABITAT brushy hillsides, thickets, farmland — usually near water. In Oregon often visits backyards.

CLOSE LOOK-ALIKES **Mongolian ring-necked pheasant,** a subspecies from colder, drier Asian regions, has been introduced; has *white* wing patch and matching rump patch, will mate with true **ring-necked pheasant.** Hybrids may have white or blue patches. **black-necked pheasant,** a subspecies long semi-domesticated in Europe, has been introduced, will also mate with **Mongolian** or **ring-necked pheasant,** so some hybrids lack the neck ring.

CAP: BARE-SKIN RED-BLUE — BREAST: PATTERNED (DARK BROWNS)

wild turkey 48″ original **wild turkey** of northern N.A. is a different subspecies from the wild turkeys of Mexico and other southern lands first taken captive to Europe for barnyard birds by the Spaniards in the time of Columbus. Difference mostly in tail tips — rusty-brown on birds from eastern U.S. and buffy on those from southwest, but almost clear white on birds from Mexico and therefore on most barnyard turkeys. All are alike in bronze and iridescent glints to brown feathers. Males have a bristly tuft of feathers on chest and more bare-skin wattles on head and neck. Only males erect tail in fan for courting display — a custom that led Spaniards to give them the name of "peacocks with the dewlap double chin". Early hunting led to swift decrease in numbers of wild flocks, but birds have now been re-introduced to old haunts and even to states in the northwest where **wild turkeys** never ventured on their own. Several states now allow limited hunting. Check with your State Game Commission or local Audubon Society for the nearest **wild turkeys.**

Ring-necked pheasants *were first brought to Oregon from China in 1881 and are now at home over much of the mid-continent. Photo, Oregon Dept. of Fish & Wildlife.*

S br · S gy · S bl · S gr · S yl · S rd · S b/w · M br · M gy · M bl · M gr · M yl · M o/b · M rd · M b/w · L br · L gy · L bl · L g/b · VL br · VL gy · VL bl · VL gr · VL r/p · VL b/w · VL bk · VL wh

Size: VERY LARGE — Color: GRAYS

Birds that are Very Large and Gray — like those that are Very Large and Brown and other colors — show such easily recognized differences in behavior that you can put them in a matching group by Actions as quickly as by Size and Color. Therefore, in this Key, as in those for most Very Large birds, you will first match the bird you want to identify with one of the four Action groups:

long-legged (or very-long-legged) waders
short-legged swimmers
hook-billed or pointed-billed hunters, fishers, scavengers
stout-billed seed-and-bug eaters

Once you have matched your bird to the right Action group, follow the usual SCANS System of matching by the color of cap and breast, then by whatever added description is given. Be sure to check the range where the bird is most likely to appear. Double-check any bird out of its usual setting. Because sizes vary more for Very Large birds than for other Key size groups, length of each species is given in inches.

VERY-LONG-LEGGED WADERS

CAP: GRAY — BREAST: PATTERNED (GRAY)

#160. sandhill crane 34–48″

CAP bare-skin red. BILL thick, medium. FRONT cheeks white; neck, breast, underparts all gray. BACK neck, back, wing, tail all gray; tail feathers *curve up* from rump and then down in a *drooping tuft* that is a clue you can see at a distance to distinguish a crane from a heron, whose feathers slope down at the back with no up-and-down curve. ACTIONS sandhill cranes are of different size in different areas — **greater sandhills** are close to 4 feet in length or height, **lesser sandhills** barely 3 feet, others in between. Those that nest in Alaska and northern Canada migrate south in winter, those in areas with milder climate (Mississippi, Florida, etc.) stay in same area year round. Now rare in some places (Mississippi) where formerly abundant, in others fairly stable population. Some have been used as foster parents to hatch and raise the chicks of rarer **whooping crane** (#195). Feed on sprouting grain or glean stubble fields, dig for roots, eat berries or small rodents or reptiles, crustaceans, insects, but are not fish-eaters like herons. (Herons are often called cranes by people who do not check with bird books for correct name. Herons fly with neck drawn back in S-shaped curve; cranes fly with *neck outstretched* — a clue to see even at a distance.) When cranes dig up food and then preen feathers, they often stain themselves with the dirt and so may look brown or sandy rather than gray. Young birds are brownish. Adults court with fantastic hop-leap dance. NOTES a ringing and resonant "hah-roo-hah", also clucks and honks. HABITAT grassy fields, marshes, mountain meadows, prairies.

GENERAL LOOK-ALIKES **great blue heron** #176. **whooping crane** #195. **great egret** #196. **wood stork** #194, **reddish egret** 27–32″ smaller than smallest **sandhill crane,** head and neck *shaggy* red-brown, body slate gray. Range Texas and Gulf Coast, may stray to California.

S br | S gy | S bl | S gr | S yl | S rd | S b/w | M br | M gy | M bl | M gr | M yl | M o/b | M rd | M b/w | L br | L gy | L bl | L g/b | VL br | VL gy | VL bl | VL gr | VL r/p | VL b/w | VL bk | VL wh

S br · S gy · S bl · S gr · S yl · S rd · S b/w · M br · M gy · M bl · M gr · M yl · M o/b · M rd · M b/w · L br · L gy · L bl · L g/b · VL br · VL gy · VL bl · VL gr · VL r/p · VL b/w · VL bk · VL wh

CAP: YELLOW — BREAST: PATTERNED (GRAY)

#161. yellow-crowned night-heron 22–28″

CAP visor yellow, fading to white for drooping nape plumes of crest, bordered by black band over eye. BILL thick, medium, pointed. FRONT face banded black-and-white (white in center); neck, breast, underparts plain gray; eye red. BACK plain gray, wing feathers edged dark and light; tail short, slopes down in typical heron fashion (not tufted like crane); smaller than smallest **sandhill.** ACTIONS feeds on crayfish, fiddler crabs, large insects, small reptiles, snails; seldom takes fish; usually walks with head held high; hunts for food by night and day; in flight feet extend well beyond tail — a clue to use at a distance. NOTES rather high-pitched "quawk". HABITAT often nests with other herons of similar size such as **black-crowned night-heron** (#182), **little blue** or **tricolored herons** (#174), spends much time in freshwater swamps or brackish bays and backwater where food is available on sandy shores and trees nearby for safe roost and nesting site.

GENERAL LOOK-ALIKE **black-crowned night-heron** 23–28″ (#182) black back and white front.

SHORT-LEGGED SWIMMERS

CAP: BROWN — BREAST: PLAIN

#162. northern pintail (m) 26–30″ (*duck* not part of name)

CAP brown hood (head and throat, not full neck). BILL flat, dark. FRONT white line curving down behind cheek to join white neck below brown throat (neck slightly longer and slimmer than for most ducks), breast and underparts white, under-tail black. Female #145 L-A. BACK brownish-gray, two center tail feathers dark, long and pointed (to give "pintail" name), small greenish patch on lower wing (shown in flight). ACTIONS holds neck in graceful arch, tail feathers tip upwards, stiff and straight; direct take-off from water, no need for running start; tips up to feed in shallow water on plants below surface; sometimes on crustaceans, insects; goes to fields to eat grain, sprouting grasses. NOTES seldom calls; male has a 2-note whistle or wheezing chuckles. HABITAT freshwater marshes, ponds, lakes, saltwater bays, grasslands, grainfields, prairies.

GENERAL LOOK-ALIKE **oldsquaw** 15–23″ only other duck with long pointed tail; in summer has black cap, white cheek, black throat and breast, brown streaked back; in winter white cap, nape and neck with brown cheek patch. Range winters on both coasts, nests in Arctic.

CAP: BROWN — BREAST: PATTERNED (SPECKLED)

#163. green-winged teal (m) 13–16″

CAP brown bordered by glossy green patch from eye to nape. Female (#145 L-A) lacks green patch. BILL flat, dark. FRONT throat dark, breast speckled buff, underparts white, sides gray with *vertical white stripe* between breast and shoulder of wing. BACK brownish-gray, glossy green patch on wing (shows best in flight), tail dark and pointed, under-tail patch yellow. ACTIONS very swift flier; feeds in shallows on plants, crustaceans, insects; in fields on grain, berries, nuts. NOTES whistles, piping cries. HABITAT marshes, lakes, ponds, rivers, bays.

hooded merganser (f) 16–19″ (#166x); cap reddish-brown.

CAP: GRAY — BREAST: PATTERNED (GRAY)

swans (y) the young of all three swan species seen in N.A. — native **tundra** (**whistling**) and **trumpeter swans** and the Eurasian **mute swan** which has escaped from zoos to breed in wild — are all feathered in gray. Adult #199.

CAP: GRAY — BREAST: PATTERNED (SPECKLED)

#164. wood duck (f) 17–20½″

CAP gray crest, drooping over nape. BILL flat, dark. FRONT *white patch all around eye,* throat white, breast speckled and streaked in brownish-gray and buff, underparts plain gray, sides spotted buff and rusty-buff. Male #180. BACK brownish-gray, wing patch blue bordered in thin black and white lines (similar to **mallard** female), blue patch and white edging show partly if duck is swimming or walking and completely in flight, tail fairly long (for a duck) and square tipped. ACTIONS makes nest in tree cavity or man-made nest box, as often in the woods as over water; young ducks drop out at mother's call, spreading wings for parachute effect and are usually unhurt even when they land on hard ground, quickly waddle off to follow her to water. Feeds on insects, water plants, nuts, seeds of water plants, berries, grain, some fish, frogs, snails. HABITAT woods near rivers, ponds (will sometimes nest close to houses, summer camps or other buildings).

CLOSE LOOK-ALIKES female **mallards, wigeons,** etc. are similar but browner and lack crest and white eye patch. **harlequin duck (f)** 15–21″ has white spots on face — one behind eye, one in front, one beneath, but not complete circular patch of **wood duck** female; also has pointed tail (not square) and no crest. Male #177. Range North, both West and East on coast and inland in West. **bufflehead (f)** 13–15″ has white patch on cheek but not complete circular eye patch, has small white wing patch (not blue). Male #177 L-A, 183x. Range cont.

CAP: GREEN — BREAST: PATTERNED (RUSTY)

#165. mallard (m) 20–28″ (*duck* not part of name)

CAP bright bottle green, a complete hood over head, neck. BILL flat, yellow. FRONT hood separated from breast and back by complete white neck ring, breast rusty, lower breast and underparts white, feet and legs orange. BACK grayish, wing patch blue with white and black borders as in female (#145), tail white with central feathers black and *curled forward at tip*. ACTION often joins tame flocks at parks and zoos, most abundant of all wild ducks and best known; seldom on salt water but on all sizes of fresh water from backyard swimming pools to Great Lakes. NOTES different from female's quack, a froglike croak. HABITAT almost anywhere near water.

CLOSE LOOK-ALIKES **northern shoveler (m)** 17–20″ same glossy green head, but breast is white (not rusty) and lower breast rusty (not white); also bill is broader, longer and "shovel shape" to match name. Range cont. **greater scaup (m)** 16–20″ same glossy green head but breast is also green; a bird of coastal bays not inland ponds, seen inland only on migration. Range, winters on both coasts, nests in Arctic, Alaska. **common goldeneye (m)** 16–20″ only head glossy green, not neck; has white patch on cheek. Range, winters across continent, nests Canada to Alaska. **common merganser (m)** 22–27″ head and upper neck glossy green, lower neck, breast and underparts white, bill is *long and narrow* and red. Range cont-exSE. **red-breasted merganser (m)** 20–26″ head and upper neck glossy green, ragged crest at nape (**mallard** head is smooth), bill is *long and narrow*. Range cont-exRockies. **common loon** 28–36″ (#183) bill thick and pointed, not flat. **yellow-billed loon** 30–36″ bill thick and pointed. Range Alaska. **wood duck** 17–20½″ (#180) head glossy green, but backward-drooping crest.

CAP: YELLOW — BREAST: PATTERNED (GRAY)

#166. brown pelican 42–54″

CAP tufted at nape. BILL thick, long dark, pouched (will hold 3–4 gallons). FRONT nape and back of long neck brown in summer and white in winter, front of neck white tinged with yellow, breast and underparts gray streaked. BACK gray streaked, tail very short. ACTIONS flies with head curved back on shoulders, dives headfirst into ocean for fish, flock often flies in a long line as they look for fish; may gather around piers where fishing boats dock and beg for fish, becoming almost tame; use pouch to hold fish until they have enough for their own meal or to feed nestlings. For very young chicks parents half-digest the food and regurgitate it into the mouths of the young; older chicks can reach into the pouch and feed themselves. NOTES usually silent, sometimes a low croaking sound. HABITAT ocean shores, inlets, bays; nest on islands or cypress groves.

GENERAL LOOK-ALIKES only a pelican looks like a pelican, but **cormorants** (#188) also have a pouch though much smaller. For **white pelican** *see* #198x.

CAP: RED — BREAST: PATTERNED (GRAY)

common goldeneye (f) 16–20″ entire head rusty-red, bushy and big-headed, white wing patches, eye yellow. Male #177 L-A. Range cont (nests E. Canada to Alaska; winters across U.S.).

Barrow's goldeneye (f) 16–20″ similar to above but less white on wings. Male #177 L-A. Range both north coasts, inland mountain northwest (rarely East).

common merganser (f) 22–27″ hood rusty-red, nape shaggy, *bill long, narrow and red,* black-and-white wing patches. Male #179. Range cont-ex SE.

red-breasted merganser (f) 20–26″ similar to above but crest more flared at nape, breast grayer. Male #179 L-A. Range cont-ex inland West.

hooded merganser (f) 16–19″ similar to above two but smaller, crest bushier and browner, breast grayer, bill shorter and darker. Male #183x. Range cont-ex SW, Far North.

redhead (m) 18–22″ hood red, lower throat and breast *black,* bill flat and gray with black tip, sides gray, underparts white, tail short and pointed. Compare with **canvasback** #183x whose back is *white.* Range cont-exArctic.

CAP: BLACK — BREAST: PATTERNED (BLACK)

lesser scaup (m) 15–19″ upper breast glossed with purple highlights. Range nests Alaska to Colorado, Iowa; winters both coasts and inland to Florida, Mexico.

CAP: WHITE — BREAST: PATTERNED (GRAY)

greater white-fronted goose 26–34″ white "front" is on the forehead, not the breast — which is gray with black scallops; *legs orange* (yellow on young birds). Range nests in Alaska and Arctic Canada, winters mainly along Pacific coastal states, also Gulf states and inland West, rare East.

blue goose 25–30″ formerly separate species, now considered a color phase of the **snow goose** (#198), head and upper neck white, under-tail white, remainder blue-gray with lighter feather edging, *legs pink.* Range, nests in Arctic, migrates through Mississippi Valley to winter in Gulf States, migrates north through Valley and along both coasts.

HOOK-BILLED OR POINTED-BILLED HUNTERS, FISHERS, SCAVENGERS

CAP: GRAY — BREAST: PATTERNED (STREAKED)

#167. northern harrier (m) (marsh hawk) 17½–24″

CAP gray, blends with head, nape. BILL hooked. FRONT breast white streaked in scattered gray and red, underparts white, face feathers radiate outward. BACK gray, darker and lighter feather edging, tail long, banded dark gray on grayish white. Clue for ID in flight: long wings, somewhat rounded tip (not pointed like falcon wings); tail long, rectangular (not fan-shaped) *rump white.* Female (#150 L-A) is brown, rump white. ACTIONS called a **harrier hawk** because it flies back and forth over a marsh or meadow hunting for small rodents like a harrier hound trying to flush out birds for its master; flies low with wings raised in V, not level with body; feeds on rodents, reptiles, birds, crustaceans, carrion; often has regular beat, cruising same area, same time, daily. NOTES whining whistle or thin scream, scolding rattle. HABITAT marshes, fields, prairies.

S br | S gy | S bl | S gr | S yl | S rd | S b/w | M br | M gy | M bl | M gr | M yl | M o/b | M rd | M b/w | L br | L gy | L bl | L g/b | VL br | VL gy | VL bl | VL gr | VL r/p | VL b/w | VL bk | VL wh

S br | S gy | S bl | S gr | S yl | S rd | S b/w | M br | M gy | M bl | M gr | M yl | M o/b | M rd | M b/w | L br | L gy | L bl | L g/b | VL br | VL gy | VL bl | VL gr | VL r/p | VL b/w | VL bk | VL wh

CLOSE LOOK-ALIKES other gray hawks have *short* rounded wings or long *pointed* wings; **gray hawk** seen along Mexican border has short rounded wings, heavily barred breast (not streaked), tail banded more widely in black and white.

#168. northern goshawk 20–26″

CAP gray bordered by *white line over eye.* BILL hooked. FRONT light gray *streaked in dark gray* throat to underparts, eye red, dark gray mask through eye back to nape, wing linings barred dark on white. BACK all gray, tail banded black on grayish white, long, rectangular; wings short and rounded, broad. ACTIONS short wings and long tail (used as rudder to make quick direction change) enable all hawks of this type **(goshawk, Cooper's, sharp-shinned)** to hunt among trees, not just over open country, and they are therefore able to capture birds, darting in to snatch them off a branch where other Very Large hawks cannot maneuver successfully; also feeds on rodents, some large insects, but mostly on birds, even those as large as pheasants. NOTES alarm call a harsh croak, conversational call with mate a questioning whine. HABITAT forests, hill country.

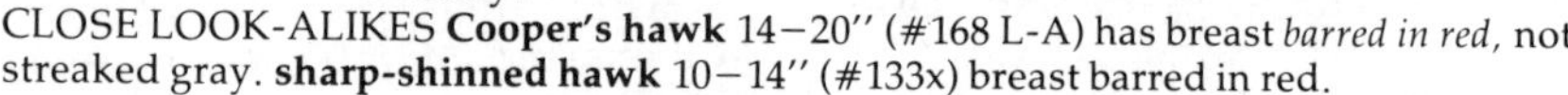

CLOSE LOOK-ALIKES **Cooper's hawk** 14–20″ (#168 L-A) has breast *barred in red,* not streaked gray. **sharp-shinned hawk** 10–14″ (#133x) breast barred in red.

great gray owl 24–33″ a round-headed owl, no ear tufts, large facial disks, *eyes yellow*, breast and back both streaked in dark and light grays. Range north and west, only occasionally comes to northeast coast. (**barred owl** of east and midwest is similar but brown and with *dark eyes* and smaller — 17–24″.)

northern gannet (y) 38″ mottled gray, *pointed bill,* long *pointed wings.* Adult #199x.

CAP: BLUE—GRAY—BREAST: PATTERNED (BARRED)

#169. peregrine falcon (duck hawk) 15–20″

CAP blends with nape and "comma" mark under eye. BILL hooked. FRONT blue-black "comma" mark under eye outlined by white "comma" mark behind it and white throat, breast shades from white to buff with few streaks and then heavily barred on to underparts. BACK blue-gray with light and dark feather edging, tail banded in black, tip narrowly white. Clue in flight: wings long and pointed, tail long and rectangular. Swept-back wings make for faster speed to put the peregrine among the fastest birds a-wing (*see* Fastest and Farthest). ACTIONS former name, **duck hawk,** came from peregrine's favorite food; also takes both land and water birds of all sizes, occasional small mammals and large insects, and has been persistently hunted by humans until recent years when federal protection was given predators as well as song birds. Now it is beginning to show signs of slow comeback, but still needs help. Most authorities on bird life believe that the **peregrine** and other birds of prey are needed to kill off diseased and injured birds and animals and so keep each species strong and healthy and at its best. NOTES seldom calls except as mates greet each other or young at nest or as they drive off invaders or sound alarm with harsh croak. HABITAT anywhere they have wing room, usually in open country, canyons and mountains, but also city rooftops, especially near water.

CLOSE LOOK-ALIKE **prairie falcon** 17″ gray-brown, similar face marks, underparts speckled, not barred. Range West.

CAP: BLACK — BREAST: PLAIN (WHITE)

terns 8 look-alike tern species (black cap, gray mantle; white face, shoulders, entire front and tail, tail deeply or slightly forked, bill stout and pointed): **Arctic, common, roseate, Forster's, Sandwich** and **elegant terns** range in size from14–17″; **Royal** and **Caspian terns** from 18–23″. Usually seen overhead showing watchers only white front and underwing; more fully described with #200; smaller terns #137, 137x.

CAP: WHITE — BREAST: PLAIN (WHITE)

#170. black-shouldered kite (white-tailed kite, now combined with two tropic species) 15–17″

CAP white hood, includes throat, nape. BILL hooked. FRONT eyes red, small black patch between eyes and bill, throat, breast and underparts white, under-wings white except for *black patch at wing shoulder* angle. BACK plain gray, *large black shoulder patch,* tail long, rectangular and white, wings long and pointed, narrow. ACTIONS has been rare for some time, now making small comeback along Pacific and Gulf Coasts from Oregon to Texas to Florida—a new species to look for even by long-time birders. Feeds mostly on small rodents, small birds, reptiles, large insects; usually stays in same area all year since winters are generally mild throughout its range. NOTES whistled cry "kee-kee-kee", sometimes brisk, sometimes plaintive. HABITAT open country, lowland or foothills, near trees for roosting and nests.

CLOSE LOOK-ALIKE **Mississippi kite** 14″ has same white hood, red eyes, but gray of back is dark, not pale, and has no black shoulder patches; *tail black,* not white. Range Texas to Florida along coast, also inland to Kansas, Tennessee, South Carolina; may wander farther north.

#171. herring gull 22–26″

CAP hood, includes head, throat, nape. BILL stout, hooked at tip, yellow (red spot on lower part). FRONT all white throat, breast and underparts, *legs pink*. BACK nape, rump and tail white, back and wings (called the mantle) gray, wings edged in white, black patch in corner, some white spots on black patch. ACTIONS scavengers on the coast or inland waterfront or on garbage dumps, also catch fish (especially herring and other small fish), probably best-known of all gulls and most widely distributed in N.A., also largest of those with similar markings of gray

S br | S gy | S bl | S gr | S yl | S rd | S b/w | M br | M gy | M bl | M gr | M yl | M o/b | M rd | M b/w | L br | L gy | L bl | L g/b | VL br | VL gy | VL bl | VL gr | VL r/p | VL b/w | VL bk | VL wh

mantle, black-and-white wing tips. May carry a shellfish high in air to drop and break open on rocks or paving below, follows ships for garbage thrown overboard, alights on city windowsills to beg for food, establishing regular schedules, may eat eggs and young of other birds, may follow farmer to get worms or rodents exposed by tractor or plow, takes fish from other birds before they can eat it; is often called **"sea gull"** although this phrase is not the official name of any gull, merely a much-used folk-name. NOTES screech of alarm, also croaks, squawks, plaintive cries, an almost catlike mewing. HABITAT ocean shores, any inland waterfront, farmland, garbage dump, golf course, field, park.

CLOSE LOOK-ALIKES **ring-billed gull** 18–21″ slightly smaller, bill ringed in black, *legs yellowish*. Range cont-exArctic. **mew-gull** 16–18″ smaller, *legs yellow-green*. Range nests Alaska-Arctic, winters Pacific Coast. **California gull** 20–23″ slightly smaller, *legs greenish*. Range West, inland and coast. GENERAL LOOK-ALIKES **western gull** 24–27″ mantle all dark slate gray, no black patch on wing tips, wings edged in white, tail white. Range Pacific Coast. **black-legged kittiwake** 16–18″ mantle gray, black patches on wing tips, but *no white spots* on black patch. Range, nests Arctic, winters on both coasts. **Bonaparte's** and other black-headed gulls 13–17″ #136. **great black-backed gull** 26–32″ #191x. **glaucous-winged gull** 24–27″ mantle so pale gray it looks white, has *gray* patches on wing tips, *no black*. Range West Coast, nests in north, winters south to Baja, goes inland along rivers. **glaucous gull** 26–32″ mantle pale gray, *wing tips white*, larger than glaucous-winged. Range Arctic, seen in winter on both coasts but seldom in south. **jaegers** 18–23″ 3 species **(parasitic, Pomarine, long-tailed)** persistent hunters (*jaeger* means hunter in German) of other birds, small rodents, have long pointed wings like falcons, ID *central tail feathers extend beyond remainder of tail*, back dark gray, cap black, underparts white or light gray. Range, nest in Arctic, winter southern seas, sometimes seen along coasts or follow rivers inland.

STOUT-BILLED SEED-AND-BUG EATERS

CAP: GRAY — BREAST: PATTERNED (BLACK)

#172. spruce grouse (m) 15–17″

CAP gray, bordered by bare-skin *red* line over eye. BILL thick, short, chicken-like. FRONT throat and breast black, throat outlined in white (not always clearly seen), breast and underparts barred gray on white, sides streaked and checked gray on white. BACK mottled and barred in grays, dark on light; rump gray, upper tail barred black on white, lower tail black (in East may have a narrow rusty tip), barring and band show in flight. ACTIONS feeds in trees more than on ground, eats needles and buds of spruce and other conifers, also berries, some seeds and grasses, mushrooms, insects; usually very tame (therefore one of grouse species called **"fool hen"** by early pioneers and modern hunters), spreads tail in courtship display but not so completely as turkey, red bare skin over eye becomes puffy in courtship. NOTES seldom calls, makes snapping noise with wings in flight and loud whir in take-off. HABITAT forests, especially spruce, jack and lodgepole pines and other conifers.

CLOSE LOOK-ALIKE **blue grouse (m)** 15½–21″ has yellow (not red) bare-skin patch over eye, throat grayish-white, not black, breast plain blue-gray, tail black with gray band across tip. Female #156 L-A. Range West, Alaska to California, inland to Arizona, Colorado, Wyoming and adjoining forested areas.

CAP: GRAY — BREAST: PATTERNED (GRAY)

#173. band-tailed pigeon 14–15½″

CAP blue-gray blends with nape and throat. BILL medium, yellow, black tip, fleshy growth at base (cere) — a feature with most doves, pigeons. FRONT head, throat, breast all blue-gray, sometimes with a lavender overtone, iridescent highlights common to all doves and pigeons; underparts paler, eye yellow with red ring, *legs and feet yellow* (**common pigeon** has pink legs). BACK white ring around nape (not throat), iridescent greenish patch below nape-ring, back same blue-gray or lavender-gray as front, wing tips darker, rump same as back (not white like rump of **common pigeon**), tail has dark band across center, *lighter gray band* across tip (**common pigeon** has dark band across tip). ACTIONS feeds on nuts, berries, insects, grains. Favorite wild berries: dogwood, cascara, elderberry, chokecherry. Will come to feeder for grain, bread, acorns, hazelnuts. Male will sit and call from top of fir tree or other tall tree, roosts and nests in trees (**common pigeon** nests and roosts on rock ledges, windowsills, seldom even alights on a tree), usually migrates south and on into Mexico for winter, but some stay in Pacific Northwest all year. NOTES an owl-like "oo-whooo, oo-whooo". HABITAT woods with oaks, hazelnut trees, water, brushy slopes with dogwood, cascara trees.

CLOSE LOOK-ALIKE **common pigeon** #134. GENERAL LOOK-ALIKE **white-crowned pigeon** 13″ cap white, remainder of body dark blackish-gray, some iridescence on nape. Range Florida Keys, occasionally farther into Florida.

CAP: GRAY/RED — BREAST: PLAIN (WHITE)

scissor-tailed flycatcher 11–15″ small red cap seldom seen, entire head usually looks light gray, throat and upper breast white, lower breast and sides washed in rosy pink, red patch on wing shoulder, back gray, wings and tail black, tail edged in white, tail is deeply forked and long — twice as long as body. Range, nests in south-central states, may wander to California, Florida, Oregon.

S br | S gy | S bl | S gr | S yl | S rd | S b/w | M br | M gy | M bl | M gr | M yl | M o/b | M rd | M b/w | L br | L gy | L bl | L g/b | VL br | VL gy | VL bl | VL gr | VL r/p | VL b/w | VL bk | VL wh

Size: VERY LARGE — Color: BLUES

Birds that are Very Large and Blue — like Very Large birds of every color — show easily recognized differences in behavior that quickly place them in groups identified by their Actions. Therefore, in this Key, as in others for this Size group, you will first match the bird you want to identify with the right group:

very-long-legged waders
short-legged swimmers

Other Color Keys for Very Large birds also contain Action groups for Hunters-and-Fishers and for Seed-and-Bug Eaters. None of the latter group is of blue basic coloring. One Hunter — the peregrine falcon — is blue-gray (or gray-blue) and is already described in the Very Large and Gray Key, #169). Once you have placed your bird as Wader or Swimmer, follow the usual SCANS System of matching ID clues by color of cap and breast first and then by other clues. Notice that the long-legged waders come in greatly varying sizes — from 42–52″ high, to 22–29″ mid-mark, to 18–22″ low. There is only one short-legged swimmer in blue.

VERY-LONG-LEGGED WADERS

CAP: BLUE-TO-PURPLE — BREAST: PATTERNED

#174. little blue heron 22–29″

CAP blends with head and neck, purplish-blue with highlights of purplish-red. BILL long, pointed, blue-gray with black tip. FRONT neck feathers somewhat shaggy at breast, *breast, underparts dark blue,* legs greenish, in courtship has slate-blue drooping plumes. BACK slate-blue, no contrasting trim, looks black at a distance or in poor light. ACTIONS slower in movement than most herons, usually feeds close to shore in shallows or on shore on fish, frogs, crustaceans, turtles, reptiles, insects; flies in typical heron style with neck curved back on shoulders, legs stretched out behind; also in typical heron pattern the feeding grounds are usually separate from roosting area. NOTES not noisy, exchange low clucking sounds while feeding together in flock,or harsh croak of alarm. HABITAT marsh, mudflats, inlets, bays—more often near fresh water than salt water but nests and feeds near both and nests in thickets and groves.

LOOK ALIKES **little blue heron** young #182 L-A are white or white-and-blue. **reddish egret** #160 L-A. **green-backed heron** #175.

tricolored heron (Louisiana heron) 24–26″ throat and front of neck, breast, rump and underparts *white* (white underparts or rump especially easy to see for ID clue), back of neck and back and wings slate-blue, cap and neck may have more tinge of rusty overtones than has **little blue heron,** head plumes in courtship are white (not blue) and rather thin and short. Range coastal areas from Gulf of Mexico to Atlantic north to North Carolina.

CAP: GREEN — BREAST: PATTERNED

#175. green-backed heron 18–22″ **(green heron,** now combined with **striated heron** of Panama)

CAP shaggy crest, dark green (may look blue or black in different light) bordered by rusty cheeks. BILL medium, pointed, dark. FRONT throat white, front of neck streaked in rusty-brown, sides plain rusty blending with cheeks, breast and underparts fading from streaked to ashy gray. BACK slate blue (in spite of name, **green-backed heron** does not often look green as it flies away and so is easily confused with **little blue heron** except for green-backed's smaller size), legs are shorter than little blue's and *bright orange-yellow* (not dull green) back may look black from a distance, especially in the glare of bright sunlight on water. ACTIONS often keeps head drawn back on shoulders so that its neck seems quite short, but then suddenly stretches out to surprising length; since legs are fairly short (for a heron) it fishes in shallows or crouches beside the water's edge, relying on keen eye-sight and instant muscle response to make darting catch; has been seen using a feather or leaf to dabble in the water as bait, making it one of only a very few birds to use a tool; has been called stupid for nesting and feeding so near people but usually knows just when to take wing and fly away (**"fly-up-the-creek"** is one of its nicknames); when courting a mate or feeling confident the male hop-steps along the sand with jaunty bob-and-bow footwork far different from the dignified slow and stately progress of longer-legged herons; often flicks its tail and raises its shaggy crest to let watchers know they have been seen; feeds on insects and small fish, small rodents, reptiles. NOTES calls out a loud "skee-ow" so often that **"skee-ow"** has become one of its nicknames; often calls as it flies away from possible enemy and to some watchers the two notes seem to be derisive "phoo-ee!" Also clucks and chuckles. HABITAT feeds and nests by fresh water and inland ponds and streams as often as by salt-water inlets and marshes; may nest away from water in dryland thickets or almost in the water among mounds of rushes and reeds or some low hummock of earth.

CLOSE LOOK-ALIKES **little blue heron** 22–29″ (#174) has same color back but longer, darker legs and darker underparts and is longer in length, no shaggy crest. **tricolored heron** 24–26″ (#174 L-A) is longer with longer legs and habitat limited to southern coasts; very white underparts, no shaggy crest. **least bittern** 11–14″ (#141x).

S br | S gy | S bl | S gr | S yl | S rd | S b/w | M br | M gy | M bl | M gr | M yl | M o/b | M rd | M b/w | L br | L gy | L bl | L g/b | VL br | VL gy | VL bl | VL gr | VL r/p | VL b/w | VL bk | VL wh

S br · S gy · S bl · S gr · S yl · S rd · S b/w · M br · M gy · M bl · M gr · M yl · M o/b · M rd · M b/w · L br · L gy · L bl · L g/b · VL br · VL gy · VL bl · VL gr · VL r/p · VL b/w · VL bk · VL wh

CAP: WHITE — BREAST: PATTERNED

#176. great blue heron 42–52″

CAP white bordered by black plumes that droop back over nape (some Florida birds lack black border). BILL long, pointed, yellow. FRONT cheek patches and throat white; neck gray at sides, streaked in center, with shaggy plumes at base of neck over breast; underparts streaked blue on white. BACK gray-blue with some lighter, fluffy feathers, *slopes at back. See* #160 **sandhill crane.** ACTIONS stalks through marsh with tall and stately tread; may stand motionless in water waiting for fish to come within reach of that long, jabbing bill, feeds by day or night (but especially at daylight and dusk as do most birds) usually catching fish crosswise in bill and then flipping in to swallow whole, but also spears large fish and stuns with blow before swallowing; also on frogs, reptiles, rodents, small birds, large insects; flies in typical heron style with long neck folded back on shoulders in S curve (but may be stretched out briefly in take-off or landing) and feet stretched out well behind short tail (legs dangle in take-off or landing), in full flight wingspread is a good 6 to 7 feet (same as **sandhill crane**); is often called **"blue crane"** by people who do not check bird books for correct name; largest heron in N.A. NOTES gruff croaks. HABITAT salt water or fresh; lakes, streams, ponds — even backyard pools or golf-course water hazards — are all of equal appeal along with marshes, sandbars, bays, ocean shores so long as they contain food; nests in trees or on rocky ledges, even on the ground, and usually in a large group of other herons, many even nesting in the same tree.

CLOSE LOOK-ALIKE **sandhill crane** #160 is the only N.A. bird of similar size and cloring. *See* #196 L-A for white phase.

SHORT-LEGGED SWIMMERS

CAP: BLUE-BLACK — BREAST: PATTERNED (BLUE)

#177. harlequin duck (m) 15–21″

CAP blue-black center stripe bordered in white at the forehead, in rusty toward nape. BILL flat, blue. FRONT face seems painted in white edged with black like the mask of an oldtime stage funnyman called a harlequin, remainder of head is blue with patches of white outlined in black (a round spot behind the eye and a crescent behind that), one white ring circles the throat and another is just below the breast, underparts blue in center, rusty patch at sides. BACK blue with white patches, white edging on wing feathers, tail fairly long and pointed. ACTIONS nests beside mountain streams and lakes or on Arctic shores, winters on both coasts; feeds on crustaceans, mollusks, insects and may swim underwater to get them, even walking along bottom; will accept handouts from hikers — bread, vegetables, fruit. NOTES male and mate exchange clucking croaks; male has a low whistling call — usually silent. HABITAT in winter usually seen only along coast or not far inland (may follow river). In summer nests in Arctic or southward in Rocky Mountains. On coast or inland mountain streams seems to prefer rough water with swirls, eddies, turbulence.

CLOSE LOOK-ALIKE female (#164 L-A) is gray with a few white "harlequin" spots on face. No other duck, male or female, has the harlequin drake's blue-black-white-and-rusty color scheme. GENERAL LOOK-ALIKES (white face patches) **wood duck** #164 17–20½". **blue-winged teal** 14–16" only *one crescent-shaped patch* between bill and eye, remainder of cheek blue, breast speckled brown and buff, back mottled browns. Range cont-exAlaska/Arctic. **common goldeneye** 16–20" one round white spot between bill and eye, remainder of head green. Range, nests Canada to Alaska, winters across U.S. **Barrow's goldeneye** 16–20" one crescent-shaped white spot between bill and eye, remainder of head purplish-black. Range both north coasts, inland mountain northwest. **bufflehead** 13–15" one triangular white patch covers entire back half of head, front half is blackish with greenish gloss, back black, breast white. Range cont. **old-squaw** 15–23" cap black, triangular white cheek patch, throat and breast black, underparts white, tail very long and pointed. Range, nests Arctic, winters both. **blue goose** 25–30" #166x.

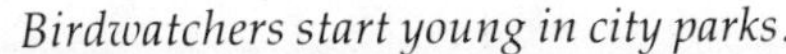

Birdwatchers start young in city parks.

S br
S gy
S bl
S gr
S yl
S rd
S b/w
M br
M gy
M bl
M gr
M yl
M o/b
M rd
M b/w
L br
L gy
L bl
L g/b
VL br
VL gy
VL bl
VL gr
VL r/p
VL b/w
VL bk
VL wh

Size: VERY LARGE — Color: GREENS

Birds that are Very Large and Green are difficult to judge for basic color clue. The green, remember, has to be on the bird's back to be considered the basic color. And it happens that most of the green back plumage looks as much like gray or blue or black as it does green, especially in changing light or in different surroundings. Also, most of the birds with greenish backs have other bright color patches elsewhere that catch your eye first and make a faster ID color clue.

After careful study, only three species have been placed in this Size-and-Color Key. All are water birds, one with fairly long legs and the other two short-legged swimmers. However, several birds — such as the mallard male — have glossy green heads or green patches that make a quick ID clue, and these are listed also with referral to more complete description in another Key. (Because sizes vary more with Very Large birds than with other Key groups, length of each species is given in inches.)

LONG-LEGGED WADERS

CAP: BLUISH-PURPLE — BREAST: PATTERNED (BLUISH-PURPLE)

#178. purple gallinule 12–14″

CAP bluish-purple, visor pale blue. BILL thick, medium, red with yellow tip. FRONT head, neck, breast and underparts all bluish-purple, eye red, legs yellow, feet yellow with *toes very long.* BACK nape bluish-purple, shoulders, wings and tail all grass-green with bronze overtones, under-tail patch white, tail short and pointed, usually cocked upright. ACTIONS walks with jaunty grace, its long toes splayed out to spread its weight so that it can even walk across lily pads in the pond without sinking; if no pads offer a bridge it will wade or swim, or may fly with yellow legs dangling or clamber over bushes and trees with easy skill; eats seeds from water plants, grain ashore, snails, frogs, worms, insects, eggs and young of other marsh birds; often bobs and bows as it walks, also twitches tail, showing the white patch, also bobs head as it swims. NOTES talkative, giving hen-like cackle as it flies, also a throaty croak. HABITAT swamps, marshy backwater, willow thickets beside stream or marsh, grain fields (especially rice).

GENERAL LOOK-ALIKES **common moorhen (common gallinule)** 12–15″ (#189 L-A) similar in shape and actions but sooty black. **American coot** 16″ (#189) similar in shape and actions but sooty black. **clapper** and **king rails** (#142x) are similar in shape and actions but are brown and have long bills; **sora** (#82) has chicken-like bill like the gallinules but is Medium.

SHORT-LEGGED SWIMMERS

CAP: GREEN — BREAST: PLAIN (WHITE)

#179. common merganser (m) 22–27″

CAP glossy bottle green hood, slight nape crest not visible. BILL *thin, long,* serrated on the sides, red. FRONT throat green (part of hood), eye red, lower neck, breast and underparts all white, long-necked, long-bodied. BACK center glossy blackish-green, white sides and collar between nape and back, wings white next to body (full width, half length) divided in three by two narrow black lines, tail grayish and pointed (green center may look black). ACTIONS dives for fish (serrated bill enables it to hold on to slippery fish), usually feeds on small fish not used by humans, also frogs, crustaceans, snails, insects, some plant roots and stems; needs running start to take off in flight. NOTES harsh croaks. HABITAT wooded lake shores, ponds, streambanks; will stay north as far as water remains open in winter; late to leave on migration and early to return.

CLOSE LOOK-ALIKE **red-breasted merganser (m)** 20–26″ (#165 L-A) similar but has shaggy nape crest plainly visible, breast speckled rusty-brown. Range cont-ex inland-west (Rockies).

CAP: GREEN — BREAST: PATTERNED (BROWN)

#180. wood duck (m) 17–20″

CAP glossy green, swept-back crest bordered in thin white line over eye. BILL flat, vari-colored — blue at tip, blue bordered in white in center, red outlined in bright yellow at base next to visor area. FRONT eye red; cheek patch encircling eye glossy green with blue highlights, outlined toward nape in white; throat white, extending to circle nape as collar; drooping green crest also has white striping; breast rusty-brown dotted in white, bordered in white and black bands next to underparts; underparts white, sides grayish with black-and-white check edging. BACK glossy bottle green, wing patches blue and violet edged with black and white, tail long, square-tipped and dark. ACTIONS often perches in trees, nest is in tree cavity or nest box (*see* female #164); feeds on water plants, especially duckweed, on insects, seeds and roots of reeds, sedges; on grain ashore and berries, acorns and other nuts; the grinding action of the gizzard, plus the action of grit and small pebbles swallowed instinctively by wildfowl (especially ducks, chicken-like birds) enables them to digest acorns shells and all; also eats frogs, snails. NOTES a warbling trill of "wheeeee", high-pitched, rising at the end as if asking a question. HABITAT wooded areas near streams, ponds, marshland; may even move into nest or feed in city parks and zoos.

CLOSE LOOK-ALIKES no other North American duck has *both* a clownlike painted face and a swept-back crest; female (#164) has crest and some "face paint" but is a drab

S br | S gy | S bl | S gr | S yl | S rd | S b/w | M br | M gy | M bl | M gr | M yl | M o/b | M rd | M b/w | L br | L gy | L bl | L g/b | VL br | VL gy | VL bl | VL gr | VL r/p | VL b/w | VL bk | VL wh

S br | S gy | S bl | S gr | S yl | S rd | S b/w | M br | M gy | M bl | M gr | M yl | M o/b | M rd | M b/w | L br | L gy | L bl | L g/b | VL br | VL gy | VL bl | VL gr | VL r/p | VL b/w | VL bk | VL wh

gray-and-white. **Harlequin duck** (#177) has clownlike face but not a crest.
SPECIAL CHECK waterfowl with green heads. Ducks and other water birds whose glossy green heads make "green" a quick color clue: **mallard (m)** #165, **northern shoveler (m)** #165 L-A, **greater scaup (m)** #165 L-A, **common goldeneye (m)** #165 L-A, **common merganser (m)** #179, **red-breasted merganser (m)** #179 L-A, **common loon** #183, **yellow-billed loon** #183 L-A, **wood duck (m)** #180.

Size: VERY LARGE — Color: RED TO PINK

Only three Very Large North American birds come in a basic color of red or pink. Each has a different shade of coloring, but each is more easily recognized by its oddly-shaped bill. All are long-legged birds of southern swamps.

Brightest among them, the scarlet ibis, is known by the typical bill of the ibis family — long and down-curved. Tallest among the three, the greater flamingo is known by its thick, short, hook-shaped bill. The oddest bill — long and flat with a wide round spoonlike tip — identifies the roseate spoonbill.

For this Key only, these birds will be listed with the bill the first ID clue, not the color of cap and breast. With birds so large and bills so odd — and so different from each other — the bill shape just has to be the next clue after basic color.

COLOR: RED — BILL: DOWN-CURVED, LONG
scarlet ibis 22–25" look at the picture of the **glossy ibis** #142 and imagine the same bird in bright red with black wing tips and you will know what the scarlet ibis looks like. You may never see one in the wild, for this species is native to South America and only a few individuals are seen in Florida swamps or along the Gulf Coast to Texas. Some of the first to arrive may have been blown north by hurricane winds or they may have escaped from zoos. However, these wanderers have mated and their young are now native North Americans.

COLOR: ROSE — BILL: LONG, FLAT, ROUNDED TIP
roseate spoonbill 32" has a white back that would place it in the Very-Large-and-White Key if the wings were not so rosy and so wide. Wing linings are rosy, too, and lower breast and underparts and the long legs, so that rose is the ID color you see, especially when the bird is in flight. There is also a shaggy tuft of rosy feathers on the white breast. The long neck is white, with a black patch just behind the grayish cap, but the long gray bill that widens out like a flat ladle on the end will be first to catch the eye. Young birds are white with a yellow bill of this same odd shape. In feeding, the bill swings from side to side, probing mud and shallows for small fish, crustaceans, slugs, insects; finds food by touch, not sight. These birds have been rare, but with protection are now making a small increase. Range Florida, occasionally Louisiana, Texas and elsewhere along Gulf Coast.

COLOR: PINKISH-RED — BILL: THICK, SHARPLY DOWN-CURVED
greater flamingo 36–50" long legs and long neck are similar to those of cranes and herons, but flamingos have webbed feet while cranes and herons have toes separated. Also, no other bird — except another flamingo — has the same oddly-shaped bill. To feed, a flamingo turns its bill upside down so that the top rests on the muddy bottom of pond, bay or marsh. As the bill moves, the water flows in and out, and tongue and bill work together to sift out anything edible — tiny plants, insects, fish. The thick, down-curved bill is light at the top, solid black on the lower half, a color scheme matched by the wings whose black lower half is usually seen only in flight.

Perhaps flamingos never were native to North America and those now seen north of the Caribbean may have been blown north by storm winds or have escaped from zoos or aviaries. However, nesting flamingo pairs have been seen in Florida almost as long as records have been kept and others are seen occasionally along the Gulf Coast from Florida to Texas. Several pairs were brought to the Hialeah Race Track in Miami, Florida, in the 1930s and stay there, since their wing feathers are clipped to prevent them from flying, and the young birds hatched there have known no other home. Occasionally a flamingo may wander north along the coast — Atlantic or Pacific — in summer and so this unusual bird may be seen far beyond its tropic homeland, even as far away as Oregon or New England. Since they are such strong fliers — and evidently like to roam — many flamingos may have come to North America from the Caribbean in times past on their own wing power without any help from humans or hurricanes. Incidentally, the first record of American flamingos came from the journals of Christopher Columbus, who in May 1494 off Cuba's south shore told of seeing birds the size and shape of cranes but bright red.

Flamingos in southern Europe and in Africa and South America are much paler than those of the Caribbean and North America, but all are generally counted the same species — just color variants. Those of Africa are almost all white except for rose and black wings.

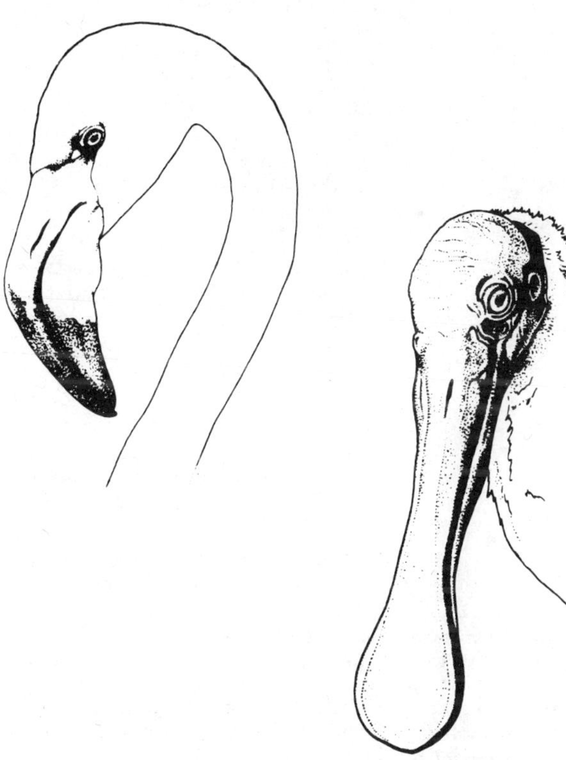

S br | S gy | S bl | S gr | S yl | S rd | S b/w | M br | M gy | M bl | M gr | M yl | M o/b | M rd | M b/w | L br | L gy | L bl | L g/b | VL br | VL gy | VL bl | VL gr | VL r/p | VL b/w | VL bk | VL wh

Size: VERY LARGE — Color: BLACK-AND-WHITE

Birds that are Very Large and come in a two-tone color scheme of black-and-white show such easily recognized differences in behavior that you can put them in a matching group by Actions as quickly as by Size and Color. Therefore, in this Key you will first match the bird you want to identify with one of these four Action groups:

long-legged (or very-long-legged) waders
short-legged swimmers
hook-billed or pointed-billed hunters, fishers, scavengers
woodpeckers

The fourth group — woodpeckers — has only two North American species of Very Large size. The others in the family are Large or Medium. Like many of their smaller kin, these two have bright red heads, but only one has the black-and-white back that puts it in this Color Key.

Once you have placed your bird in the right Action group, follow the usual SCANS System of matching by colors of cap and breast first, then by further description. (Because sizes vary more for Very Large birds than for other Key groups, length is given in inches for each species.)

LONG-LEGGED OR VERY-LONG-LEGGED WADERS

CAP: BROWN — BREAST: PATTERNED (BUFFY-BROWN)

#181. American avocet 17–20″

CAP buffy-brown (summer) buffy-gray (winter) bordered in front by white visor and chin patch, in rear cap color blends with cheek and nape. BILL long, slender, up-curved. FRONT long neck is all buffy-brown, breast and underparts all white, long legs gray-blue. BACK center of back white, sides black, outer wings solid black, white next to body divided in three by crosswise slanting band of black, rump and tail white. ACTIONS sweeps long bill back and forth as it feeds in shallows of marsh or lake or salt-water pond on crayfish, snails, insects, small fish, seeds of water plants; also feeds on insects ashore; nests near water, both parents protect nest and young, often putting on vigorous display of pretended lame leg or lame wing or both, shrieking and calling to attract attention of any intruder while commanding young to hide or run. NOTES long-drawn "whee-eek" or "plee-eek" or "klee-eek" repeated in frenzied or plaintive tone. HABITAT marshes, mudflats, inland ponds, lakes, sloughs or salt-water bays (but more inland nests).

CLOSE LOOK ALIKE **black-necked stilt** 13–17″ similar, but bill is *straight* and cap is *black* with white visor, front of neck white, nape and back of neck black, *back all black including wings,* no white pattern to show in flight, legs red. Range West, Gulf Coast Texas to Florida and up coast to Delaware, may be returning elsewhere on East Coast. GENERAL LOOK-ALIKES **whooping crane (y)** brown head and neck, brownish-buff streaking on neck and back *but no black,* legs dark, bill medium thick and *straight.* Range, most **whooping crane** young are hatched in northern Canada where avocets do not occur, but **whooping cranes** hatched by **sandhill crane** foster parents (on government preservation program) may some day be seen in avocet territory; however, well-grown young cranes will be twice the 17–20″ height of avocets. **cattle egret** 19–21″ (#193) has buffy cap and buffy breast and back markings in nesting season but *no black,* legs are yellow and shorter, body chunkier, neck shorter and usually hunched back on shoulders, bill straight, not up-curved.

CAP: BLACK — BREAST: PLAIN (WHITE)

#182. black-crowned night-heron 23–28″

CAP bordered by white visor, white cheek and nape, 2 or 3 drooping white nape plumes in nesting season. BILL medium (short for a heron) pointed. FRONT eye red, breast and underparts all white, legs yellow (short for a heron). BACK nape white, back black, nape and neck white, wings and rump grayish-white, body chunky. ACTIONS usually sits with head hunched back on shoulders and not stretched out in typical heron pose; feeds mostly by night, but also by day; often wades into water to fish, waiting motionless for fish to come within reach, or may swim out to deeper water; also feeds on water plants, frogs, reptiles, rodents, crustaceans, young birds, insects; nests in trees, usually with several other pairs near by. NOTES harsh croaking "quark" or "quawk" (led to oldtime name of **night raven, night crow**). HABITAT marsh, swamp, wooded areas near water, even city parks, coastal sea islands and shores, inland lake shores.

CLOSE LOOK-ALIKES adults have no close look-alike but young birds are streaked brown and resemble **American bittern** (#144) and young **yellow-crowned night-heron** (#144 L-A) or **limpkin** (#144 L-A). GENERAL LOOK-ALIKE **little blue heron (y)** 25–29″ the young are white and change gradually to the dark blue of the adult, a patch here, a streaking there. Since the blue looks black at a distance or in poor light, one of these "calico pattern" youngsters almost in full plumage might be mistaken for an adult **black-crowned night-heron.** But check the cap (solid black with white visor for the night-heron) and the breast (white with no patches or streaking for the night-heron).

American oystercatcher 17–21″ shorebird with long, flat red bill (3–4″), black hood that includes head, neck and upper breast, lower breast and underparts white, back black, rump and upper tail white, wide white bands across lower wings, legs and feet pink; can pry oysters and other shellfish from rocks, cut muscle that holds shell closed and pry shell open with strong bill tip. Range Atlantic and Gulf Coasts. On Pacific Coast the very similar **American black oystercatcher** (#186x) with no white on back has the same role, same long red bill.

SHORT-LEGGED SWIMMERS

CAP: GRAY — BREAST: PLAIN (WHITE)

red-throated loon 24–27″ cap, cheeks and sides of throat gray, throat red, nape striped black and white, breast white (in winter back is mottled gray and white, throat white), usually silent except on nesting ground in Arctic. Winter range both coasts and Great Lakes.

Arctic loon 23–29″ cap and nape gray, sides of neck striped black and white, throat black. Range, nests in Arctic, winters on Pacific Coast south to Baja.

CAP: BLUE — BREAST: PLAIN (WHITE)

king eider (m) 19–25″ cap pale blue, visor large and orange outlined in black, cheek greenish-white, shoulders white, shows wide white wing patched in flight. Range, nests in Arctic, winters both coasts to midline.

CAP: GREEN — BREAST: PLAIN

spectacled eider (m) 20–23″ visor also pale green, cheek white outlined in

S br · S gy · S bl · S gr · S yl · S rd · S b/w · M br · M gy · M bl · M gr · M yl · M o/b · M rd · M b/w · L br · L gy · L bl · L g/b · VL br · VL gy · VL bl · VL gr · VL r/p · VL b/w · VL bk · VL wh

black, upper breast white, lower breast and underparts black. Range Alaskan coast.

common goldeneye (m) #177 L-A; #165 L-A.

common merganser (m) #179.

red-breasted merganser (m) #179 L-A.

northern shoveler (m) #165 L-A.

#183. common loon 28–36″

CAP glossy blackish-green in summer (winter, blackish-gray). BILL medium, dark, pointed. FRONT throat blackish-green, neck striped narrowly black-and-white, banded in dark green above breast, breast and underparts white, sides speckled white on black (winter, throat and neck white). BACK dappled white on black in summer (winter, mottled grayish-black), long-bodied. ACTIONS nests in northern U.S. and Canada, stays north so long as water remains unfrozen and fish available, may sleep on water or land, salt water or fresh; needs to make running take-off from water for flight, dives to escape enemies, does not like to nest near active humans; feeds on reptiles, crustaceans, insects as well as fish; cannot walk well on land because legs set so far back on body and so usually nests near water, usually uses same nest site every year and thought to keep same mate for life. NOTES tremolo call in various tones, called laugh or yodel or wail, often heard at dusk or dawn or during night; also "yak-yak" conversational notes to mate or to flock members on migration. HABITAT nests northern U.S. to Alaska and Arctic, winters on both coasts south to Gulf Coast, nests on sheltered shores, often on islands or jutting points of land among reeds, grasses, underbrush.

CLOSE LOOK-ALIKES all loons have similar long-bodied, short-necked silhouettes. **red-throated loon** #182x. **Arctic loon** #182x. **yellow-billed loon** 30–36″ largest of the loons, most like **common loon** but identified by yellow (not dark) bill. Range, nests in Alaska and Arctic Canada west of Hudson's Bay, winters on Pacific Coast south to U.S. border, may occasionally stray farther south.

CAP: RED — BREAST: PLAIN (GRAYISH-WHITE)

canvasback (duck) 19–24″ bill long, sloping down from red hood, neck longer than most ducks also to give different silhouette, back *whiter* than gray back of similar **redhead** (#166x), breast and shoulders black, tail black and pointed; a favorite with gourmets and hunters and has been banned or limited for hunting to preserve species. Nests on northwest plains of U.S. and Canada, usually winters along coasts (Pacific, Atlantic, Gulf).

CAP: BLACK-AND-WHITE — BREAST: PLAIN (WHITE)

bufflehead 13–15″ (as for the **canvasback** and **redhead** and several other species in this family, the word *duck* is not part of the official name). Black hood is divided by a triangular white patch from eye and cheek over the top of the head to nape, black may look greenish in certain light, looks "big-headed" but does not have a flared crest like the **hooded merganser.** Female #164 L-A. Range, nests in northwest, winters all across the U.S. and both coasts.

hooded merganser (m) 16–19″ long, narrow bill is best ID, but first look goes to the beautiful flared crest, part of a black hood marked with a center triangular patch of white; whether raised or lowered, the crest is still eye-catching. Female #166x. Not an abundant species but nests all across the continent except southwest and far north; winters on Atlantic, Pacific and Gulf Coasts.

Barrow's goldeneye (m) 16–20″ big-headed but no upright crest, small white crescent patch between eye and bill. Female #166x. Range both north coasts, inland mountain west.

common eider (m) 23–27″ center of cap black bordered by white of cheeks and white and green of nape, bill sloping and yellow, breast white, underparts solid black, rump, tail and lower wing edges black; a sea bird usually seen with others floating together. Range, nests Alaska to Arctic East Coast, winters off both north coasts.

CAP: BLACK — BREAST: PATTERNED (BLACK)

#184. anhinga (m) 32–36″

CAP blends with black of nape and neck. BILL long, pointed, yellow. FRONT eye red, bare-skin eye patch blue, red bare-skin patch under chin, neck very long and black, breast and underparts all black, (female has brown head, neck and upper breast, otherwise black). BACK black, wings streaked in white, large bands of white midwing, tail tipped in white, long, wide, and square-tipped, barred in black. ACTIONS feathers are not waterproof and so **anhingas** must sit with wings outspread to dry in sun and air; expert swimmers and divers, often swim with only head and neck above water and so resemble a snake that **"snakebird"** is a common nickname; also called **"water turkey"** because the tail spread to dry is somewhat like a turkey's white-tipped dark tail; may dive from air into water or from surface while swimming or swim underwater after fish which it usually flips into air and swallows headfirst; also feeds on insects, crustaceans, reptiles, young alligators and turtles; flies with neck outstretched, often soars with wings outspread buoyed by rising air currents; has unusual neck structure which enables it to stab with extreme strength and swiftness and so is also nicknamed **"darter".** (*Anhinga,* an Amazon Indian name, was the first name in print.) NOTES rapid clicking. HABITAT marsh, swamps, backwater bays; often nests in same colony as **herons** and **egrets,** may fish in same area as **cormorants.**

CLOSE LOOK-ALIKES **cormorants** (#188) also spread wings to dry but have all-black plumage or only small white wing patch.

CAP: WHITE — BREAST: PATTERNED (BLACK AND GRAY)

emperor goose 26–30″ cap, cheeks and nape white, throat and front black-and-gray with scalloped edges in white, legs orange. Range Alaska, may stray south in winter along Pacific Coast to California.

S br S gy S bl S gr S yl S rd S b/w M br M gy M bl M gr M yl M o/b M rd M b/w L br L gy L bl L g/b VL br VL gy VL bl VL gr VL r/p VL b/w VL bk VL wh

Steller's eider (m) 17–19″ head and neck white with black spot around eye, greenish tuft on nape, blurred spot between eye and bill, black collar, buffy underparts. Named to honor the German physician-naturalist Georg Steller who sailed to Alaska with the Russian expedition under Bering and spent months of shipwreck studying Alaskan wildlife. Two other namesakes are **Steller's jay** (#141) and **Steller's sea-eagle,** rare visitor to Alaska's offshore islands and coast, which is much like the **bald eagle** but with a brown head, white shoulders, white legs and white tail. Range Alaska, occasional strays elsewhere (native from Scandinavia to Siberia).

oldsquaw (m) 15–23″ in *winter* head and neck are *white* with curved brown mask over eyes and cheeks; breast black, underparts white, tail long, black and pointed. In *summer* has *black* cap, nape and neck with white cheek patch; breast black, sides and underparts white. Female similar with brown instead of black. Range, nests in Arctic, winters both coasts and around Great Lakes.

HOOKED-BILLED OR POINTED-BILLED HUNTERS, FISHERS, SCAVENGERS

CAP: BLACK — BREAST: PATTERNED (BLACK)

#185. black-billed magpie 18–22″

CAP hood including head, neck, throat, upper breast. BILL medium, sturdy, *black,* pointed. FRONT throat and upper breast black, lower breast and underparts white. BACK center black, sides white, outer wing feathers streaked in white with black tips, wing shoulders white and feathers between iridescent green-black-purple, tail feathers also iridescent greenish-black, half of over-all length is tail. ACTIONS bold, aggressive, often takes food from campers or farm animals; gleans ticks and other insects from backs of wild and farm animals and may then peck at sores; feeds on dead animals, rodents, birds, eggs, insects, grain, reptiles, some fruit. NOTES in flight, flocks keeps up give-and-take chatter, calls with rising inflection as if asking question using a harsh croaking "yak-yak" or a whining "ma-ag" that evidently led to the name given by English farmfolk centuries ago — the *pie* is from the old English term for a black-and-white pattern. HABITAT ranch country, streamside thickets, open prairie and grassland.

CLOSE LOOK-ALIKE **yellow-billed magpie** 16–18″ similar but slightly smaller and with bill yellow instead of black. Range usually seen only in California but has been seen in Oregon, possibly elsewhere nearby.

crested caracara 20–25″ cap black, cheeks and throat white, breast and tail barred black on white, bill hooked, red with gray tip. Mexico's national bird, usually known there as **Mexican eagle.** U.S. range near U.S.-Mexican border, Florida.

CAP: WHITE — BREAST: PLAIN (WHITE)

#186. snowy owl 20–27″

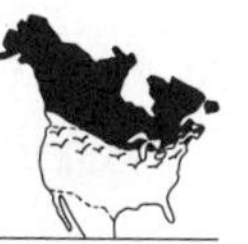

CAP white, center flecked in black, no ear tufts. BILL hooked. FRONT throat white, breast and underparts white barred in black, eye yellow. BACK white, barred and flecked in black, tail white flecked lightly in black near tip, some individuals are almost all white with few black markings. ACTIONS hunts by day, often perches on ground or rock or small hummock of earth rather than in tree since few trees exist in its northern nesting ground, many go south for winter when food not available; feeds on rodents (mice, lemmings), birds, fish or any other available animal, alive or dead; a good year for watching **snowy owls** south of Canada means it has been a poor year for animals of the Arctic tundra. NOTES seldom heard away from nesting grounds, calls to mate with throaty growl or clicking sound or whistling hoot. HABITAT north country fields, beaches.

CLOSE LOOK-ALIKE no other owl — no other white bird of any kind — has the bulky, big-bodied shape of the **snowy owl,** but the **common barn owl** (#153) smaller at 14–20″ looks all white underneath and could be mistaken for a snowy by someone who does not judge size or get a view of the back or of the barn owl's heart-shape face.

gyrfalcon 20–25″ cap white, throat white, breast and back flecked with black, wings long and pointed, tail long and rectangular (not fan-shaped). Also comes in a gray color phase and a darker blackish-brown phase. Range, nests in the Arctic, winters in northern Canada and southern Alaska, rarely wanders farther south.

red-billed tropicbird 36–42″ pointed bill, streamer tail half of over-all length; fishing bird of tropics sometimes seen off southern California coast, rarely off Atlantic Coast.

white-tailed tropicbird 28–32″ orange-to-red bill, streamer-tail, black-and-white body pattern; sometimes seen off the Florida or Gulf Coast.

WOODPECKERS

CAP: RED — BREAST: PATTERNED (BLACK)

ivory-billed woodpecker 20″ this species, largest of North American woodpeckers, is probably extinct, or at least very close to extinction. A few birds have been sighted in recent years in Texas, Louisiana and South Carolina, but were not seen again. A large triangular red crest with center black feather and large white wing patches and the ivory-colored bill distinguish this rare species from the slightly smaller **pileated woodpecker** (#192) with dark bill and all-black back.

Size: VERY LARGE — Color: BLACK

Birds that are Very Large and Black — like most of the other Very Large species — show such easily recognized differences in behavior that you can put them in a matching group by Actions as quickly as by Size and Color. Therefore in this Key you will first match the bird you want to identify with one of these four Action groups:

long-legged wader and walker
short-legged swimmers
hook-billed or pointed-billed hunters, fishers, scavengers
woodpeckers

Once you have placed your bird in the right Action group, follow the usual SCANS System of matching by colors of cap and breast first, then by further description. (Because sizes vary more for Very Large birds than for other Key groups, length of each species is given in inches.)

LONG-LEGGED WADER AND WALKER

CAP: BLACK — BREAST: PATTERNED (BLACK)

American black oystercatcher 16½ – 18½″ long, flat, red bill; pinkish legs and feet, yellow eye, body plumage all black. *See* #182x for Atlantic Coast species, **American oystercatcher.** Range Pacific Coast, Alaska to Baja.

SHORT-LEGGED SWIMMERS

CAP: BLACK — BREAST : PLAIN (WHITE)

#187. western grebe 22–29″

CAP slight crest, bordered by white of cheek, throat. BILL medium long, pointed, yellow. FRONT eye red; cheeks, throat, neck, breast and underparts all white, neck long and swanlike. BACK nape, back of neck and back, wings, tail all black, some gray feather edging on back, white bands on wings show in flight, toes separate and padded (lobed). ACTIONS feeds largely on fish, eats some insects, crustaceans; known for elaborate courting "dance"' in which mates bob and bow then rise upright as if walking on water and then race off together side by side, wings fanning furiously to maintain balance, necks arched gracefully (the graceful neck has led to the nickname **"swan grebe"**); all grebes are expert divers, swimmers. NOTES trilling croak, shrill whistle. HABITAT nests among reeds and rushes near water or on a floating mound of marsh reeds and mud in inland lakes, sloughs; often winters on Pacific Coast from mid-Canada south.

GENERAL LOOK-ALIKES **red-necked grebe** 17–22″ smaller, cap black, cheeks white as in **western grebe,** but neck rusty — and shorter, though still longer than usual duck's neck. Winter birds *gray* necked. Range, nests in northwest to Alaska, winters both coasts. **horned grebe** 12–15″ winter birds like **western grebe** in coloring but much smaller, summer birds have rusty throats and underparts, shaggy black throat and cap, buffy-yellow ear tufts or horns drooping along cap. Range, nests northwest to Alaska, winters both coasts. **eared grebe** 12–14″ winter birds like **western** in coloring (neck gray) but much smaller, summer birds have black cap and neck, buffy yellow drooping ear tufts. Range West.

common puffin 14″ the thick, parrot-like, brightly-colored bill long ago gave all puffins the nickname of **"sea parrot"**, and their white faces give them an amusing clownlike appearance. Range North Atlantic Coast — they feed at sea and come ashore only to nest in underground burrows.

horned puffin 14–15″ the so-called horn is a black fleshy spikelet over each eye during courting season. The thick bill is yellow with red tip. Range North Pacific Coast all year.

tufted puffin 14½–15½″ white face patch is more triangular than in other puffins, in courting season has long blond tufts drooping back from cap over nape, at all seasons can be told from other puffins by *black* breast and underparts (both the others are white). Range Pacific Coast, nests in north, winters Alaska to California-Baja border.

black skimmer 16–20″ black cap bordered by white visor and cheeks, throat, breast, underparts and wing lining; cap, nape, back and wings black (wings bordered in white on lower edge); bill medium, *bright red* with black tip; legs and feet red; skims low over water scooping up small fish and crustaceans with lower bill (only bird with lower bill longer than upper half); usually feeds at dusk and dawn and rests on beach by day. Range Atlantic Coast south from Long Island, Gulf Coast, recently a few seen on shores of Southern California.

common murre 16–17″ black hood and back, white breast and underparts; seabird that sits upright on the rocks when it comes ashore — a pose that reminds watchers of penguins; bill medium long, black, slender, pointed; winters at sea but comes ashore to nest on north coasts (south to Nova Scotia — and rarely Long Island — on Atlantic; to California on Pacific).

thick-billed murre 17–19″ similar to **common murre**, bill only slightly thicker, has nested inland on shores of Hudson Bay, Great Lakes, but usually coasts.

CAP: BLACK — BREAST: PATTERNED (BLACK)

#188. double-crested cormorant 29–36″

CAP in spring, small black tuft each side of cap. BILL medium, slight hook at tip. FRONT bare-skin orange patch around eyes and under bill (expandable pouch), all black on long neck, breast and underparts (young birds lighter breasted). BACK all black, no white shows even in flight; tail looks wedge-shaped in flight, not square-tipped like **anhinga's** (#184). ACTIONS feathers not waterproof so perch after swimming with wings spread out to dry; dive from surface to catch fish (usually small bony species not wanted by humans), also feeds on crustaceans, small reptiles, mollusks; nests on rocks, shore, trees; only cormorant seen regularly on *both coasts and inland*. NOTES grunting croaks on nesting ground, otherwise usually silent. HABITAT shores of both oceans, bays, inland lakes and rivers.

CLOSE LOOK-ALIKES **anhinga #184. great cormorant** 34–40″ white cheeks and throat patch, white wing patch. European species seen in winter on North Atlantic Coast. **Brandt's cormorant** 33–35″ blue and yellow throat patch, drooping neck plumes in nesting season. Range Pacific Coast only, not inland. **pelagic cormorant** 25–30″ small ear tufts like **double-crested** but has red bare-skin face patch and white wing patch. Range Pacific Coast.

#189. American coot 16″

CAP blends with black of head and throat, bordered by white visor that extends to bill. BILL thick, short, chicken-like, white, dark ring on tip. FRONT throat and neck black shading to blackish-gray on underparts, eye red, legs greenish-black. BACK neck, back and wings black, tail black, pointed and usually cocked upright showing white under-tail; over-all length 16″ so is small for this Size group. ACTIONS has long toes padded with flesh (lobed) to make for easy walking over lily pads and marsh; dives from surface to fish — like a duck and is often called **"black duck"** — has to make running, pitter-patter take-off to get airborne and so was called **"black patterer"**, which somehow changed to **"Blue Peter"**. Also known as **"mud hen"** and many other nicknames that come to birds often seen over a wide area. NOTES mates call to each other with stuttering croak or tremolo coo and many other cackling, grunting noises. HABITAT inland ponds, lakes, marshes and nearby fields; coastal bays.

CLOSE LOOK-ALIKE **common moorhen (common gallinule)** 14½″ similar but has *red* visor, bill red with yellow tip (not white), legs yellow, sides of underparts bordered with broken line of small white patches. Range East, also California, Arizona and New Mexico, occasionally strays farther north. GENERAL LOOK-ALIKE **ring-necked duck** 14½ – 18″ head, back, upper breast black (brown neck ring seldom seen), male grayish white underparts, female dark brown. Range, summers northern U.S. and Canada on lakes, winters all coasts and inland from Canadian border south. **black scoter (American scoter, common scoter)** 17 – 21″ only all-black duck in North America, only color is *orange knob* on bill. A sea duck that nests in Arctic, winters on both coasts, Great Lakes. **surf scoter** 17—21″ all black except for white visor patch, three-colored bill (white, red, yellow tip), white nape patch and orange legs. Nests in Canada and Arctic, winters on both coasts, Great Lakes and occasionally on other large lakes. **white-winged scoter** 19 – 24″ all black except for small white eye patch and white wing patches on lower wing next to body. Nests from Alaska and northern Canada south to North Dakota, nonnesters wander in summer on both coasts and inland, in winter on both coasts and Great Lakes and occasionally on other large lakes.

HOOK-BILLED AND POINTED-BILLED HUNTERS, FISHERS, SCAVENGERS

CAP: YELLOW — BREAST: PATTERNED (BLACK)

California condor 43 – 55″ close to extinction, remaining birds only in Los Padres National Forest in California. Largest of the North American vultures, wingspread 8 to 10 feet. Bare skin of head and throat orange-yellow (sometimes pinkish-yellow) bordered by black breast ruff, breast and underparts black but underwings *white on upper half,* back and tail black, wings black with some white streaking. Young birds similar but have gray bare-skin heads.

#190. turkey vulture 26–32″

CAP bare-skin red hood over head, neck. BILL hooked. FRONT breast and underparts black, underside of wings *black on upper half,* gray or grayish-white on lower half, wing-spread up to 6 feet. BACK black, tail long, extends well beyond feet in flight (not short and fan-shape like tail of black vulture). ACTIONS like all vultures, uses wide wings to soar aloft on rising air currents while watching for carrion on ground below, has extremely keen eyesight; on ground is clumsy, hops awkwardly, stomps up and down in one place when angry or driven from food by eagles or other predators; talons are not strong enough to give the killing grip of hawks and eagles and so must rely on carrion for most of its food, gathers in flock to feed on carcass, also eats grasshoppers, fish, newborn birds and mammals, eggs — even fruit and vegetables if hungry enough — anything killed on the highway — mammal, reptile, rodent, bird; usually moves slowly in the air or on the ground and so was given the name **buzzard** — which means "slow bird" — by early English colonists in America, although in England this name is given only to slow-flying hawks of the genus Buteo. The word *turkey* was used because it has a bare-skin red head like the turkey and similar dark plumage. NOTES hisses, grunts — usually silent. HABITAT garbage dumps, ranch country, highways with long, straight stretches in open country where speeding cars kill many animals. More abundant in South than North because of year-round food supply; its return to Hinckley, Ohio, is celebrated as the first sign of spring on March 15 each year.

CLOSE LOOK-ALIKES **black vulture** 23–27″ smaller, wingspread 5 feet, tail fan-shaped, short, (not long, rectangular), wings have broad white patches on underside at the *tips,* rest of underwing dark; does not usually migrate so far north as **turkey vulture** in summer, seldom seen in West except Southwest but does reach Kansas, Ohio, Washington, D.C. though not in large numbers. **crested caracara** 20–25″ #185x.

magnificent frigatebird 37–41″ wide-winged (84–96″) sea bird of southern coasts and tropic waters recognized in flight by long, sharply angled wings and *deeply-forked* tail; female has white upper breast, remainder black, male all iridescent black except for red patch under bill which expands like a huge red balloon during courtship; often takes fish from gulls, terns and other sea birds, dive-bombing them until they drop or disgorge their catch. Nests on islands of Florida Keys, Gulf Coast, Baja Coast; seen on Pacific Coast north to Oregon (occasionally) and on Gulf Coast and Atlantic Coast north to New England, Nova Scotia (occasionally). Also called **man-o'-war bird.**

S br | S gy | S bl | S gr | S yl | S rd | S b/w | M br | M gy | M bl | M gr | M yl | M o/b | M rd | M b/w | L br | L gy | L bl | L g/b | VL br | VL gy | VL bl | VL gr | VL r/p | VL b/w | VL bk | VL wh

#191. American crow (common crow) 17–21″

CAP blends with head, body. BILL stout, medium, pointed, black. FRONT all black, neck feathers under throat smooth (not ruffed like raven throat feathers). BACK all black, tail *fan-shaped* when spread in flight, looks square-tipped when bird is on perch or ground (not wedge-shaped like raven tail). ACTIONS often takes eggs and nestlings of smaller birds, also eats corn and other grain but eats many harmful insects, mice, small reptiles and rodents that do much damage to farm crops, also eats carrion, garbage, almost anything; is very alert and wary, posts a sentinel to keep watch for danger while flock is feeding and will warn all birds in area with its danger call; can be taught to imitate whistles, words; when can't break open a clam shell or similar hard-shelled food, will carry it aloft to drop and break on rocks or pavement below (may even try to break open a golf ball this way, with frustrating results), has survived by its wariness and wits in spite of continual persecution by humans; northern flocks go south in winter but others stay year round. NOTES besides the usual "caw", crows have many variations in tone and tempo, each with its own meaning and message that flockmates understand. They "talk" as they gather in the roost at night and before they leave each morning as if exchanging news or advice on best feeding places, dangers, etc.; also mimics other animal calls, other sounds, words. HABITAT woods, farms, waterfronts, city golf courses and parks — anywhere there's food and nearby roosting places.

CLOSE LOOK-ALIKES **fish crow** 16–20″ slightly smaller crow of Atlantic and Gulf Coasts, gives a chopped-off "cah" or "car" instead of full-toned "caw", otherwise typical. **northwestern crow** 16–17″ smaller bird of Pacific Coast. **common raven** 21–27″ larger than any crow; throat feathers shaggy, tail wedge-shaped, not square-tipped like crow tail, soars with wings level with body (crow usually has wings slightly lifted in V-shape), bill is more arched than crow bill, thicker; has retreated from cities and people, no longer common in East, usually seen only in remote hill country, still fairly abundant in northwest and north ranch country and Far North wilderness; call a throaty "crrroak" rather than a caw, a menacing and eerie sound when heard amid forest stillness; other call notes also deep and hoarse; like the crow a scavenger and eater-of-almost-anything.

snail kite (m) (Everglade kite) 16–18″ bluish-black all over except white of upper tail and narrow tail tip band, wings broader than those of other kites and not so sharply pointed, bill deeply hooked, a special tool for opening small shells. Feeds almost exclusively on one snail of fresh-water marshes. Female (#150x). Range Florida, Central and South America.

CAP: WHITE — BREAST: PLAIN (WHITE)

American swallow-tailed kite 19—25″ head, neck, breast and underparts all white, back, wings and tail black, wingspread 45–50″, tail long and deeply forked (more than half its length), underside of wings white on upper half, black on lower; easily recognized in overhead flight because of black-and-white pattern and deeply-forked tail; supremely graceful in swallow-like flight as it swoops and glides; feeds on the wing, skimming low over ground to snap up grasshoppers and other insects, small reptiles and birds, eats on the wing, bending to bite food held in claws. Now seen mostly in Florida and adjoining areas of Gulf and South Atlantic Coast, but once ranged north and inland to the Great Lakes and strays may still be seen there for a rare birding treat.

great black-backed gull 26–32″ head and shoulders white, tail and rump white, mantle (spread wings and back) *black*, wings bordered in narrow white tips on lower edges; largest of any North American gull except the silvery-white **glaucous gull** (both about same length with 60–66″ wingspread), legs pinkish. No other gull except the smaller (20–22″) and much rarer **lesser black-backed gull** has a really black mantle (lesser has yellowish legs). Range North Atlantic Coat south to New Jersey, may wander farther south, inland to Great Lakes (**lesser black-backed gull** same range).

WOODPECKERS

CAP: RED — BREAST: PATTERNED (BLACK)

#192. pileated woodpecker (m) 16–19½″

CAP triangular red crest bordered by white line over eye, black line through eye. BILL sturdy, medium, pointed, dark. FRONT cheek white, bordered by red line from bill to mid-cheek meeting black line that curves down white neck to edge black breast, side of neck white, breast and underparts black, edged in white at sides, *underwings white on upper half*, black on lower edge and feather tips. BACK black except for small white patch on wing (not always seen), tail black; in flight a pointed wedge shape. ACTIONS digs a large oval or oblong nest hole (not round as do most woodpeckers), also digs nearby roosting holes; feeds on tree-boring insects such as beetles and carpenter ants, on flying insects, and on grubs, acorns and other nuts, seeds, some fruit; will come to feeder for suet, nuts, if yard has enough open space to give "wing-room" for so large a bird (28–30″ wingspread). NOTES similar to "flicka-flicka" of flicker but louder, throatier, also a brisk "chuck-chuck". HABITAT dense forests of tall trees especially older trees and conifers and hardwoods, also wooded streambanks and marshes, lakes. Lack of such areas due to logging and cleared farmland has cut down on population of this species, but recently it has shown a slight increase in some areas.

CLOSE LOOK-ALIKES **pileated woodpecker (f)** resembles male except has *black visor* on red crest and chin line is all black, not red and black as in male. **ivory-billed woodpecker** (#186x) slighty larger (20″) has buffy-white bill (not dark) and black visor on male with red crest, all-black crest on female, large white wing patches for both.

Size: VERY LARGE — Color: WHITE

Birds that are Very Large and White — like most of the other Very Large species — show such easily recognized differences in behavior that you can put them in a matching group by Actions as quickly as by Size and Color. Therefore, in this Key you will first match the bird you want to identify with one of these three Action groups:

long-legged (or very-long-legged) waders
short-legged swimmers
hook-billed hunters, pointed-billed fishers

Once you have placed your bird in the right Action group, follow the usual SCANS System of matching by colors of cap and breast first, then by further description. (Because sizes vary more for Very Large birds than for other Key groups, length is given in inches for each species.)

LONG-LEGGED, VERY-LONG-LEGGED WADERS

CAP: ORANGE-BUFF — BREAST: PLAIN (WHITE)

#193. cattle egret 19–21″

CAP short shaggy crest (orange-buff in courting-nesting seasons, pale buff or white in winter) bordered by white over eye, on cheeks. BILL medium long, yellow-orange, pointed. FRONT shaggy tuft of buffy-orange plumes on breast in courting-nesting seasons, pale buff or white in winter, head, neck, breast and underparts all white otherwise, neck long (but not so long as other egrets), legs pink (yellow on young birds); smallest of North American egrets — about size of **green-backed heron** (#175). BACK buffy plumes on shoulders in courting-nesting season, not winter (like crest and breast tuft not always easily seen even in summer), otherwise all white. ACTIONS given name for habit of following herds (or grazing wild animals) to glean insects stirred up by moving hoofs or to perch on back to feed on ticks; also eats frogs, toads, spiders and earthworms; not a native North American species — first reached northern South America from Africa, evidently blown by storm winds, around the late 1880s; first in Florida 1941-2, soon spread north and west; first in Oregon 1965, now almost continental in range wherever it finds cattle. NOTES not talkative, throaty croaks and squawks around nest. HABITAT pastures and grazing land for feeding, woods and streambank thickets for nesting.

LOOK-ALIKES all other long-legged white birds are larger. *See* #196 and L-As.

CAP: GRAY — BREAST: PLAIN (WHITE)

#194. wood stork (wood ibis) 35–45″

CAP dark bare-skin hood covers head and upper neck, lighter gray patch as visor. BILL long, thick, dark, slightly down-turned at tip. FRONT all white from mid-neck on down to underparts; underwings *black* on lower half, white on upper — an ID clue to tell them in flight from **great egret** or **great white heron** when bill cannot be seen. BACK all white except for black tips of wing and tail feathers that show as bird walks or perches and the full band of black that shows in flight all across lower half of wings and entire tail, wingspread 65″. ACTIONS flies with neck outstretched (like a crane, not hunched like a heron), walks in shallows, probing in mud and water for fish, frogs, reptiles, insects, any small creature to make a meal. NOTES usually silent, but hiss at intruder; nestlings have usual begging cry. HABITAT mangrove and cypress swamps, backwater and bay — most nest in Florida sanctuaries but adults and young wander in late summer north and west, regular visitor in California; population declining because of loss of suitable habitat.

GENERAL LOOK-ALIKE No other North American bird has dark bare-skin head and white plumage, but check **white ibis** #197 (smaller, bill more curved and slender, black of wings on tips only) and **whooping crane** #195 (larger, bill straight, black of wings on tips only). Other white long-legged birds show no black on wings, others with black wing tips have short legs #198x **white pelican,** #198 **snow goose,** #199x **northern gannet.**

CAP: RED — BREAST: PLAIN (WHITE)

#195. whooping crane 49–56″

CAP cap and visor red, area between bill and cheek red, cheek white, blending with nape and neck. BILL medium long, straight, pointed. FRONT all white, throat to underparts, underwings show wide black patch on tips in flight, wingspread 6½–7½′, tallest North American bird. BACK all white except black wing tips, tail feathers curve *up* from rump and then curve *down* in dropping tuft (as do **sandhill crane's** #160) for crane or heron ID clue (heron feathers slope down with no up-down curve). ACTION formerly nested in North Central States and Canada, now only in Canada; retreated from people; in 1941 only 23 found nesting in Canada, wintering on Texas Gulf Coast (formerly wintered all across South to Florida). Through hard work by conservationists in Canada and U.S. flock increased to 124 by 1981; eggs taken from Canada nests and placed in **sandhill crane** nests in central U.S. may eventually lead to **whooping cranes** in other nesting areas and lessen danger that entire flock might be wiped out by natural disaster in the nesting area or in migration. Feeds on small fish and crustaceans, snails, toads, frogs, reptiles, acorns, grains, wild grassses and marsh plants. Pairs perform fantastic hop-and-

S br
S gy
S bl
S gr
S yl
S rd
S b/w
M br
M gy
M bl
M gr
M yl
M o/b
M rd
M b/w
L br
L gy
L bl
L g/b
VL br
VL gy
VL bl
VL gr
VL r/p
VL b/w
VL bk
VL wh

S br | S gy | S bl | S gr | S yl | S rd | S b/w | M br | M gy | M bl | M gr | M yl | M o/b | M rd | M b/w | L br | L gy | L bl | L g/b | VL br | VL gy | VL bl | VL gr | VL r/p | VL b/w | VL bk

leap mating dance. NOTES a trumpeting "kurr-loo, kurr-ler-loo". HABITAT remote marshes.

GENERAL LOOK-ALIKE **wood stork** (#194) comes closest, but **whooping crane** has white tail (not black) and is larger (56 vs. 45″) and has black only on forepart of wings not all the way across; other birds with black wing tips are smaller and shorter-legged, such as **white pelican** (#198x), **snow goose** (#198), **gannet** (#199x), **white ibis** (#197); other white long-legged birds have no black in wings, as **great egret** (#196).

CAP: WHITE — BREAST: PLAIN (WHITE)

#196. great egret (American egret, common egret) 37–41″

CAP white blends with head and neck, no crest, plumes. BILL long, pointed, *yellow*. FRONT all white plumage, *legs and feet black,* wingspread 55″. BACK all white, in courting-nesting seasons has long frothy white *plumes on back* extending beyond tail (but not in bustle-like tuft of cranes). ACTIONS flies with neck hunched back in S-curve like herons (**egrets** are members of **heron** family) not outstretched like cranes; feeds only during day and returns to community nesting, roosting area at night; feeding grounds often some distance from roost; feeds in salt or fresh-water marshes, ponds on fish, frogs, reptiles, crustaceans, small rodents, large insects such as grasshoppers; usually nests in trees with other egrets, wood storks, herons. NOTES loud hoarse croak or stuttering series of croaks. HABITAT marshes, willow thickets along streambanks, cypress and mangrove swamps, mudflats, back-water bays.

CLOSE LOOK-ALIKES **great white heron** 42–52″ color phase of **great blue heron**, larger than **great egret** , wingspread 6½–7′, has white plume on cap over nape, bill *and legs yellow* (**great egret** has black legs and feet). Range southern Florida only nesting area, very occasional stray wanders northward. **snowy egret** 22–26″ smaller than **great egret** in length and wingspread (38–45″), in courting-nesting season has long frothy *plumes on crest, neck and back,* extremely beautiful; before taking of plumes was banned by federal law this species was driven close to extinction by plume hunters; ID clue — bill is *black*; legs black but *feet bright yellow* (nicknamed **"bird with golden slippers"**). Young **little blue heron** much same size and all white, but has bluish bill, greenish legs and no frothy plumes. Range inland and coast over most of continent except Canada and adjacent border area of U.S. in marshes, ponds for nesting but has wandered even to Alaska in late summer when ponds and marsh dry up and food is scarce for eater of fish, crustaceans. **reddish egret** 27–32″ all white phase sometimes seen, bill pinkish with dark tip, shaggy crest and neck and back plumes in courting-nesting season (*see* #160 L-A for normal dark phase). Range, nests in Baja and along Gulf Coast to Florida, winters in southern Florida and may wander west to California or north inland and on Atlantic Coast. **cattle egret** (#193) smaller, may lack any hint of buffy crest and plumes, bill and legs both yellow. **little blue heron (y)** (#182 L-A) smaller, bill bluish, legs and feet greenish, adult #174. **roseate spoonbill (y)** young birds are all white, bill yellow, long, *with round tip like adult's* (#180x). **white ibis** (#197).

#197. white ibis 22–28″

CAP white bordered by bare-skin red visor and patch surrounding eye. BILL long, slender, down-curved, red or pinkish-red. FRONT except for bare-skin red face patch, entire front is white, in flight show underwings tipped in black, legs red. BACK all white except for black wing tips, back slopes down to short tail like heron's, may not show black wing tips when perched or walking. ACTIONS walks with neck extended probing in mud and shallows for crustaceans, frogs, fish, slugs, small reptiles, water beetles and similar insects; seldom goes far from salt water; feeds by day, returning to roost at night, often at some distance from feeding marsh, returning flock often in long straggly line. NOTES often makes low grunting sound while feeding, also a throaty "kuh-roo" and a loud honk in alarm. HABITAT coastal and inland marsh, mangrove and cypress swamps, palmetto groves, never far from coast.

CLOSE LOOK-ALIKE **white ibis (y)** similar red down-curved bill with dark tip and red face patch but head and neck are streaked brown, back plain brown, underparts and rump white. Resembles **white-faced** or glossy **ibis** (#142) more than adult **white ibis** except for white underparts and rump. GENERAL LOOK-ALIKES in flight, any Very Large white bird with black wing tips: **wood stork** (#194), **whooping crane** (#195), **Ross' goose** (#198x), **snow goose** (#198), **northern gannet** (#199x), **white pelican** (#198x). For ID, each has a very different bill.

SHORT-LEGGED SWIMMERS

CAP: WHITE — BREAST: PLAIN (WHITE)

#198. snow goose 25–38″

CAP white. BILL red or pinkish red, "lip" edges black. FRONT all white, black tips of underwing feathers show in flight, only 3–4″ larger than a **mallard**, formerly separated by size into two species as **greater** (25–38″) and **lesser** (25–31″) **snow goose,** now one species which also includes the former **blue goose** (#166x) as a color phase of the **snow goose. Blue goose** has head and upper neck white, under-tail patch white, front and back blue-gray with lighter edging on body plumage, darker on wings. BACK white except for black wing tips which usually show even when wings are folded and are very obvious when bird is in flight, white of both back and front may be stained with buffy or rusty tones from mud of feeding grounds but natural color is all white. ACTIONS nests in Arctic usually close to sea coast and often in large colonies (at times a thousand or more pairs within the square mile), feeds on sprouting grasses and wheat in spring, on grain left in stubble fields in fall and all year on certain tender roots and marsh plants. NOTES loud hacking honk or conversational mumbling. HABITAT Arctic tundra near coast in summer; marshes, ponds, bays, grain fields in winter. **Greater snow goose** nests in Greenland areas, winters on Atlantic Coast to South Carolina. **Lesser snow goose** (more abundant) nests in western

Canada Arctic, winters California to Texas and inland along Mississippi River and tributaries. CLOSE LOOK-ALIKE **Ross' goose** 21–25½" slightly smaller, similar white plumage with black wing tips, but bill shorter (no black edges), neck shorter, head smaller in proportion to body. Range, nests in Canada Arctic, migrates in fairly direct diagonal line to central California valleys for winter, occasionally seen in Alaska and elsewhere in West, almost never in East. GENERAL LOOK-ALIKES any Very Large white bird with black wing tips may look similar in flight. *See* Look-Alikes for #197.

American white pelican 50–70" same general big-bill-with-pouch shape as **brown pelican** (#166) but longer and with wider wingspread (8–9½'), bill orange or pinkish-orange, including pouch, body plumage white with black wing tips, but black may not show when bird is at rest with wings folded. Does not dive for fish from air like brown pelican, but fishes from surface and several pelicans may fish together, circling to drive fish into shallows for easier catching. Young birds have grayish streaking on head and neck and gray bill. Young and adults fly with head hunched back on shoulders — an ID clue since other Very Large white birds with black wing tips fly with neck outstretched. Nevertheless, gunners often shoot white pelicans, claiming to mistake them for **snow geese,** although big pouch bill makes a second clue, and population is declining. Range, nests on islands in lakes in northwest U.S. and Canada and on Texas coast, winters from California to Florida on coast, and inland lakes occasionally on Atlantic Coast.

#199. tundra swan 47–58" (**whistling swan,** now combined with European **Bewick's swan**)

CAP white blends with head, neck, body. BILL flat, black. FRONT usually has bare-skin yellow patch between eye and bill (**trumpeter swan** lacks this patch), bill, legs and feet black, long neck usually held straight (not curved like a **mute swan**) otherwise all white. BACK all white, wingspread 6–7' (less than **trumpeter's** wingspread by over a foot; slightly less than **mute swan's**). ACTIONS feeds mostly on marsh plants and underwater plants, dipping head under and rooting them out with its bill; favorites include wild celery, eelgrass and similar plants; sometimes eats thin-shelled mollusks but not reptiles and rodents as herons do; flies with long neck outstretched, flocks often in V-shaped wedge on long-distance migration flight and very high; nests on Alaskan and Canadian tundra, winters on both coasts, migrating inland via Great Lakes area to Atlantic Coast and southward to Pacific Northwest and California, occasionally to Gulf Coast. NOTES usual call is closer to a high-pitched tremolo "coo" than a whistle, but its thinner, higher tone (compared to the bugle call of the **trumpeter swan**) led explorers Lewis and Clark to choose "whistling" name when they first saw and heard the two species together on the Columbia River in 1805; the new name of **tundra swan** reminds you not to expect a true whistle — listen instead for a high-pitched, laugh-like "whoa-ho, ho-ho, woo-hoo" in soft and musical tone; also has other cries, but its windpipe (not so long and twisted as that of the trumpeter) does

not allow it to equal the trumpeter's deep and resonant tone, and so the voice of either is an ID clue. HABITAT lakes, rivers, bays — especially those with islands, since islands usually have fewer people and animal predators.

CLOSE LOOK-ALIKES **trumpeter swan** 58–72″ is larger, calls with deeper, more resonant voice, does not have yellow bare-skin patch between eye and bill but does have a thin pinkish-orange stripe at the "lip" edge of the lower bill near the base for ID clue (not always easy to see). The longest bird in North America, though not the tallest, and top weight of 38 pounds makes it the heaviest; its wingspread of 6′ for the female, over 8′ for the male, falls behind that of the **California condor** (10′) and the **white pelican** (9½′) but is greater than the **tundra swan's** and barely equalled by the largest **mute swan's.** Like the **tundra swan**, the **trumpeter** carries its neck straight, not relaxed in the graceful curve of the **mute swan**. **Trumpeters** were nearly driven to extinction by over-hunting but patient work by conservationists has increased their numbers and nesting places in recent years. Most nests still in Alaska but others now in Canada's western provinces and in Montana, Wyoming, Oregon, Nevada and South Dakota, with perhaps others soon to be established in the West. Winters on ice-free waters from Alaska to Oregon to Minnesota. **mute swan** 56–62″ can be told from either **trumpeter** or **tundra swan** by color of its bill — bright orange with a black knob at its base and black bare skin between bill and eye in triangular patch. The **mute swan** is an Old World species, not native to the Americas, but brought here for zoos and parks and private estates because it is more easily tamed and accustomed to humans than either **tundra swan** or **trumpeter.** Nevertheless, it still has wild instincts and has escaped to establish wild flocks in several places including New England, New Jersey, Virginia, Ohio, Pennsylvania, West Virginia, Michigan, and Minnesota and will probably do so elsewhere. Besides the bill-color clue, the **mute swan** can be identified by the graceful curve of its neck — a typical pose copied for many a greeting card and picture. In spite of its name it is not completely mute and will hiss loudly at intruders and sometimes give a sort of grunting bark — no louder sound is possible because of its non-curving windpipe. **swan young** — all three species — are gray, not white, as many will remember from Hans Christian Anderson's famous story of "The Ugly Duckling" that didn't know he was a swan.

HOOK-BILLED HUNTERS, POINTED-BILLED FISHERS

CAP: YELLOWISH BUFF — BREAST: PLAIN (WHITE)

northern gannet 35-40″ a bird of ocean and ocean shore with a "cigar shape" body that looks pointed at both ends (pointed gray bill, pointed white tail) as it sails and soars; entire head washed with yellowish-buff, black bare skin between eye and base of bill, body white except for black wing tips plainly visible above and below when bird is in flight, barely visible tips when wings are folded, legs short, feet webbed and dark; nests on North Atlantic cliffs (especially around Gulf of St. Lawrence), winters at sea from Massachusetts to Florida and around Gulf Coast to Texas; feeds by diving from midair into water for fish, will also swim underwater. Because it is a Very Large white bird with black wing tips may be confused with all others of similar size and coloring as noted with #197. For each the distinctly different bill is most useful ID clue, and for the gannet the cigar-shaped body. In the South the **wood stork** (#194) is often miscalled a gannet, adding further confusion.

CAP: BLACK-AND-WHITE — BREAST: PATTERNED (BLACK-AND-WHITE)

snowy owl, 20–27″ (#186) although it may look all white from a distance, back, breast and cap of snowy owl are well-flecked with black.

gyrfalcon 20–25″ (#186x) may look all white from a distance but is well-streaked and flecked with black.

#200. Forster's tern 14–16½″

CAP black (white in winter with black eye mask). BILL medium, *pointed,* orange-red with black tip. FRONT white, underwings white or silvery-gray-white, legs and feet orange-red. BACK mantle (back and spread wings) very pale gray that looks white in bright sunlight over water, tail silvery, *deeply forked* with white outer edge and darker inner edge of fork, wing tips silvery white, wingspread 30″. ACTIONS **Forster's tern** (named for naturalist Johann R. Forster who sailed with British Captain James Cook on his second round-the-world voyage) follows typical tern behavior in flying over water to hunt for fish and diving head first with graceful plunge to catch its dinner; the dive is an ID clue to distinguish terns from gulls, which usually swim about on fishing expedition and dive from surface; also flies over marsh or dry land hunting insect food, frogs, and swoops down to snatch them up with that sturdy pointed bill without having to alight; may nest alone or in colonies with terns and other shore-nesters. NOTES fuzzy, raspish "zhurr" or shrill stuttering cry, brisk nasal "k-yarr". HABITAT inland marshes and lakes or salt marshes, nests in south-central Canada and adjacent northern U.S., winters on California and Gulf Coasts and on Atlantic from Delaware south.

CLOSE LOOK-ALIKES 6 other tern species are much like **Forster's** in size and coloring, 2 others are similar in coloring but larger, 1 similar coloring but smaller (**least tern** #137x). For beginners the first step is identifying any tern from gulls of same waterfront habitat (*see* #171). Summer gulls have *white heads* or black hoods (not just caps) and most have *rounded* or square tails (not forked) and medium bills with *hook tips* (not pointed). No white-breasted tern wears a dark hood (just a cap); all have deeply or slightly forked tails and pointed bills. To tell one tern from another, look chiefly for color of bill and legs, tail shape, and range.

Arctic tern 14–17″ bill and legs *bright red,* tail deeply forked. Summers in Arctic, winters in Antarctic, making the world's farthest flight (*see* Fastest and Farthest), usually migrates well offshore, seldom seen on east coast U.S. and only occasionally on west coast.

common tern 13–16″ *bill red with black tip,* legs red, tail deeply forked but shorter than tail of **Forster's**; nests in south-central Canada and adjacent U.S. also along Atlantic Coast, winters on Pacific Coast, southern Atlantic and Gulf Coasts.

elegant tern 16–17″ black cap is a crest, *bill yellow* and very slender, tail moderately forked, only on Southern California coast.

gull-billed tern 13–15½″ bill is *black,* thick like a gull but pointed (not hook-tipped), mantle white (not as gray as other terns), legs black. Nests in southern California, on Gulf Coast, inland and coastal Florida and Atlantic Coast north to Long Island.

S br S gy S bl S gr S yl S rd S b/w M br M gy M bl M gr M yl M o/b M rd M b/w L br L gy L bl L g/b VL br VL gy VL bl VL gr VL r/p VL b/w VL bk VL wh

roseate tern 14–17″ mantle very pale gray, looks white; tail long, white and deeply forked, *bill black with red base,* legs red, breast has pinkish flush in courting-nesting season. Nests on Atlantic Coast and Florida Gulf Coast, winters north to North Carolina, rare inland.

Sandwich tern 14–16″ *bill black tipped with yellow,* legs black, tail moderately forked. Nests along Atlantic and Gulf Coasts, uncommon. Named for town of Sandwich in England where first recorded.

Caspian tern 19–23″ largest of these look-alike terns, bill red, tail slightly forked. Nests on Atlantic Coast from Virginia south, on Gulf Coast, around Great Lakes and other inland lakes and marshes in Canada and U.S. West and on Pacific Coast from Oregon south, winters on Gulf Coast and southern coasts of both Atlantic and Pacific.

royal tern 18–21″ second largest of these look-alikes, *bill orange,* tail moderately forked, seen usually only on coast, not inland — Atlantic, California, Gulf Coasts.

From Alexander Wilson's American Ornithology, *the 1840 edition edited by Thomas Brewer, which includes the first seven volumes published by Wilson (1808-1813) and the six completed after his death by fellow-ornithologists George Ord and Charles Lucien Bonaparte.*

Part Four

BIRDS FOR THE RECORD BOOK

LARGEST AND SMALLEST

Ostriches, the world's largest birds, are found now only in Africa. A full-grown male ostrich may stand eight feet tall and weigh up to 300 pounds. An ostrich egg is about 9 inches long — the equal of 13 to 18 hen eggs. The shell is so sturdy that it can be used for a cup or a canteen to carry water on desert journeys.

The bee hummingbird, the world's smallest bird, is just 2¼ inches long. It lives only on Cuba and nearby Isle of Pines, but there are other hummingbirds almost as small elsewhere in the Americas, north and south. Each weighs from 1/10th to 1/15th of an ounce and their eggs are barely ½ inch long.

Honors for the largest bird in North America must be split three ways The tallest is the whooping crane (#195). Full grown males stand 56 inches tall, nearly 5 feet. Their wingspread of 7½ feet is impressive, but the California condor (#190x) outranks them with a 10-foot spread. Heaviest and longest is the 38-pound trumpeter swan (#199 L-A) at 58–72" inches bill-to-tail.

All three of these record-makers have been threatened with extinction. The condor is closest to vanishing, for no more than 30 individuals remain — all in Los Padres National Forest in California. In 1941 only 23 whooping crane were found in northern Canada nesting grounds or their winter home on the Texas Gulf Coast, but hard work by conservationists brought the total to 124 in just 40 years. Trumpeter swans have made the best comeback and are no longer on the endangered list although they are normally seen only in the northwest from Alaska to Oregon, Nevada and Wyoming.

The smallest bird in North America is the Calliope hummingbird, 2¾ inches long (#52). Both male and female wear shining emerald-green coats and the male is the only North American hummer with a striped gorget — purplish-red and white. They winter in Mexico and nest through western states and on up into British Columbia but are not an abundant species. The smallest birds most watchers are likely to see in their own backyards are only slightly larger — 3 to 3½ inches. In the West this will be the rufous hummingbird (#7m, 53 L-Af) and in the East the ruby-throated hummingbird (#51m, 57f)

The ruby-throated is the only species of hummingbird seen regularly in the East, but a dozen more besides the rufous and the Calliope are seen in the West. All but two of them are under four inches in length, and those two scarcely reach five inches, even including a long needle-like bill. There are 321 species of hummingbirds and all of them live only in the Americas. Since they feed on flower nectar, flower pollen and insects they live mostly in the tropics from Mexico to Brazil and Peru where flowers bloom all year and insects abound. All of the species that nest in the north usually return to the tropics for the winter — except one. This hardy mite is the Anna's hummingbird (#54), living year-round in California. A few are also at home as far east as Arizona and as far north as Oregon and Washington.

The Anna's hummers can endure northern winters because they have the ability to go into a torpid state — something like hibernation — in which they need no added food or warmth. Body heat, heart beat and breathing rate are all reduced as they stay in this sleeplike torpor. Just how long they can remain torpid and still recover has not yet been determined. All hummingbirds can torpidate for a time and still recover normal functions, but the Anna's can do so for a longer period — at least 18 hours — than some other tested species. A few birds of other families have this ability also, including swifts, swallows and the poorwill. Even chickadees have been found in a state of torpidation during an extremely cold night, but active again next morning. Perhaps many of the smaller birds have this ability, for small bodies scarcely have room for the amount of fat needed to see them through a long night of severe cold. Research on this safety factor has only recently begun and more is needed.

Hummingbirds also make the record books for their flying skill. No other kind of bird can fly backward or hover in midair as expertly as they do. They have endurance, too. Ruby-throated hummingbirds that nest in eastern North America and cross the Gulf of Mexico on southern journey to a winter home in Mexico make an almost unbelievable non-stop flight over water of some 500 miles. The rufous hummingbirds will also be among the record-holders for birds that fly fastest and farthest.

FASTEST AND FARTHEST

The world record for the fastest bird on the wing is usually given to the peregrine falcon (#169). It is at home all around the world in almost all countries north of the equator. It has been clocked at speeds of from 170 miles per hour to over 200 on short dashes.

Perhaps no bird has ever been clocked at its fastest pace, for a person can't stand, stop-watch in hand, and tell a bird to fly its fastest because this race is for the record book. Birds fly fastest when they are being pursued by an enemy, or when they are trying to drive an enemy away from mate, nest or young, or when they are showing off in courtship. They also go faster when they have a strong wind behind them. To have all conditions for swiftest speed just right — and a stop-watch handy besides — isn't likely to happen very often.

But birds of several kinds have been clocked at surprising speeds. Runners-up — or "fliers-up" — for the peregrine's title include eagles, swifts, swallows, sandpipers and that pirate of the tropic seas called the magnificent frigatebird. They have all been timed at well over 100 miles per hour on short flights.

The world record for the bird that goes fastest on foot, rather than on the wing, is claimed for the ostrich. Records of 35 to 50 miles an hour — and some even higher — have been claimed. This matches the speed of a good race horse.

In North America the honors for the fastest bird on foot go to the greater roadrunner of the southwest (#151). So far, most roadrunner speed claims go no higher than 15—18 miles an hour, but no one knows how fast this unusual bird could go if it really had a reason for all-out speed, with no place to hide from its pursuer. It slips away from its enemies as often as it outruns them, and its track is difficult to follow because it leaves a two-way footprint that seems to be going both ways at once. It can play this trick without conscious effort because it has two toes pointing forward and two toes pointing back. Most birds have three toes pointing forward and just one toe behind, so their footprints clearly point just one way.

Records for birds that fly farthest, rather than fastest, are more easily measured. The Arctic tern (#200 L-A) that nests in our summertime near the North Pole, is rated as farthest flier of all, for its goes south each autumn to find a second summer at the South Pole. The full course measures 11,000 miles or more each way.

Several large shorebirds — sandpipers, plovers, curlews — are also honored as far fliers. Their yearly migration route each autumn from northern North America to South America's southern regions is measured at 8,000 to 10,000 miles each way.

The farthest fliers among small and medium land birds are the barn swallow, cliff swallow and common nighthawk. Some individuals among all three will make an 8,000 mile trip from Canada or Alaska to Argentina or Chile. The blackpoll warbler tallies 7,000 miles as it flies from western Canada nesting grounds to Ecuador or Brazil, going eastward to the Atlantic Coast before it heads south. Fifteen or so songbirds travel 5,000 to 7,000 miles each way on migration flight.

Among them are the yellow warbler, Swainson's thrush, bobolink, scarlet tanager and northern (Baltimore) oriole. Some rufous hummingbirds travel 4,000 miles between Mexico and Alaska. Ruby-throated hummers that nest farthest north in Canada travel almost as far.

One other small bird — the northern wheatear (#27 L-A) — may be rated among the farthest fliers, too, when its full route is learned. This species formerly stayed in the Old World year round. All of them wintered in Africa, and in spring some headed north to western Europe and others to India and Asia. Several years ago some of the birds nesting in Europe began drifting across Greenland to Canada and northern states to nest. Others from Asia began nesting in Alaska. Someday a northern wheatear wearing a little metal leg band proving it hatched in Alaska may be found in some faraway land to give it a record for long-distance mileage.

Banding birds with these metal markers is one of the most important ways of getting accurate information on a bird's life-span, range and migration route. Only trained workers are permitted to apply such bands and official records are kept by the U.S. Fish and Wildlife Service in their Bird Banding Laboratory at Laurel, Md., and by the Canadian Wildlife Service in Ottawa, Ontario. Other countries have similar banding offices and international records are exchanged by those in charge. No matter how much we know about birds, there is always more to learn.

Unrolled bird band. "Avise" means "inform" to Latin Americans.

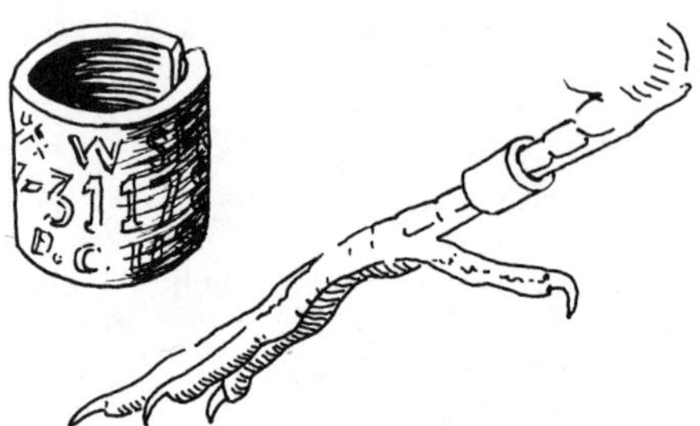

MOST BEAUTIFUL TO SEE AND HEAR

Beauty cannot be added up like numbers in a column with only one right answer. But surely any list of the most beautiful North American birds would give first place to those whose feathers gleam with jewel-like brilliance. Even so, it is difficult to choose among these:

ring-necked pheasant cock
wood duck drake
rufous hummingbird male
Anna's hummingbird male
magnificent (Rivoli's) hummingbird male

Indeed, almost any hummingbird, male or female, could be included. And for those who feel that graceful carriage and the purity of all-white plumage count more than jewel tones, add the swans:

tundra (whistling) swan
trumpeter swan
mute swan

If choice must match a favorite color, add the northern cardinal, the eastern, western and mountain bluebirds or the goldfinch. Or name the painted bunting whose coat of many colors includes red, blue, yellow, green, brown.

Naming the bird with the sweetest song is as much a personal choice as naming the one with the most beautiful plumage. In Old World fairy tales the nightingale was usually named sweetest singer, but there are no nightingales in North

America. However, thrushes are not too distant cousins of the nightingales and among them our hermit thrush (#77) is often mentioned as having our loveliest song. The Swainson's thrush should share the honor. Both are known coast to coast. As usual, only the males sing and only in springtime, and both males and females are feathered alike in woodsy brown backs and speckled fronts. Listening females hear a clear and flutelike carol — and so do listening humans.

Since both thrushes are usually shy and seldom sing in city backyards, many watchers will name more sociable birds as their favorite — especially the song sparrow or house finch or house wren. It's your choice.

MOST UNUSUAL IN ACTIONS

The brown-headed cowbird (#112) is named for the color of the male's hood and the way this species follows cattle to glean the insects stirred up by moving hooves. Cowbirds also perch on the back of cattle to pick up any insects pestering the beasts — a service cows usually appreciate. But the action that places the cowbird on this list is its custom of using baby-sitters to rear its young. The female cowbird always lays her eggs in the nests of another species, never builds a nest of her own, never sits on an egg or tends her chicks in any way. Of course the male shirks all parental responsibility, too. The female usually stays around long enough to see the chosen baby-sitter taking over the job, but then she's likely to disappear. Sometimes she will lay two eggs in the same nest, but usually only one.

Sometimes the baby-sitter refuses to accept the strange egg. She may build a new nest atop the old one so that the alien egg will get no heat as she broods the new-laid clutch of her own depositing. Sometimes she builds a new nest in a completely different site. But most of the time any female already sitting on eggs will accept the strange egg as if it were her own.

Usually the cowbird chooses a smaller bird for baby-sitter, and so the cowbird chick, when it hatches, will be the largest and noisiest in the nest and with the widest-open mouth. Therefore it will probably be fed first and oftenest, perhaps will even push its foster siblings out of the nest completely. It grows so fast that it is soon bigger than its foster parent. So if you see a mother bird stretching up on tiptoe to feed a baby bigger than herself, you can guess what happened. You may also see a young cowbird fledgling running after its baby-sitter squawking at the top of its voice, then squatting down on the ground to make itself more her size, more easily reached with whatever tidbit she holds in her bill. I have seen a song sparrow baby-sitter hop up on the edge of a flowerpot saucer to make herself tall enough to reach a foster-chick's open mouth.

Cuckoos of the Old World demand baby-sitters, too, but North American cuckoos usually build their own nests and tend their own young. Of course a bird of any kind may occasionally lay an egg in a nest not her own. Sometimes this happens when the female is caught far from her chosen nesting site at egg-laying time. Sometimes it happens when nesting sites or nesting materials are hard to find. Once in a while two females—even two females of different species — will use the same nest for the entire incubation period and then raise all the babies together, share and share alike. But usually the larger or stronger bird of the two will drive the other one away and take over all the eggs — or all the babies — herself.

Another candidate for "most unusual action" is the American dipper (#86) known and named for its habit of going under water for its food and walking around on the bottom of creek or stream bed until it finds a meal. It is the only songbird to seek its food underwater. Water insects and their eggs and larvae, snails and small fish and fish eggs make up most of the dipper menu. And since it has a short bill, short neck, short legs, the only way to get this food is to plunge beneath the surface. One moment you will see it there beside a mountain stream — trilling its lovely song or snatching at a passing moth — and then with a flip of its gray wings, under it goes head first and starts gleaning among the sand or pebbles on the bottom.

The American dipper is a bird of the western high country, but it ranges from Alaska to Panama wherever there are rippling streams and waterfalls. Look for a plump gray bird of medium size with a very short stub tail. In silhouette it reminds you of a bob-tailed robin, but it holds its tail erect, wren-fashion. It builds a dome-shaped nest, often trimmed with fronds of moss, which is usually placed beside a waterfall where the flying spray will keep the moss alive and green. This camouflage trim may convince a passing crow or jay or other egg-hunter that the bulge is only a clump of moss, not a nest at all.

Instead of the official name, American dipper, you may know it as a water ouzel, a name given to its relatives in England. *Ouzel* is an old name that seems to have some kinship to *drossel*, an old German name for birds of the thrush family. A dipper does look something like a thrush — except for that cocky wrenlike tilt to its tail — and it also has a thrushlike song, so perhaps the connection is not without reason, even though scientists today place the dippers in a family of their own. Anyone who watches a dipper doing its underwater walking will surely set this bird apart from all others, too.

MOST HONORED AS EMBLEMS

The bald eagle is our national bird emblem. It was chosen by vote of the U.S. Congress on June 20, 1782. Since that date its likeness has appeared on our national seal, on gold and silver coins and paper bank notes, on military insignia and on postage stamps and in political cartoons and in designs and handicrafts of all kinds. The bird itself was once seen in abundance, too, but is now scarce almost everywhere except Alaska and a few other places with protected waterways where it may fish for food and have some privacy for its nest. (*See* #154)

The bald eagle was chosen because it is found only in North America, and a native bird seemed the only right choice for a new nation just declaring its independence from European rule. The golden eagle would have been just as imposing an emblem, but golden eagles nest in every land north of the equator all around the globe and were once the symbol of imperial Rome and of many European families.

Benjamin Franklin once declared that he thought the American wild turkey was a better choice, since it has a more dignified and admirable nature, never robbing other birds of their food as bald eagles are seen to do now and then. But Europeans knew the turkey only as a barnyard bird, not a wise and crafty and dignified wild bird, and they would have made endless jokes about the young United States being ready for carving like its turkey emblem. So it is a good thing that others did not agree with Franklin. Almost everyone now agrees that the bald eagle is a fitting symbol for a nation that prizes freedom.

An emblem for each State

In the twentieth century when birdwatching was fast becoming a popular national pastime, each state — and the District of Columbia also — chose an official bird to serve as its emblem. Usually the selection was made by the vote of school children or by garden clubs and then approved by the governor or by official action of the state legislature. Sometimes an early choice has been changed for a species that seemed more fitting or because too many others had chosen the same bird.

Some birds won the honor because the name of the state had become part of their own names — such as Carolina wren, California quail. But the State of Utah chose the California gull, in spite of its name, because birds of this species had saved Utah's early settlers from starvation by devouring huge swarms of locusts that were destroying the grain fields. Delaware also let history guide its vote, for its emblem is a certain blue hen and all her chicks that had been mascots of state regiments in the Revolutionary War.

Most states, especially where children did the voting, chose the most familiar bird of farm and dooryard, one that was easy to recognize and remember for its bright colors and cheery song. Others tried to name a bird that was at home in their state but not often seen elsewhere.

Since several birds were chosen by more than one State, the ones named oftenest can surely claim the record for most popular birds in the land. First place goes to the cardinal (now officially northern cardinal) chosen by seven states: Illinois, Indiana, Kentucky, North Carolina, Ohio, Virginia, West Virginia. Second place goes to the western meadowlark named by six states: Kansas, Montana, Nebraska, North Dakota, Oregon, Wyoming. Third place belongs to the mockingbird (now northern mockingbird) named by Arkansas, Florida, Mississippi, Tennessee and Texas.

Three states honor the American goldfinch (Iowa, New Jersey,Washington). Two states apiece honor the mountain bluebird (Idaho and Nevada) and the eastern bluebird (Missouri and New York) and the black-capped chickadee (Maine and Massachusetts). Each of the other birds represent just one state and the complete list names 29 species:

Alabama–northern flicker
(known there as "yellow-hammer")
Alaska–willow ptarmigan
Arizona–cactus wren
Arkansas–northern mockingbird
California–California quail
Colorado–lark bunting
Connecticut–American robin
Delaware–blue hen's chickens
District of Columbia–wood thrush
Florida–northern mockingbird
Georgia–brown thrasher
Hawaii–nene goose
Idaho–mountain bluebird
Illinois–northern cardinal
Indiana–northern cardinal
Iowa–American goldfinch
Kansas–western meadowlark
Kentucky–northern cardinal
Louisiana–brown pelican
Maine–black-capped chickadee
Maryland–northern (Baltimore) oriole
Massachusetts–black-capped chickadee
Michigan–American robin
Minnesota–common loon
Mississippi–northern mockingbird
Missouri–eastern bluebird
Montana–western meadowlark
Nebraska–western meadowlark
Nevada–mountain bluebird
New Hampshire–purple finch
New Jersey–American goldfinch
New Mexico–greater roadrunner
New York–eastern bluebird
North Carolina–northern cardinal
North Dakota–western meadowlark
Ohio–northern cardinal
Oklahoma–scissor-tailed flycatcher
Oregon–western meadowlark
Pennsylvania–ruffed grouse
Rhode Island – Rhode Island red hen
South Carolina–Carolina wren
South Dakota–ring-necked pheasant
Tennessee–northern mockingbird
Texas–northern mockingbird
Utah–California gull
Vermont–hermit thrush
Virginia–northern cardinal
Washington–American goldfinch
West Virginia–northern cardinal
Wisconsin–American robin
Wyoming–western meadowlark

Part Five

ABOUT BIRD NAMES AND LATIN LABELS

WHY LATIN?

As you have already discovered, most bird books list each bird by two names. In many magazines, also, any bird name — blue jay, barn swallow, mallard — is usually followed by a second name put in parentheses or printed in italics or both. This second name is the scientific name, a two-word label in Latin, and it is accepted as the official name for scientific use in every land and language all around the world.

An official name for worldwide use is needed because most birds are seen in many different countries and so acquire many everyday names in many languages. And while scientists cannot be expected to know every language in the world, they can learn enough Latin to understand the labels. Also, even in English — or any other language — any common bird may be known by several different names and nicknames. And the same name may even be given to two very different birds, even in the same country. So the only way to be absolutely sure which bird is meant is to add the scientific label.

This scientific label is in Latin for two reasons. First, Latin is no longer the everyday spoken language in any country and so it is a "second language" for everyone. But it was once the everyday language of Rome. And when Roman armies conquered most of Europe centuries ago, they forced each conquered land to make all its official records and writings in Latin. At last, when Rome itself was conquered, the European countries could go back to using their own languages. But Latin was then the only language that all educated Europeans understood, and so for several centuries more it remained the one language for international use. All text books were written in Latin; all university classes were taught in Latin. So the language of ancient Rome became the language of learning, the language of science, for all Europe.

When European authors finally began writing scholarly books in their own language, most of them continued to use Latin names for animals, plants and minerals. But there wasn't any central authority to force them all to use the same Latin word in the same way. Most writers felt the name should be a complete description, four, five or six words long, and each one coined whatever label he thought best, no matter what other labels might be used in other books.

In 1758 the great Swedish naturalist Carl Linnaeus urged everyone to give up all their lengthy Latin labels and use just the two-word labels he had published. Everyone realized that a two-word Latin label — always the same in every book — was a very practical idea, but most writers were reluctant to give up their own creations and let Linnaeus get all the credit. So it was over a century before naturalists met for an international conference and agreed to follow the two-word system Linnaeus had devised. Each nation now has its own committee to approve one official everyday name in its own language (U.S. bird names are approved by the American Ornithologists' Union) and the same authority approves any needed changes or additions for the scientific names.

In the Latin of ancient Rome it was the rule to put the main word first, ahead of any describing word — saying "bird big", for instance, rather than "big bird". This same rule is followed in coining the scientific labels. It is also the rule that the first word of each label is the name of the group to which the species belongs. This group is called a *genus* — Latin for "kind" or "sort" — and its Latin plural *genera* is still used. The second word of the label describes in some way the individual kind of bird, called the species. Usually the description is by size or color or actions or notes or setting or by the name of its discoverer or of someone the discoverer wanted to honor with a namesake. The common pigeon, for instance, is labeled *Columba livia* — *Columba,* Latin for dove, to name the genus and *livia,* Latin for bluish, to identify the species by its typical color.

Species that are very similar in appearance, actions and anatomy (especially anatomy) are placed in the same genus and so have the same first word in their Latin label. The band-tailed pigeon, for example, is labeled *Columba fasciata* (meaning, dove banded). Even if you don't know what the Latin words mean, you know at once that *Columba fasciata* and *Columba livia* must be very much alike since they are in the same genus, sharing the same first word for scientific label.

Birds of one genus may be like those of another genus in a rather general way — as small doves are like the larger pigeons — and these genera are listed together in a group that scientists call a family. The family name for all the different genera of doves and pigeons is *Columbidae* — the word for doves plus the *-idae* ending that means "like" or "similar". Every family name ends in these same letters, so it is easy to recognize a family name when you see one, even if you don't know a word of Latin. You also know that birds in the same scientific family are much alike, but not so much alike as birds in the same genus.

Families that share certain likenesses are grouped together in a category called an order. The word for each order of birds ends in the letters *-iformes.* All families of dovelike birds are in the order *Columbiformes.*

At present, all the birds of the world are catalogued in 28 orders and 154 families. The number changes from time to time as scientists who study bird ways gain new knowledge. Then some groups are divided and others combined. Or an entirely new category may be identified and labeled. But all species, all families and orders of birds are still in the Class Aves, the class for animals with feathers. Every other class of animals — and every class of plants — is arranged in similar scientific groups, each species in its own genus, family, order and class. Identifying each species by its proper scientific groups and labels is called classifying.

Anyone who expects to make a serious study of birds will want to know more than this book tells of classifying and the use and meaning of scientific terms. But at least you know all the good reasons why Latin labels are used for scientific records.

NORTH AMERICAN BIRDS BY ORDER AND FAMILY

Even birdwatchers with only a casual interest in classifying and Latin labels may want to know a little about the way North American birds are arranged by order and family. Those who also want to know some of the genus-plus-species Latin labels will find them listed with the 200 birds of the color portraits.

Following here is a list of the 21 orders and 66 families of North American birds in the official sequence approved July 1982 by the American Ornithologists' Union for publication in the *A.O.U. Check-list* of 1983. Orders and families are listed by Latin names and species by common name. (The *-iformes* of each order label is pronounced *if-or-meez.* The *-idae* of each family label is pronounced *id-ee.*) A brief explanation of the root word for each Latin term and something about group traits is included.

1. *GAVIIFORMES* 1 family: **Gaviidae**, loons. *Gavia* is an old Latin name for webfooted water birds, especially those that dive and swim under water as loons do.
2. *PODICIPEDIFORMES* 1 family: **Podicipedidae**, grebes. *Podici* is Latin for rump; *pedi* for foot. Grebe feet are set back toward the rump, giving a strong swimming stroke. Each toe is separate and padded (lobed), not webbed.
3. *PROCELLARIIFORMES* 3 famiies: **Diomedeidae,** albatrosses; **Procellariidae**, fulmars, shearwaters, diving petrels; **Hydrobatidae**, storm petrels. *Procella* is Latin for storm. These birds have tubular nostrils, horny hooked bills and are fish-eaters, strong fliers roving the ocean even during storms.
4. *PELECANIFORMES* 6 families: **Phaethontidae**, tropicbirds; **Sulidae**, boobies and gannets; **Pelecanidae**, pelicans; **Phalacrocoracidae**, cormorants; **Anhing-**

idae, anhinga; **Fregatidae**, frigatebirds. *Pelecan* is Latinized Greek for axe-shaped, describing the pelican's beak and pouch. All except tropicbirds have pouches (but smaller than pelicans') and all have long bills and four toes united.

5. *CICONIIFORMES* 3 families: **Ardeidae,** herons, egrets, bitterns; **Threskiornithidae**, ibises, spoonbill; **Ciconiidae**, jabiru, wood stork. *Ciconia* is Latin for stork. All are like the storks in being long-billed waders feeding largely on aquatic life. Toes are separate, not webbed.
6. *PHOENICOPTERIFORMES* 1 family: **Phoenicopteridae**, flamingo. *Phoeniceus* is Latinized Greek for Phoenicians, the traders who first brought bright red or purple dyes to Rome, and for the color itself. The "pter" is from *pteron*, Greek for wing. Flamingos of the Mediterranean were largely white with red wings. Their webbed feet put them in a different order from herons, though earlier classifiers put them with the Ciconiiformes.
7. *ANSERIFORMES* 1 family: **Anatidae**, 8 tribes — whistling-ducks, swans, geese, wood duck, marsh ducks, diving bay-ducks, diving sea-ducks, stiff-tailed ducks. *Anser* is Latin for goose. All North American species have webbed feet, thick down feathers. All but the thin-billed mergansers of the diving sea-ducks tribe have broad, flat bills.
8. *FALCONIFORMES* 3 North American families: **Cathartidae**, vultures and condor; **Accipitridae**, osprey, kites, hawks, eagles; **Falconidae**, caracara, kestrel, merlin, falcons. *Falco* is Latin for hook or sickle, describing the curved bill and hooked talons of these meat-eating predators. All have keen vision and strong wings.
9. *GALLIFORMES* 2 North American families: **Cracidae**, chachalacas; **Phasianidae** (4 subfamilies), partridge, chukar; pheasants; grouse, ptarmigan, prairie chickens; wild turkey; quail. *Galli* is Latin for roosters, *gallina* for hens, so the order name means chicken-like. All have plump bodies and strong feet like the Asian jungle-fowl, ancestors of today's barnyard chickens.
10. *GRUIFORMES* 3 North American families: **Rallidae**, rails, gallinule, moorhen, coots; **Aramidae**, limpkin; **Gruidae**, cranes. *Grus* is Latin for crane. All are like the cranes in marsh and prairie habitat, but neither of the other two families has the extremely long legs of the cranes.
11. *CHARADRIIFORMES* 8 North American families: **Burhinidae,** thick-knees; **Charadriidae**, lapwing, plovers, dotterel; **Haematopidae**, oystercatchers; **Recurvirostridae**, avocet, stilt; **Jacanidae**, jacana; **Scolopacidae** (8 tribes) sandpipers, yellowlegs, willet; curlews, whimbrel; godwits; turnstones; knots, sandpipers, dunlin; dowitchers; snipe; woodcock; and a subfamily for phalaropes; **Laridae**, jaegers, skuas, gulls, kittiwakes, terns, noddies, skimmer; **Alcidae**, murres, auks, guillemots, murrelets, auklets, puffins. *Charadrius* is Latinized Greek for an old word for shore birds. All are strong fliers as well as waders or swimmers, and feed on shores of fresh or salt water.
12. *COLUMBIFORMES* 1 North American family: **Columbidae**, doves and pigeons. *Columba* is Latin for dove. Both doves and pigeons have plump bodies, short legs, short bills with a soft skin overlay called a cere at the base. Both males and females can turn their partially digested food into a milk-like substance to feed the young.
13. *PSITTACIFORMES* 1 family: **Psittacidae**, budgerigars, parakeets, parrots. *Psittacus* is Latinized Greek for parrot. All species have hooked bill with hinged upper beak, yoked toes (two forward, two to rear) with grasping claws.
14. *CUCULIFORMES* 1 North American family: **Cuculidae**, cuckoos, roadrunner, anis. *Cuculus* is Latin for cuckoo, imitating the call. All have yoke-toed feet, with outer hind toe reversible.
15. *STRIGIFORMES* 2 families: **Tytonidae**, heart-faced owls; **Strigidae**, round-faced owls. *Tyto* is Greek for owl; *striga* is Latin for owl and for a night-flying witch. All are meat-eaters, hunting mostly by night or at dusk and dawn, though some species hunt by day. All have large heads with both eyes front.
16. *CAPRIMULGIFORMES* 1 family: **Caprimulgidae**, nighthawks, pauraques, poorwill, chuck-will's-widow, whip-poor-will. *Capri* is Latin for goat; *mulgi* for

suck. The ancients believed that these birds fluttered around the goat herds in order to get a suck of milk. But they were after insects stirred up by moving flocks, not milk, and did not deserve the goatsucker name that has clung to them so long. All birds of this order have small bills and wide mouths with hinged jaws that make them expert at gulping down insects in midair flight. They have strong wings, very weak feet, often fly by night or at dusk or dawn, but also at midday.

17. *APODIFORMES* 2 families: **Apodidae**, swifts; **Trochilidae**, hummingbirds. *Apod* is Latin for footless. These birds have feet, but too small and weak to be of much use in walking or hopping. It has been suggested that the order name be changed to *Micropodiformes*, meaning small footed, but such action has not been taken. *Trochilos* is an ancient Greek name for a bird exceptionally agile and exceptionally small. It was given to several Old World species, including the winter wren, before finally being assigned to the hummingbirds by the Swedish classifier Linnaeus in 1758. Some classifiers suggest that hummingbirds be placed in an order of their own, *Trochiliformes*, but that has not yet been done.
18. *TROGONIFORMES* 1 family: **Trogonidae**, trogons. *Trogon* is Greek for gnawer, chosen because these birds have toothlike edges on the bill.
19. *CORACIIFORMES* 1 North American family: **Alcedinidae**, kingfishers. *Corax* is Latinized Greek for raven, imitating the harsh, raven-like voices of this order. *Alcedo* is a Latinized form of the Greek word for kingfishers. All have strong bills, nest in cavities, have 2 or 3 toes partially joined.
20. *PICIFORMES* 1 North American family: **Picidae**, woodpeckers, sapsuckers, wryneck. *Picus* is Latin for woodpecker, and for a legendary god turned into a woodpecker by a jealous goddess. All members of the order have strong bills, strong toes, a coiled "shock absorber" in their heads and nest in tree cavities.
21. *PASSERIFORMES* 24 North American families: **Tyrannidae**, flycatchers, pewees, phoebes, kingbirds, becard; **Alaudidae,** skylark, horned lark; **Hirundinidae**, swallows, martins; **Corvidae**, jays, nutcracker, magpies, crows, ravens; **Paridae**, chickdees, tits, titmice; **Remizidae**, verdin; **Aegithalidae**, bushtit; **Sittidae**, nuthatches; **Certhidae**, brown creeper; **Pycnonotidae,** bulbuls; **Troglodytidae,** wrens; **Cinclidae**, dippers; **Muscapidae** (3 subfamilies), kinglets, Old World warblers, gnatcatchers; thrushes, bluethroat, wheatear, bluebirds, solidaire, robin; wrentit; **Mimidae**, catird, mockingbird, thrashers; **Prunellidae**, accentor; **Motacillidae**, wagtails, pipits; **Bombycillidae,** waxwings; **Ptilogonatidae,** phainopepla; **Laniidae**, shrikes; **Sturnidae**, European starling, mynas; **Vireonidae**, vireos; **Emberizidae**, (6 subfamilies), American warblers, ovenbird, waterthrushes; bananaquit; tanagers; cardinals, grosbeaks, buntings; towhees, sparrows, seedeater, buntings, juncos, longspurs; bobolink, blackbirds, cowbirds, grackles, meadowlarks, orioles; **Fringillidae**, brambling, finches, grosbeaks, crossbills, redpolls, siskin, canary; **Passeridae**, house sparrow, Eurasian tree sparrow.

    Passer is an old Latin word for sparrow and an even older word for any bird that walks or hops on the ground. It comes from Latin *passus,* meaning step or stride, and so separated sturdy-legged birds from swifts and swallows and other birds almost continually on the wing. In modern usage *passerine* has come to be the label for all birds whose feet are especially adapted for perching — three toes to the front, one to the rear, and with an automatic leg-lock muscle that enables the percher to keep clinging to a branch even in sleep. Many have good singing voices and are sometimes referred to as Oscines, from the Latin word for songbird.

Any book published before 1983 has a somewhat different listing. Most of them do not place flamingos in a separate order and many groups now rated as subfamilies are given full family status and some groups come in a different sequence. Both common names and Latin labels have been changed for a number of species also. In this book the Keys list the new name, but give the former name in parentheses so that you can find any species by either old name or new in any text.

Some names have been changed because the scientific rule says that the official name must be the oldest name in public print with proper description. Quite often a name thought to be the oldest is put aside when a still older one is discovered. A new name may also be needed when a subspecies is changed to full-species rank or when birds formerly classified as two or more species are later combined into one. Of course no two species can have the same name, common or scientific, and so if two species have been called mockingbirds — one in North America and one in the West Indies, for instance — each will be given a new name that is unique, all its own. From now on, birders in North America will list the *northern* mockingbird, not just mockingbird, on their records for this very good reason, remembering that "northern" refers to the entire continent, not just our northern states. Instead of just cardinal, bobwhite, cowbird, catbird — as most of us have said so long — the official names now are more complete — northern cardinal, northern bobwhite, brown-headed cowbird, gray catbird. There are several other changes on the 1982 list and all of them will be published for reference in the A.O.U. *Check-list of North American Birds,* 6th edition, 1983, which replaces the 5th edition of 1957.

Part Six THE COLOR PORTRAITS

Birds portrayed in color are listed first by Key number so that you can locate each one quickly on the color page or in the text. Each one is also identified by the common name and scientific label published in 1982 by the American Ornithologists' Union. If a different name or label was published in the 1957 *A.O.U. Check-list,* it is given in parentheses so that you can locate each bird in older books.

PLATE I

1. house sparrow (f)
   Passer domesticus
2. Bewick's wren
   Thryomanes bewickii
3. house wren
   Troglodytes aedon
4. winter wren
   Troglodytes troglodytes
5. bank swallow
   Riparia riparia
6. northern waterthrush
   Seiurus noveboracensis
7. rufous hummingbird (m)
   Selasphorus rufus
8. grasshopper sparrow
   Ammodramus savannarum
9. brown creeper
   Certhia americana
10. song sparrow
    Melospiza melodia
11. Savannah sparrow
    Passerculus sandwichensis
12. pine siskin
    Carduelis pinus (Spinus pinus)
13. vesper sparrow
    Pooecetes gramineus
14. least sandpiper
    Calidris minutilla
    (Erolia minutilla)
15. elf owl
    Micrathene whitneyi
16. house sparrow (m)
    Passer domesticus
17. ovenbird
    Seiurus aurocapillus
18. chipping sparrow
    Spizella passerina
19. American tree sparrow
    (tree sparrow)
    Spizella arborea
20. lark sparrow
    Chondestes grammacus
21. purple finch (m)
    Carpodacus purpureus
22. house finch (m)
    Carpodacus mexicanus
23. white-crowned sparrow
    Zonotrichia leucophrys
24. white-throated sparrow
    Zonotrichia albicollis
25. Lapland longspur (sm)
    Calcarius lapponicus

4
3
2
15
19
18
17
1
8
12
13
9
22
21
16
7
14
25
10
5
23
24
6
11
20

PLATE II

26. bay-breasted warbler (m)
Dendroica castanea
27. dark-eyed junco
(slate-colored)
Junco hyemalis
28. least flycatcher
Empidonax minimus
29. solitary vireo
Vireo solitarius
30. red-eyed vireo
Vireo olivaceus
31. tufted titmouse
Parus bicolor
32. chimney swift
Chaetura pelagica
33. magnolia warbler (m)
Dendroica magnolia
34. Philadelphia vireo
Vireo philadelphicus
35. golden-crowned kinglet (m)
Regulus satrapa
36. yellow-rumped warbler
Dendroica coronata
(myrtle warbler now combined
with Audubon's warbler,
Dendroica auduboni)
37. ruby-crowned kinglet (m)
Regulus calendula
38. black-capped chickadee
Parus atricapillus
39. white-breasted nuthatch
Sitta carolinensis
40. dark-eyed junco
Junco hyemalis
(Oregon junco, *Junco oreganus*)
41. red-breasted nuthatch
Sitta canadensis
42. blue-gray gnatcatcher
Polioptila caerulea
43. lazuli bunting (m)
Passerina amoena
44. indigo bunting (m)
Passerina cyanea
45. northern parula (m)
(parula warbler)
Parula Americana
46. cerulean warbler
Dendroica cerulea
47. black-throated blue warbler (m)
Dendroica caerulescens
48. cliff swallow
Hirundo pyrrhonota
(Petrochelidon pyrrhonota)
49. tree swallow
Tachycineta bicolor
(Iridoprocne biocolor)

41
39
31
37
35
40
27
38
28
26
30
34
33
32
36
46
49
47
48
29
43
44
42
45

PLATE III

50. magnificent hummingbird (m)
(Rivoli's hummingbird)
Eugenes fulgens
51. ruby-throated hummingbird (m)
Archilochus colubris
52. Calliope hummingbird (m)
Stellula calliope
53. ruby-throated hummingbird (f)
Archilochus colubris
54. Anna's hummingbird (m)
Calypte anna
55. Tennessee warbler
Vermivora peregrina
56. mourning warbler (m)
Oporornis philadelphia
57. painted bunting (m)
Passerina ciris
58. common yellowthroat (m)
(yellowthroat)
Geothlypis trichas
59. black-throated green warbler (m)
Dendroica virens
60. lesser goldfinch (f)
Carduelis psaltria
(Spinus psaltria)
61. yellow warbler
Dendroica petechia
62. orange-crowned warbler (m)
Vermivora celata
63. palm warbler
Dendroica palmarum
64. lesser goldfinch (m)
Carduelis psaltria
(Spinus psaltria)
65. American goldfinch (m)
Carduelis tristis
(Spinus tristis)
66. Wilson's warbler (m)
Wilsonia pusilla
67. hooded warbler (m)
Wilsonia citrina
68. red crossbill (m)
Loxia curvirostra
69. black-and-white warbler (m)
Mniotilta varia
70. lark bunting (m)
Calamospiza melanocorys
71. American redstart (m)
Setophaga ruticilla
72. killdeer
Charadrius vociferus
73. horned lark
Eremophila alpestris
74. cedar waxwing
Bombycilla cedrorum
75. sage thrasher
Oreoscoptes montanus

53
51
54
55
50
52
71
59
69
56
70
58
67
61
65
64
66
62
60
68
63
57
75
74
72
73

PLATE IV

76. fox sparrow
Passerella iliaca
77. hermit thrush
Catharus guttatus
(Hylocichla guttata)
78. spotted sandpiper
Actitis macularia
79. rose-breasted grosbeak (f)
Pheucticus ludovicianus
80. common nighthawk
Chordeiles minor
81. northern saw-whet owl
(saw-whet owl)
Aegolius acadicus
82. sora
Porzana carolina
83. northern mockingbird
(mockingbird)
Mimus polyglottos
84. loggerhead shrike
Lanius ludovicianus
85. eastern phoebe
Sayornis phoebe
86. American dipper
(dipper)
Cinclus mexicanus
87. American robin
(robin)
Turdus migratorius
88. varied thrush
Ixoreus naevius
89. eastern screech-owl
(screech owl)
Otus asio
90. western kingbird
Tyrannus verticalis
91. gray catbird
(catbird)
Dumetella carolinensis
92. barn swallow
Hirundo rustica
93. purple martin (m)
Progne subis
94. blue grosbeak (m)
Guiraca caerulea
95. mountain buebird (m)
Sialia currucoides
96. eastern bluebird (m)
Sialia sialis
97. European starling
(starling)
Sturnus vulgaris
98. scarlet tanager (f)
Piranga olivacea
99. orchard oriole (f)
Icterus spurius
100. yellow-breasted chat
Icteria virens

76
91
85
77
88
79
87
95
94
97
93
98
96
80
99
90
81
92
84
100
83
78
86
82
89

PLATE V

101. evening grosbeak (m)
Coccothraustes vespertinus
(Hesperiphona vespertina)
102. western tanager (m)
Piranga ludoviciana
103. Scott's oriole (m)
Icterus parisorum
104. northern oriole (m)
(Baltimore oriole)
Icterus galbula
105. northern oriole (m)
Icterus galbula
(Bullock's oriole *I. bullockii*)
106. black-headed grosbeak (m)
Pheucticus melanocephalus
107. orchard oriole (m)
Icterus spurius
108. northern cardinal (m)
Cardinalis cardinalis
(cardinal, *Richmondena cardinalis*)
109. scarlet tanager (m)
Piranga olivacea
110. pine grosbeak (m)
Pinicola enucleator
111. eastern kingbird
Tyrannus tyrannus
112. brown-headed cowbird (m)
Molothrus ater
113. rufous-sided towhee (m)
Pipilo erythrophthalmus
114. rose-breasted grosbeak (m)
Pheucticus ludovicianus
115. bobolink (m)
Dolichonyx oryzivorus
116. red-winged blackbird (m)
Agelaius phoeniceus
117. Brewer's blackbird
Euphagus cyanocephalus
118. three-toed woodpecker
(northern 3-toed)
Picoides tridactylus
119. yellow-bellied sapsucker
Sphyrapicus varius
120. red-headed woodpecker
Melanerpes erythrocephalus
121. red-bellied woodpecker
Melanerpes carolinus
122. downy woodpecker
Picoides pubescens
123. yellow-billed cuckoo
Coccyzus americanus
124. brown thrasher
Toxostoma rufum
125. American kestrel
(sparrow hawk)
Falco sparverius

101
106
102
103
104
105
107
124
108
109
110
114
113
120
123
119
125
122
115
118
121
112
111
117
116

PLATE VI

126. northern bobwhite (m)
(bobwhite)
Colinus virginianus
127. mourning dove
Zenaida macroura
(Zenaidura macroura)
128. lesser golden plover
(American plover)
Pluvialis dominica
129. common snipe
Gallinago gallinago
(Capella Gallinago)
130. burrowing owl
Athene cunicularia
(Speyotyto cunicularia)
131. eastern meadowlark
Sturnella magna
132. northern flicker
(yellow-shafted flicker)
Colaptes auratus
133. California quail
Callipepla californica
(Lophortyx californicus)
134. rock dove
(common pigeon)
Columba livia
135. gray jay
Perisoreus canadensis
136. Bonaparte's gull
Larus philadelphia
137. black tern
Chlidonias niger
138. belted kingfisher
Ceryle alcyon
(Megaceryle alcyon)
139. blue jay
Cyanocitta cristata
140. scrub jay
Aphelocoma coerulescens
141. Steller's jay
Cyanocitta stelleri
142. glossy ibis
Plegadis falcinellus
143. long-billed curlew
Numenius americanus
144. American bittern
Botaurus lentiginosus
145. mallard (f)
Anas platyrhynchos
146. Canada goose
Branta canadensis
147. ruddy duck (m)
Oxyura jamaicensis
148. American wigeon
Anas americana
(American widegon,
Mareca americana)
149. golden eagle
Aquila chrysaetos
150. red-tailed hawk
Buteo jamaicensis

135
140
139
141
132
131
134
137
130
126
150
127
133
146
136
149
148
138
145
147
144
128
129
143
142

PLATE VII

151. greater roadrunner (roadrunner) *Geococcyx californianus*
152. great horned owl *Bubo virginianus*
153. common barn-owl (barn owl) *Tyto alba*
154. bald eagle *Haliaeetus leucocephalus*
155. osprey *Pandion haliaetus*
156. ruffed grouse *Bonasa umbellus*
157. sage grouse (m) *Centrocercus urophasianus*
158. ring-necked pheasant (f) *Phasianus colchicus*
159. ring-necked pheasant (m) *Phasianus colchicus*
160. sandhill crane *Grus canadensis*
161. yellow-crowned night-heron *Nycticorax violaceus* *(Nyctinasa violacea)*
162. northern pintail (m) (pintail) *Anas acuta*)
163. green-winged teal (m) *Anas crecca* *(Anas carolinensis)*
164. wood duck (f) *Aix sponsa*
165. mallard (m) *Anas platyrhynchos*
166. brown pelican *Pelecanus occidentalis*
167. northern harrier (m) (marsh hawk) *Circus cyaneus*)
168. northern goshawk (goshawk) *Accipiter gentilis*)
169. peregrine falcon *Falco peregrinus*
170. black-shouldered kite *Elanus caeruleus* (white-tailed kite, *Elanus leucurus*, now combined with two tropical species)
171. herring gull *Larus argentatus*
172. spruce grouse (m) *Dendragapus canadensis*
173. band-tailed pigeon *Columba fasciata*
174. little blue heron *Egretta caerulea* *(Florida caerulea)*
175. green-backed heron *Butorides striatus* (green heron, *Butorides virescens*, now combined with striated heron of Panama)

169
155
167
154
168
153
156
170
152
158
159
151
172
157
173
164
163
175
162
165
160
171
161
174
166

PLATE VIII

176. great blue heron
Ardea herodias
177. harlequin duck (m)
Histrionicus histrionicus
178. purple gallinule
Porphyrula martinica
179. common merganser
Mergus merganser
180. wood duck (m)
Aix sponsa
181. American avocet
Recurvirostra americana
182. black-crowned night-heron
Nycticorax nyticorax
183. common loon
Gavia immer
184. anhinga
Anhinga anhinga
185. black-billed magpie
Pica pica
186. snowy owl
Nyctea scandiaca
187. western grebe
Aechmophorus occidentalis
188. double-crested cormorant
Phalacrocorax auritus
189. American coot
Fulica americana
190. turkey vulture
Cathartes aura
191. American crow
(common crow)
Corvus brachyrhynchos
192. pileated woodpecker (m)
Dryocopus pileatus
193. cattle egret
Bubulcus ibis
194. wood stork
(wood ibis)
Mycteria americana
195. whooping crane
Grus americana
196. great egret
(common egret, American egret)
Casmerodius albus
197. white ibis
Eudocimus albus
198. snow goose
Chen caerulescens
(*Chen hyperborea* — blue goose and snow goose now one species as *C. caerulescens*)
199. tundra swan
Cygnus columbianus
(whistling swan, *Olor columbianus*)
200. Forster's tern
Sterna forsteri

185
190
186
191
200
199
192
187
183
198
179
180
178
181
182
177
193
184
189
188
176
196
195
194
197

Band-tailed pigeons *find grain on the feeding rock, water in a handy bowl and shelter beneath a hedge of firethorn and Oregon grape.*

Part Seven

INVITING BIRDS TO YOUR YARD

Most of us who enjoy looking at birds and learning their ways wish we could live amid woods and wilds with birds of all kinds always at the door. Not many see that wish come true, but anyone who has a yard — even a small yard in the midst of a crowded city — can make it a place where birds of some kind will come and feel at home. In these days of ever-increasing urban spread and highway sprawl, a city backyard may be the closest that many a small bird can come to the wildwood thickets and grassy meadows its ancestors once knew as homeland.

Each spring, all across the continent, robins and wrens and other migrant birds come on northbound wings seeking the place where they had nested the year before — only to discover that it has vanished. In its place may be a new shopping mall, supermarket, warehouse, apartment, marina, parking lot or highway — ashpalt, brick and concrete instead of grassland and thicket and untouched waterfront.

On a nearby highway a sign may direct tourists to a fine wildlife sanctuary fifty miles farther on, but birds follow instincts, not highway signs. And instinct tells them that this is the place where they belong. So they start looking for some nearby patch of greenery, some sheltered ledge, a nook or cranny that will do for nesting site. And if they cannot find such a place soon enough, while their bodies still have springtime readiness for mating and nesting and rearing young, then there will be no nest this year, no nestlings to grow up and become the parents of next year's broods. And if this happens another year — and still another — the danger is clear. The oftener it happens, the greater the threat that one more species is on the dark road to extinction. Like the frantic rider in Benjamin Franklin's moral tale who lost everything for want of a nail to fasten his horse's shoe, a whole species of birds could be lost for want of a hedge or bush in which to build a nest — a hedge or bush that could have been planted in some city backyard if only enough caring people knew the need.

Even a very large city yard will not have room for some of our most endangered species — whooping cranes, California condors, bald eagles. But you do have room for robins, don't you? And a pair of song sparrows, chickadees, wrens? Even if you have only a balcony and no yard at all, you could have a box of nasturtiums for hummingbirds, a suet ball for chickadees, a water bowl for any bird that wings by. And if you have neither yard nor balcony, you could help establish or support a mid-city sanctuary elsewhere, perhaps in a park or churchyard or in a place sponsored by the Audubon Society or some other group dedicated to preserving wildlife.

To turn your yard or any other place into a bird sanctuary you want to provide the three things we all need for survival — food, water, shelter. For birds, shelter means more than just putting up a house or two for springtime nesting. Shelter is a year-round need. Above all it means providing the natural hide-aways that birds seek instinctively when threatened by their enemies — by cats, hawks, people with guns, traps, poisons, by winter's cold and snow or summer's heat and by stormy wind and rain any time of year. And the best natural shelter is just this — a hedge or thicket, even a single bush or tree, that is thick-growing and evergreen. And if it is thick-growing and evergreen and thorny besides, then it offers the best protection of all.

So when you choose shrubbery and trees for your yard, keep the birds' need for shelter in mind. Any hedge that shelters them will also protect you from traffic noises and give you privacy from neighbors and passersby as well as a pleasant view. Among the best choices are firethorn, barberry, catbriar, yew, cedar, juniper, privet, holly, hawthorn, wild rose, Oregon grape.

If you haven't room for hedge or thicket, try pruning some small tree or tall shrub so that it will be thicker growing, the branches so compact and interlaced that even the fiercest hawk cannot penetrate its maze to snatch a trembling wren or chickadee from its perch. Even if no hawk threatens, birds need such a fortress for nest or night roost, especially winter night roost. Of course, you cannot provide such thick growth with one pruning and hedges don't grow in a single season. So while you and the birds are waiting for full protection, you might make a temporary corner brushpile. In January you can use discarded Christmas trees. In spring and fall save the lopped-off branches from your own pruning chores or ask to take some from parks and roadsides. November cornstalks make a tepee shelter, too. Be sure any pile has more than one opening — always an escape route if a cat or other predator is lurking nearby. Remove and replenish the pile as needed so that it does not dry out and become a fire hazard.

In spring you can provide nesting materials — feathers from an old pillow to make up for the ones birds used to find in handy chickenyards; lengths of string (but no nylon fishing line or anything longer than 5 inches that might get twisted around a bird's neck and strangle it as it struggles); little wads of lint from your electric clothesdryer; cotton from pill bottles. When you put up a bird house, make sure it has the over-all dimensions and size doorway to suit the bird you hope to attract. If you live in a rainy area, face the house away from prevailing storm winds. Drill a small drain hole in the floor so that water won't collect and flood the nest.

If you have large picture windows that reflect sky and greenery, birds may mistake them for clear air space and fly into them at full speed, breaking their necks or at least dealing themselves a stunning blow. Break up the reflected image somehow — with dangling chimes or with pinwheels mounted on the sill or with the life-size image of a falcon with wings wide spread (cut it from black construction paper following the picture in any bird book). The small songbird swerves to avoid the threatening falcon and avoids the glass, too. Squiggles of soapsuds or beer foam break up the image, too, and may be used during spring and fall migration when forest and shore birds are passing through the city on old fly-ways and are most likely to make a fatal mistake.

Some of the plants you choose for shelter serve double duty by providing food, too. All of the hedgerow plants suggested above have berries or seed pods birds enjoy. The northern spread of mockingbirds in recent years is almost exactly matched by increased use of wild rose (*Rosa multiflora*) in roadside and garden planting, for rose hips are excellent winter food.

If you have room for more than one food-bearing plant, choose those that ripen at different times — some in midsummer, some in autumn, some that are hardy enough to hang on all winter. Check with a local nurseryman or county agricultural agent to learn what plants do best in your area and the dates when their fruits or seeds will ripen. Among favorites found in many areas across the continent are blackberry, serviceberry, elderberry, firethorn, mountain ash, mulberry, wild cherry, wild grape, barberries (including the variety known as Oregon grape), cascara, dogwood, cedar, juniper, yew, cotoneaster, holly, hawthorn, sumac, wild rose, Russian olive, autumn olive.

For seed-eating birds the top favorites are sunflower seeds, especially the small black-oil variety which has a softer shell than the old-fashioned striped seed usually used. Even pine siskins can crack the black-oil seed's softer shell. Siskins and all the seed eaters also relish the new seed mixes which are pre-hulled before packaging. They not only save the birds from the hard job of cracking the shells but save you from the task of cleaning up the husks that litter the ground beneath the feeder. They are especially welcomed by birdwatchers who live in apartment houses where messy feeders are forbidden. Peanuts and other nut bits are sometimes included in these mixes. Birds relish all kinds of nuts from the fanciest pecans purloined from some orchard to acorns, but nuts served whole can be used only by birds with bills strong enough to crack the hard shells — or strong gizzards to digest the entire nut as turkeys and pheasants and other chicken-like birds do. By actual laboratory test, turkeys have digested pecans, shell and all, in only an hour.

Harder shelled hickory nuts and acorns soften in strong stomach juices within 8 hours and are fully digested by the next day. The grit and pebbles turkeys swallow grind against the nut to aid the softening, of course, and the whole process seems almost unbelievable.

Besides the feeding shelves and fruit and nut trees, you will want to set aside a special corner for a hummingbird garden. All species feed on flower nectar and pollen, as well as insects, and their favorites are the tube-shaped flowers with deep cups to hold large quantities of nectar. Many of these favorites are bright red or orange, but others are pastel shades and some are white. In our yard the all-time favorites are fuchsias, especially the varieties with red single blossoms. Nasturtiums and impatiens (both the wild *Impatiens capensis* or jewelweed and the smaller garden variety, *Impatiens balsamia*) attract hummers, too. So do honeysuckle, trumpet vine, Oswego tea (*Monarda didyma*), salvia, nicotiana, columbine, penstemons and all the flowering gooseberry-currant clan. Flowering currant, which blooms early in March in Oregon is especially welcomed by the first rufous hummingbirds returning from their winter in Mexico and other southlands. Pussywillow pollen also gives them good protein — important when insects are still scarce.

When any natural food isn't available, the backyard sanctuary should be ready to offer a substitute at any time of year. For hummingbirds, prepare a sugar-water formula using 3 parts water to 1 of white sugar. You can make a feeder for this syrup from a pill bottle — just punch a hole in the lid — or buy one at any garden center. Usually the ready-made ones have a red frill at the opening to imitate flower petals and so catch the hummer's eye.

Almost every kind of bird — except hummingbirds and insect eaters such as swifts and swallows — will eat plain white bread scattered in bits either on the ground or on a feeding board or windowsill. Most kinds of birds also relish beef suet as a substitute for grubs and caterpillars and such not available in winter. Peanut butter and the crumbs of dry dog food are also welcomed by many species. Only the seed-eaters with bills strong enough to crack the shells will feast on wild-bird seed mixes and chicken-feed mixes, and they'll eat almost everything else, too. Serve the suet in a chunk, just as it comes from the butcher, but wrapped in wide-mesh nylon netting and tied to a branch or porch railing so that some prowling four-footed raider can't carry it off. Or put the raw suet through a meat grinder and press it into the crevices of a pine cone. Twist a length of garden wire around the top of the cone and hang it from any handy hook or branch. For an extra treat, mix the ground suet with peanut butter and/or crumbled dog food or bread or cracker crumbs. Never serve plain peanut butter without some dry mix. Some birds digest it without harm, but it can clog the digestive system and birds have died as a result.

As an aid to digestion, whatever the menu, make sure there is a patch of bare earth where birds may pick up bits of grit, sand or gravel. Most of the year the birds find it on their own, but may need help in snow-time.

In spring, female birds getting ready to lay eggs need added calcium in their diet to make sure the shells are firm. Save a few egg shells from your own breakfast, dry them in a slow oven, then run them through the blender or crush them with a rolling pin. Scatter the powdery result in the garden. What the birds don't eat will provide extra nourishment for your plants.

Water, of course, is needed for drinking and bathing all year, but especially in warm weather. Birds do get thirsty and often pierce your favorite fruit to quench that thirst. Since they usually prefer wild berries to cultivated ones, keeping a patch of elderberries or blackberries near your orchard rows or grapevines may save you from losing your own crop. Your water bowl may be the most expensive marble fountain you can find or a plastic flower-pot saucer or the lid of a trash can, a hubcap or any other container — the birds will be equally pleased so long as the water is kept fresh and clean. However, a metal bowl attracts heat in summer, and the water will be cooler in a ceramic or concrete bowl. Whether on a pedestal or on the ground, a water bowl should be in the open — so that cats can't lie hidden in surrounding greenery and leap out to pounce on a bird with feathers too wet to make quick flight. But some tall hedge or bush should be near enough for the bather to take a quick refuge when danger threatens.

If cats are a persistent problem in your yard, you might encircle feeders and bird bath in a wire-fence fortress too high for cats to leap over. You can also hang moth balls in a nylon net bag beneath feeding board or bath. Most cats hate the camphor odor and most birds have little or no sense of smell. A small patch of loose earth for dust-bathing might be a welcome addition, too. Many birds enjoy a good dusting as much as a water bath.

No one yard can provide everything for every kind of bird. But even if you have only a corner to spare for their welcome, you will find birds of some kind accepting your invitation. Like an oasis in the desert, your backyard refuge can be a giver of life, one small link that keeps Nature's great chain unbroken.

BIRD HOUSE CONSTRUCTION SIZES

Species	A	B	C	D
Bluebird	8″	5×5″	1½″	6″
Chickadee	8–10″	4×4″	1-1/8″	6–8″
Titmouse	8–10″	4×4″	1-1/4″	6–8″
Nuthatch	8–10″	4×4″	1-1/4″	6–8″
House Wren	6–8″	4×4″	7/8″	1–6″
Flicker	16–18″	7×7″	2-1/2″	14–16″
Downy Woodpecker	8–10″	4×4″	1-1/4″	6–8″
Purple Martin	6″	6×6″	2-1/2″	1″
Tree Swallow	6″	5×5″	1-1/2″	1–5″
Barn Owl	15–18″	10×18″	6″	4″
Sparrow Hawk	12–15″	8×8″	3″	9–12″

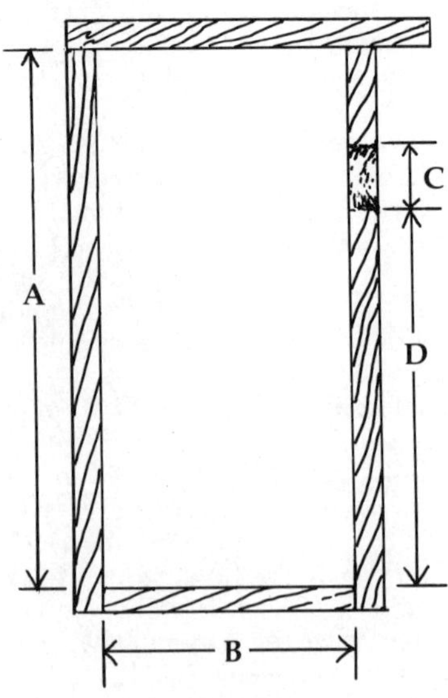

Reprinted with the permission of the Oregon Fish and Wildlife Department.

Part Eight

FOR THE BIRDWATCHER'S BOOKSHELF

BOOKS

Before you buy any kind of bird book or choose one from the library, always check the copyright date (printed on the reverse of the title page) so that you know whether you have a recent publication. Books ten or twenty years old — even older — may have much useful and accurate information on bird descriptions, but they will not always have the latest official name or correct information on where the birds can be seen and whether they are scarce or abundant. Don't pass up these older books — some of them are treasures — but do be aware of publication date if you're concerned with up-to-date information. Check, too, on the area the book covers. Some book titles do not reveal that they are about European birds or birds of only one section of North America. Check again to make sure that the book has the kind of information you want, whether birdwatching in general or some one particular phase.

There are hundreds of books to choose from, but some of the best are listed here in each group along with a selection of magazines and recordings of bird songs.

For general reference:

American Ornithologists' Union. A.O.U. Check-list of North American Birds. 1957 5th edition; 1983 6th edition. Contains common and scientific names of species and subspecies, data on first records and range. No descriptions.

Austin, Oliver L. Jr. (il. Arthur Singer) Birds of the World. 1961. Golden Press. Excellent over-all view of world birds.

Bent, Arthur Cleveland. Life Histories of North American Birds. 1919–1936. Smithsonian (now available in reprint paperback, Dover Publications) 26 volumes (available separately). Fascinating details on everyday bird life; some black-and-white photographs.

Pearson, T. Gilbert. (il. Louis Agassiz Fuertes) Birds of America. 1917, 1936. Doubleday. Old but still of much interest to birders.

Peterson, Roger Tory. The Birds. 1968. Time-Life Nature Library. Good background material on bird behavior, migration, etc.

Stokes, Donald. A Guide to the Behavior of Common Birds. 1980. Little, Brown. Thorough study of 25 common birds, well told.

Skutch, Alexander F. The Life of the Hummingbird. (il. Arthur Singer) 1973. Crown. The well-researched story of hummingbird life-style with color portraits of the most abundant species.

Terres, John K. The Audubon Society Encyclopedia of North American Birds. 1980. Knopf. Excellent. The best and most complete book of birding information yet published. Details for each species on clue marks, behavior, range, origin and meaning of names and scientific labels, general articles on song, migration, etc. One volume, 1109 pages, fine color photographs.

Wallace, George J. and Harold D. Mahon. An Introduction to Ornithology. 1975 (revised edition) Macmillan. Widely used as a college text; excellent for the serious birder who studies at home.

For identification:

Audubon Society Field Guide to North American Birds: Eastern Region. John Bull and John Farrand. 1977.
Western region. M. D. F. Udvardy, 1977. Knopf.
Each volume well illustrated with color photographs, excellent text, unusual arrangement by habitat and color.

Peterson, Roger Tory. A Field Guide to the Birds (East of the Rockies) 1980. Houghton Mifflin. Excellent revision of both text and pictures for original 1934 edition, the standard bird guide for hundreds of watchers.

__________ A Field Guide to Western Birds. 1969 (revision in preparation) Houghton Mifflin. Excellent — and the expected revision will be better still.

Robbins, Chandler, and Bertel Bruun, Herbert S. Zim. (il. Arthur Singer) Birds of North America. 1966 (revision in process). Golden Press. Handy-sized bird guide to cover the entire North American continent. Excellent.

Wetmore, Alexander. Song and Garden Birds of North America. 1964. National Geographic Society. Excellent for both color photographs and text; includes small album of recorded songs.

__________ Water, Prey and Game Birds of North America. 1965. National Geographic Society. Excellent for both color photographs and text; includes small album of recorded songs and calls.

Attracting birds:

Arbib, Robert, and Tony Soper. The Hungry Bird Book. 1971. Taplinger (also Ballantine paperback reprint). Excellent information on what to feed birds in the yard, how to build feeding shelves and houses, prepare water bowls, protect against predators, care for orphans or injured birds.

Harrison, George. The Backyard Birdwatcher. 1979. Most of the things most backyard birdwatchers want to know, well told.

McKenny, Margaret. Birds in the Garden and How to Attract Them. 1939. University of Minnesota Press. Good suggestions.

Marriage, L. Dean. Invite Birds to Your Home. 1975. U.S. Government Printing Office (Soil Conservatiom Service). Brief but well told, well illustrated. Trees and shrubs to attract birds in northwest. (Similar booklets for northeast, southeast, southwest, midwest.)

Martin, Alexander C. and Herbert S. Zim, Arnold L. Nelson. American Wildlife and Plants. 1951. McGraw Hill (Dover paperback reprint) Detailed listing of which birds and mammals feed on which plants, wild or cultivated.

Terres, John K. Songbirds in Your Garden. 1953. Crowell. Good detailed suggestions for attracting birds.

For pleasure reading:

Arbib, Robert. The Lords' Woods. 1971. Norton. A sensitive birdwatcher's account of 30 years of birding.

Bodsworth, Fred. Last of the Curlews. 1954. Dodd Mead (Apollo paperback reprint). Accurate but fictionalized tale of what may have been the last Eskimo curlew.

Bowers, Mary Beacom, ed. Stories About Birds and Birdwatchers. 1980. Atheneum. Reprinted articles from *Bird Watcher's Digest.* A varied selection to please beginners and experts.

Harwood, Michael. View from Hawk Mountain. 1973. Scribner. The story of what you may see at the best place to watch the spectacular fall migration of hawks.

Holmgren, Virginia C. Bird Walk Through the Bible. 1972. Seabury. All the birds named in 273 Bible passages, with details on those also seen in North America.

_________ The War Lord. 1969. Follett. Accurate but fictionalized account of the first Chinese pheasants to nest successfully in North America.

_________ Chinese Pheasants, Oregon Pioneers. 1964. Oregon Historical Society. Factual account of the first Chinese pheasants to nest successfully in North America (reprint from Oregon Historical Quarterly, Sept. 1964).

Horsfall, R. Bruce, and Carra E. Bluebirds Seven. 1978. Aubudon Society of Portland (Oregon). A charming combination of pictures by a famous bird artist for a story of baby bluebirds told by his wife.

Ogburn, Charlton. The Adventure of Birds. 1975. Morrow. Readers who are birders themselves will feel they are with the author sharing every adventure.

Sutton, George Miksch. Bird Student. 1980. The autobiography of this artist-naturalist makes fascinating reading for artists and birdwatchers alike.

For listening:

Borror, Donald J. Songs of Eastern Birds (12-inch, 33⅓). Songs of Western Birds (12-inch, 33⅓). Ohio State University. Dover Publications.

Cornell University Laboratory of Ornithology. American Bird Songs, vols I, II (or both as Anthology of American Bird Songs, including Dawn in a Duck Blind, An Evening in Sapsucker Woods–(12-inch), (3-record set).

_________ A Field Guide to Western Bird Songs. 3 records (or 3 cassette tapes) to accompany Peterson's book (records or tapes for the revised guide to eastern birds not yet available).

Droll Yankees, Inc. Birds on a May Morning. (12-inch) 36 most-often-seen-and-heard eastern birds, most of which are also seen in the West.

_________ Song Sparrow. (7-inch)

_________ Songs of the Forest. (12-inch) Thrushes — singers identified on one side, uninterrupted songs on reverse.

Matthews, F. Schuyler. Book of Wild Birds and Their Music. 1921 Putnam (Dover reprint 1967).

MAGAZINES:

American Birds. National Audubon Society.

Audubon. National Audubon Society, 950 Third Ave. N.Y. N.Y. 10022

Bird Watcher's Digest. Box 110, Marietta, Ohio 45750

Living Bird. Laboratory of Ornithology, Cornell University, Ithaca, N.Y. 14850

National Geographic. National Geographic Society, Washington, D.C. 20036

National Wildlife. National Wildlife Federation, 1412 16th St. N.W., Washington, D.C. 20036

(Your local Audubon Society may also publish a monthly magazine or newsletter.)

Index of Birds

Entries are followed by Key reference numbers (#), where applicable, and then by the page numbers of additional information.

f = female x = extra unnumbered species
m = male L-A = look-alike species
y = young S-A = sound-alike species

General Index